Modeling with UML

Bernhard Rumpe

Modeling with UML

Language, Concepts, Methods

 Springer

Bernhard Rumpe
Software Engineering
RWTH Aachen University
Aachen
Germany

ISBN 978-3-319-81635-7 ISBN 978-3-319-33933-7 (eBook)
DOI 10.1007/978-3-319-33933-7

Translation from the German language edition: Modellierung mit UML – Sprache, Konzepte und Methodik by B. Rumpe, © Springer-Verlag Berlin Heidelberg 2004, 2011. All Rights Reserved.

Printed on acid-free paper

This Springer imprint is published by Springer Nature
The registered company is Springer International Publishing AG Switzerland

Foreword[1]

Designing large software systems is one of the big technical challenges of our time. The scope and complexity of software have now reached dimensions that push all established approaches and methods for its development to its limits.

In this situation, software developers have increasingly discovered the established concept of model creation in the engineering sciences. In the past, a large number of different approaches have worked out under the concept model-based software development, which aims at extensive model creation to support development of software systems. Model creation enables specific representations of important properties and aspects of a software system to be analyzed or designed. One objective is an appropriate abstraction leading to decreased complexity and improved controllability of software systems. Despite all the progress made in this field and its clear practical maturity, there are still many questions that need to be answered by research.

The additional development effort required is certainly a critical factor in model creation. The question here is how much effort should be invested in model creation and how model-based procedures, which are often heavyweight, can be made flexible enough to better consider the profiles of the development projects.

Besides model orientation, use of so-called agile methods has become another trend in software engineering in recent years, especially around the concept of "Extreme Programming". This term encompasses lightweight process models for software development that secure a reduction of software bureaucracy and support a much greater flexibility in software development. For projects with a certain profile, agile methods can facilitate a considerably more effective process. However, preconditions for this are sufficiently competent developers as well as a clearly limited project size. Thus, such agile methods can only be used successfully in small projects with a handful of developers over a manageable period of time so that feedback can actually work to achieve faster communication within the project.

---

[1]Translated from the Foreword of the German Edition.

At first sight, it seems that model-based approaches, with their strong systematics and their modeling techniques explicitly detached from the actual coding, are not compatible with agile methods, which are usually code-centered. This book impressively shows that it is still possible to combine model-based approaches with agile methods by using well-known modeling languages such as UML. However, one must then carefully consider which UML constructs can be used as modeling, testing, and implementation description tools and what the methodical procedure should look like.

This book provides an answer to this question, aiming to use relevant practical approaches such as the agile approach and the widespread language UML without leaving out a proper scientific foundation and well-documented process. In particular, it is clearly shown which UML constructs are suitable for, e.g., rigorously developing test cases or launching an evolution by applying perfect transformation rules.

The book demonstrates how the quite different paradigms of agile methods and model orientation correspond to and supplement each other. The result is an approach that equally satisfies the requirements for a practically relevant, well-usable procedure as well as the demand of a precise scientific foundation.

This text reads very well without giving up the claim of providing a solid content and technical representation. Bernhard Rumpe has successfully tested the process suggested in this book in a number of smaller projects.

Thus, this work represents a valuable contribution, providing useful guidance for practitioners and additional information on how to combine current trends in software engineering—such as agile procedures and model-based development—successfully and with reasonable additions. Students will receive a comprehensive introduction to the topic, and the book serves as a sound foundation.

This, as well as the consecutive book "Agile Modeling with UML" are equally well suited for practitioners interested in such an approach for their development projects as well as for lectures dealing with practical questions while not neglecting a fundamental scientific foundation.

Garching, Germany
February 2004

Manfred Broy

Preface to the Second Edition[2]

Ten years ago, it could be foreseen that agile methods would prevail, at least for a substantial subdomain of software development, even though they were smiled at by many developers at that time. Today, agile methods have become an established part of the software engineering portfolio. In many places, they have been extended and adjusted to specific domains.

At the same time, the Unified Modeling Language started its triumph and has since practically absorbed or eliminated all other wider used modeling languages, with the exception of Matlab/Simulink, which we do not see as a proper modeling language but as a graphical programming language. UML is quite large and still suffers from the multiple options and interpretation possibilities that, due to its various fields of application, cannot be clarified that easily. Instead, it might be better to create a more explicit variability model for syntactical, methodical, and semantic differences and to configure UML for single projects by suitable selection [Grö10].

The programming language Java has prevailed even more successfully as the primary web and business system language, as well as a teaching language for computer science students.

Therefore, in this as well as the second book "Agile Modeling with UML" UML and Java are consolidated, moderately supplemented and enhanced to allow smooth and integrated use. UML is available in version 2.3 and Java in version 6. UML/P introduced in this book represents a relatively independent and adapted version, a so-called profile of UML, but this profile has been adjusted in some parts by modifications from UML 1.4 to UML 2.3. Because we use Java as the target of generation and test activities, it is certainly of interest to refer to new concepts in Java such as the generics and the assert statement.

Despite or maybe particularly because of the success of both approaches, the gap between the worlds of the model-based software development with UML and agile methods has not really decreased. While agile methods definitely prefer to generate

---

[2]Translated from the Preface of the German Edition.

code instead of writing it manually, many developers regard the hurdle to successful generation to remain relatively high. Often, the reason for this is the inconvenient and the heavyweight character of the generation process and the relatively high initial effort required to introduce generation tools into the development process. This gap still needs to be closed.

A number of people have directly or indirectly contributed to the creation of the first, and the revision to the second, version of this book. My particular thanks go to Manfred Broy, whose support made this book possible. I would also like to thank my employees and students, especially Christian Berger, Marita Breuer, Angelika Fleck, Hans Grönniger, Sylvia Gunder, Tim Gülke, Arne Haber, Christoph Herrmann, Roland Hildebrandt, Holger Krahn, Thomas Kurpick, Markus Look, Shahar Maoz, Philip Martzok, Antonio Navarro Pérez, Class Pinkernell, Dirk Reiss, Holger Rendel, Jan Oliver Ringert, Martin Schindler, Mark Stein, Christopher Vogt, Galina Volkova, Steven Völkel, and Ingo Weisenmöller who used this book as a basis for their work or who helped to supplement and improve it for the second edition. I would like to thank the former Bavarian Minister for Science, Research, and the Arts, Hans Zehetmair, for the habilitation scholarship award and my appreciated colleague and predecessor Prof. Dr. -Ing. Manfred Nagl for his benevolent support in establishing the chair at Aachen.

My sincere thanks are due to my friends and colleagues, my scientific staff, and the students from Munich for constructive discussions, collaboration in the application examples and reviews of intermediate results of this book in its first edition: Samer Alhunaty, Hubert Baumeister, Markus Boger, Peter Braun, Maria Victoria Cengarle, David Cruz da Bettencourt, Ljiljana Döhring, Jutta Eckstein, Andreas Günzler, Franz Huber, Jan Jürjens, Ingolf Krüger, Konstantin Kukushkin, Britta Liebscher, Barbara Paech, Jan Philipps, Markus Pister, Gerhard Popp, Alexander Pretschner, Mattias Rahlf, Andreas Rausch, Stefan Rumpe, Robert Sandner, Bernhard Schätz, Markus Wenzel, Guido Wimmel, and Alexander Wisspeintner.

Aachen, Germany   Bernhard Rumpe
June 2011

Preface to the English Edition

Colleagues have asked when the English version of this book would be published. Finally, here it is. I wish all the readers, students, teachers, and developers fun and inspiration for their work.

I would like to thank all the people that helped me translating and quality checking this book, namely Sabine Blumensath, Robert Eikermann, Timo Greifenberg, Julia Gunder, Sylvia Gunder, Arne Haber, Robert Heim, Lars Hermerschmidt, Gabi Heuschen, Katrin Hölldobler, Andreas Horst, Steffi Kaiser, Carsten Kolassa, Thomas Kurpick, Achim Lindt, Markus Look, Klaus Müller, Antonio Navarro Pérez, Pedram Mir Seyed Nazari, Dimitri Plotnikov, Alexander Roth, Christoph Schulze, Michael von Wenckstern, and Andreas Wortmann.

Aachen, Germany
February 2016

Bernhard Rumpe

Contents

1

Introduction

> The quest for knowledge is a natural
> tendency of all human beings.
>
> Aristotle

In recent years, software engineering has become an effective engineering discipline. Due to the constantly increasing complexity of its tasks and the diversity of its application domains, a portfolio of software engineering techniques has been constructed, offering a customized range of suitable methods and concepts for the application domain, criticality, and complexity of each system to be developed. Techniques for management of projects, configuration, variant and quality, as well as software product lines, development processes, specification techniques, analysis and design patterns, and best practices for specific tasks are only some elements of this portfolio.

On the one hand, this portfolio offers competing approaches with problem-specific advantages. On the other hand, the evolution of the languages, frameworks, and tools used allows and requires continual supplementation and enlargement of this portfolio. Today, programming languages such as Java, well-engineered class libraries, and permanently improving software development tools admit methods which were inconceivable just a few years ago. For example, tool-based evolution or modification of a software architecture already in operation has become considerably easier in the meantime.

Further material:

http://www.se-rwth.de/

© Springer International Publishing Switzerland 2016

B. Rumpe, *Modeling with UML*, DOI 10.1007/978-3-319-33933-7_1

The rapidly changing technology, the flexibility expected by users, e.g., in the E-service domain, and the extensibility of systems as well as the high criticality of business applications require constant optimization and adjustment of development processes and their associated methods. Only by using available software development techniques can a high-quality system which suits the desires of the customer be developed in an agile way and complemented steadily with regard to given temporal and personnel resources.

The widespread use of the Internet also facilitates increasing integration of business applications across company boundaries together with user integration through feedback mechanisms via social networks. Thus, complex networks of E-service and E-business applications arise, especially in the field of Internet-based software. This requires appropriate software engineering techniques. In this domain, mainly object technology is used, and the Unified Modeling Language (UML) standard is applied for modeling purposes.

1.1 Goals of Book 1 and 2

Mission Statement: The primary goal is to provide foundational model-based development techniques for the mentioned portfolio. In doing so, this book presents a variant of UML which is especially suitable for efficient development of high-quality software and software-based systems.

UML Standard: The UML standard has to meet many requirements resulting from differing circumstances and is, thus, inevitably overloaded. Many elements of the standard are not useful for our purpose, or they are not applicable in their given form, while other language concepts are missing. Hence, an adjusted language profile of UML, called UML/P, is introduced in this book. In this regard, UML/P is being optimized for the recommended development techniques in terms of its design, implementation, and maintenance to facilitate its application in agile development methods.

This book focuses mainly on introduction of the language profile. In a second book called "Agile Modeling with UML," we concentrate on model-based methods for generation, test case definition, and evolution.

UML/P resulted from several basic research and application projects. The application described in Appendix D, for example, was developed using the principles described in this book as far as practicable. The delineated auction system is ideal for demonstrating the techniques developed in the two books, as changes of the business model or environment occur particularly often in this application domain. Flexible yet high-quality software engineering is essential for this sector.

Object Orientation and Java: Today, object technology is primarily used for new business applications. Its existing varieties of class libraries and frameworks, available tools, and not least the largely successful language design explain the prosperity of the programming language Java. The UML language profile UML/P explained in this book and the development techniques based thereon are thus based on Java.

Bridge Between UML and Agile Methods: At the same time, both books form an elegant link between the approaches of agile methods not yet integrated optimally and the modeling language UML. Agile methods such as Extreme Programming are equipped with a range of interesting techniques and principles enriching the software engineering portfolio for certain types of projects. Characteristics of these techniques include sparse use of documentation, concentration on flexibility, optimization of time to market and, minimization of necessary personnel resources together with concurrent retention of the desired quality. Therefore, agile methods are well suited as a foundation for the targets of this book.

Agile Methods Based on UML/P: UML is used as a notation for a number of activities such as use case modeling, target performance analysis, as well as architectural and detailed design at different levels of granularity. UML artifacts represent an essential foundation for planning and controlling milestone-driven software engineering projects. Therefore, UML is mostly implemented in plan-driven projects with relatively high documentation and the inflexibility resulting from that. However, UML is more compact, semantically more ample, and better suited to describe complex facts than a programming language. That is why it has crucial advantages for modeling of test cases and transformational evolution of software systems. Based on a discussion of agile methods and the concepts contained therein, the second book will outline an agile method which uses the UML/P language profile as a base for several activities without importing the inflexibility of typical UML-based methods.

1.2 Overview

Chapter 2 includes a definition of the components of class diagrams, a discussion on the deployment of views and representations, and a proposal for the definition of stereotypes and tags.

Chapter 3 introduces the design of the Object Constraint Language (OCL) in all its semantic facets and syntactically adjusted to Java. For specification purposes, a two-valued logic is introduced and the expressiveness of OCL discussed. Constructs for set comprehension, introduction of local functions, and special OCL operators for flattening of data structures and transitive closure of an association are presented.

Chapter 4 contains the introduction of object diagrams as an independent notation in UML/P. A bilateral integration of OCL and object diagrams permits use of diagrams as OCL predicates and also the description of complex constraints within a diagram through OCL. OCL logic operators are used to describe unwelcome situations, alternatives, and the composition of object diagrams.

Chapter 5 gives a detailed introduction to the Statecharts of UML/P. Here, first of all, simple automata are studied as a semantic model. The results gained from this study are transferred to UML/P Statecharts with regard to nondeterminism, subspecification, completion, and expressiveness. For the description of the preconditions, we use OCL; for actions we use either OCL or Java. By using a collection of transformation rules, we can derive simplified Statecharts which can be translated into OCL or are suitable for code generation.

Chapter 6 describes a simple form of sequence diagrams for description of linear processes.

Appendixes A–C describe the abstract syntax of UML/P.

Appendix D describes the application example from the E-commerce domain. In parts of the book, the Internet-based auction system will be intensively referred to for examples.

1.3 Notational Conventions

This book introduces several types of diagrams and textual notations. In order to immediately realize which diagram or textual notation is shown, a label is given at the top right. Deviating from UML 2.3., this label is given in one of the forms depicted in Fig. 1.1. This form can also be used for marking textual parts and is more flexible than UML 2.3 markings. On the one hand, a label is used as a guideline and on the other hand as part of UML/P as the diagram's name, and properties in the form of stereotypes can be added. Occasionally, special forms of labels are used, which are mostly self-explanatory.

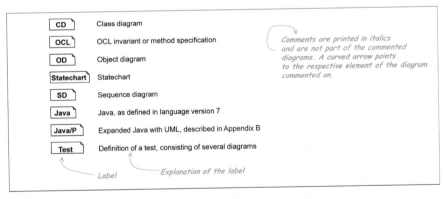

Figure 1.1. Labels for diagrams and text parts

Textual notations such as Java code, OCL descriptions, and textual parts in diagrams are all based on the ASCII character set. For better legibility, single keywords are highlighted or underlined. For stereotypes, transformations, test patterns, and refactoring rules, a template is presented in Table 2.19, which allows for a systematic description of the element introduced. The following additional characters are used in the text:

- The representation indicators "..." and "©" are formal parts of UML/P and describe whether the representation shown in a diagram is complete or not.
- Stereotypes are given in the form «StereotypeName». Tags have the form {TagName=Value} or {TagName}.
- Nonterminals are shown as ⟨Name⟩. We add the definition number of the nonterminal, as in ⟨OCLConstraint$_{C.7}$⟩, when we use a nonterminal in another section.

1.4 Placement of UML/P

1.4.1 Importance and Scope of UML

Especially for developer communication, there are a number of advantages of graphical notations compared with textual forms of expression. They enable the viewer to get a quick overview and simplify the perception of the system's parts and their relations. But due to their two-dimensional character, graphical description methods also have disadvantages. They need, for instance, considerably more space when shown or printed. This lower *information density* easily leads to a lack of overview, especially with regard to large models. Furthermore, precise definition of the syntax and semantics of a graphical language is generally regarded to be more difficult.

With the dominance of the object-oriented programming paradigm in almost every field of software and system development, and systems becoming increasingly complex, quite a number of object-oriented modeling approaches have been defined.

The Unified Modeling Language (UML) [OMG10a] was successful in integrating different notations and, thus, became a standard modeling language for software engineering. UML is now widely used. To allow this, the separation of methodological considerations and the notations used within methods was crucial. The aim of UML is to offer a modeling technique for preferably all application domains in software engineering. Accordingly, UML/P language profile defined in this book is partly methodically neutral, although it is especially suited for generative projects with Java as target language. Similar approaches are shown in recent books working on the relationship between UML and a programming language such as Java [Lan09, Lan05].

With UML, integration of several existing modeling languages has been achieved. Syntactic differences have been harmonized and concepts from differing fields have been integrated into the core language. Although this created a rather large and partly overloaded language, it can be expected that UML will claim to be the essential language standard for at least one more decade.

1.4.2 UML Language Profiles

UML is no longer understood as a language defined completely in all its syntactic and semantic details but as a language framework or language family [CKM+99, Grö10, GRR10] which allows, due to extension mechanisms and semantic variation possibilities, creation of *language profiles* that can be adjusted to the respective purpose of the application. Thus, UML has the characteristic of a colloquial language such as English which also allows for adjusting the vocabulary in the form of technical language and dialects.

[OMG99] already defined the essential requirements for UML profile concept, and [CKM+99] discussed how this affects the manifestation of business- or project-specific language profiles.

[Grö10, GRR10] reveal how the organization of syntactic and semantic variations of a part of UML in the form of features and language configurations can be shown and how it can be applied for the configuration of a language which suits the project.

Example language profiles include the specialization of UML to real-time systems [OMG09], Enterprize Distributed Object Computing (EDOC) [OMG04], multimedia applications [SE99b, SE99a], and frameworks [FPR01]. The [SE99b, SE99a], and frameworks [FPR01]. vocabulary is introduced directly into the model through the definition of classes, methods, attributes or states. In addition, profiles offer lightweight extension capabilities for UML syntax, such as the stereotypes and tags discussed in Fig. 2.17, and heavyweight extensions with new modeling constructs.[1]

According to [OMG99], the concept for defining a UML profile has, among others, the following purposes:

- Precise definition of tags, stereotypes, and constraints is possible.
- Description of semantics using natural language is allowed.
- A more specific profile can adjust a more general profile to the desired form.
- The combination of profiles allows for simultaneous use of multiple profiles.
- Mechanisms for managing the profiles' compatibility are provided.

However, the goal of simple exchangeability and combinability of language profiles cannot be fulfilled that easily. On the contrary, tool-based lan-

---

[1] Common languages also allow for the imprint of new vocabulary through the definition of terms. New modeling constructs would correspond to grammatical extension but are not common in other languages.

guage profiles can usually be combined only when they are explicitly aligned with one another.

1.4.3 Notations in UML/P

UML/P consists of six subnotations (see Fig. 1.2). Thereby, some subnotations of the UML standard are left out. UML/P is a language profile which in particular supports the activities of *design, implementation,* and *evolution,* because UML/P can also be used as a complete programming language. This explains the suffix "/P", which stands for "usable for programming."

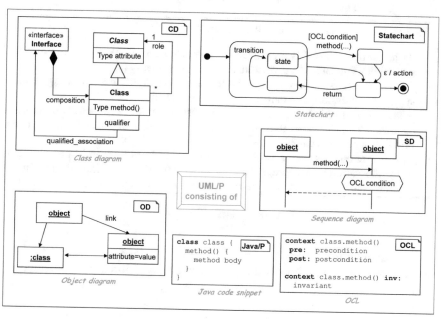

Figure 1.2. The sublanguages of UML/P

Not least, the programming language's applicability can be ascribed to the integration of Java code snippets into UML/P and the harmonization of textual parts of UML/P with the Java syntax.

The necessity of introducing further specializing language profiles discussed in the previous paragraph is facilitated in UML/P through the concrete definition of stereotypes and tags. Both forms of adapting language elements are used for defining UML/P itself but are also available for further adjustments, so that UML/P can act as a starting point for defining further application-, domain- or technology-specific language profiles.

1.4.4 The Terms "Modeling" and "Model-Based Development"

The Term "Modeling"

In software engineering, the term "model" is used for several different concepts. Among others, there are product models, process models, and test models. For a thorough classification, please see [SPHP02, Sch00]. Figure 1.3 gives an overview on some general definitions of the term "model." It is generally accepted that a model is an abstraction of a modeled item, for instance, by reduction in detail. Furthermore, it is reasonable, although not in all definitions present, to demand that a model has a purpose.

The definition of "modeling" in the literature:

- By its nature, a *model* is a reduced or abstracted representation of the original system in terms of scale, precision, and/or functionality (see [Sta73]).
- A *model* is an abstraction of a system that aims to simplify the reasoning about a system by omission of irrelevant details (see [BD00],
- A *model* is a simplified, goal-oriented representation of the function, of an item or a sequence of events that makes their examination or study easier or even possible at all (see [Bal00]).
- In software engineering, a *model* is the idealized, simplified, and in a way, similar presentation of an item, system or other part of the world with the aim of enabling the better study of certain properties of the original (see [HBvB$^+$94]).

Figure 1.3. Definition: model

However, there is disagreement about the granularity of a model. [Bal00], on the one hand, talks about a complete *product model* and associates it with a collection of diagrams; on the other hand, he regards the model as an *artifact* which equates a model with a single diagram. We also use the term "model" in a broader sense and regard a class diagram or a Statechart as a model of a part of the system to be realized.

Principally, a model is a model of an *ideal* or an *original*. In software engineering, however, models are often designed prior to the original. Besides, due to the immateriality of software, it is possible to create a complete system out of a model without manual support but by *automated* adding of details.

Model-Based Software Engineering

In Sect. 2.4, the term "view" is identified as a representation of, e.g., a *product model* accessible to the developer. The two-stage model abstraction from the system to the complete model and, in the end, to the developer view taking place in this process is caused by the size and complexity of the modeled system. Usually, a complete product model has a complexity which does not easily allow one to understand its relationships. Thus, extracts of the product model are created using views that highlight certain aspects but leave out others at the same time. A view is also a model and therefore has a purpose. A view is created in order to communicate a "story." A product model can be understood as the sum of its views. In comparison, [SPHP02], for example, defines the term "model concept" more restrictively by not regarding views as independent models. Correspondingly, all test and refactoring techniques discussed there are formulated directly on the product model, which contains everything.

While these levels of abstraction of modeling are generally accepted by developers, two approaches for their technical realization nowadays prevail among toolmakers:

- The *model-based approach* requires administration of a complete and consistent model of the system in the respective tool and only allows development of steps that are consistently carried out on this model and all the views contained therein.
- The *document-oriented approach* permits editing of each single view as an autonomous document. Inconsistencies among as well as between documents are accepted at first and only recognized using respective analysis tools.

Both approaches show specific advantages and disadvantages. The advantages of the model-based approach are as follows:

- A model's consistency can only be preserved automatically in a model-based form. In the document-oriented approach, the analysis is time-consuming and therefore, for instance, slows down code generation.
- Due to the fact that tools need not offer techniques such as weaving of several class diagrams or Statecharts for the same class, their implementation is easier.

On the other hand, there are certain benefits of the document-oriented and drawbacks of the model-based approach:

- Experiences with syntax-driven editors for programming languages have shown that support is helpful while syntax-driven editors disturb the developer's flow of thought and efficiency. The document-oriented approach better tolerates temporary inconsistencies and syntactically deficient documents.
- In large projects with many developers, model-based tools are necessary to take measures in order to ensure consistency of the model that is handled in parallel. This includes a shared repository with synchronization or locking mechanisms. While synchronization implies inefficiency, the locking prevents common model ownership and prohibits agility.
- Permanent model synchronization using a repository forbids local testing of alternatives. Hence, a transaction concept, version control or a similar

mechanism has to be provided by the repository. But this also leads to the de facto problem of integrating model versions.

- In comparison, the document-oriented approach requires the usage of integration techniques for model parts modified in parallel, such as those used in version control systems. This integration becomes necessary when the developer commits the locally modified version into the version control system and, thus, makes it accessible to other project participants. Therefore, local experiments do not have consequences when they remain unpublished.

- For self-developed special tools, it is generally easier to process single, file-based documents instead of the complete models which are held in the repository and are subject to version or transaction control.

- An incremental, modular approach for model processing, especially for generation, can considerably increase the efficiency of the development because models only need to be loaded and code generated if the models have changed. But this requires a modularity of UML models in the sense that information that is to be exchanged between models has to be clarified in terms of interfaces and also separately filed analogously to programming languages.

In practice, a synergistic compromise of both approaches might prove to be the ideal approach. This already becomes apparent in integrated development environments (IDEs) for programming languages. An IDE contains an editor with syntax-driven highlighting, navigation, and replacement possibilities up to automatic analyses and code generation in the background. But storage of information happens in an artifact-based way in single files supported by additional and automatically calculated tables where applicable. Thus, single files remain accessible to other tools, but the developer gets the impression of a model-based development environment. It is also beneficial that developers can choose which files and, therefore, which part of the "model" they want to load and manipulate in the tool.

Model-Driven Architecture (MDA)

The model-driven architecture (MDA) approach [OMG03, PM06, GPR06] is a continuation of the standardization ideas of the Object Management Group (OMG) based, among others, on UML. One of the key ideas of this approach is to define *platform-independent* models of business applications with UML in the first step of the development. A second step follows with mapping of this platform-independent model to an implementation on concrete hardware, a given operating system, middleware, and framework components.

As a result, the development of the platform-independent UML model is decoupled from platform-specific concepts. The implementation then consists of a mapping of the platform-independent to a platform-specific UML model formulated in a distinctive UML language profile. For this purpose, for example, Common Object Request Broker Architecture (CORBA)-specific UML profiles should be available. Next, a preferably automated mapping of this model onto an implementation and corresponding interface definitions follows. Beside technology-specific mappings, MDA also involves standardization efforts for application domains. This, e.g., includes XML-based communication standards for E-commerce, telecommunications, or the data model for the finance industry.

On the one hand, MDA is based on the observation that business applications have, on average, a much longer lifespan than technological platforms and that, thus, quite often migration of applications is necessary. On the other hand, MDA is grounded on the hope that this observation will simplify the reutilization or evolution of application-specific models for similar applications and the interoperability between systems.

As a whole, MDA is an approach that intends to revolutionize the tools for software engineering as well as the process of their definition, and that especially deals with company-wide and cross-company interconnection of systems [DSo01, GPR06]. Interestingly, a significant reduction of effort for software development through generation is intended, but suitable methods to achieve this goal are discussed only very little.

The approach discussed in the second volume can also be understood as a concretization of a part of MDA. In contrast to MDA, we do not present an all-embracing approach, taking into account, e.g., metamodeling, available middleware techniques or the interoperability between applications. Instead, we suggest the simple but more effective solution here in the sense of XP, in which only those interfaces are served, those middleware components used, and those operating systems taken into account for which the system is to be developed *now*. We have to take into account that the availability of standardized mappings of platform-independent models on the respective technology will be unlikely for many areas. In general, those mappings are to be developed on the basis of predefined patterns by the developers themselves, and thus, the code generators need to be parameterized correspondingly. Accordingly, simplicity, and not the attempt to meet many unnecessary standards, should come first.

1.5 The Future: Agile Modeling with UML

In order to increase the efficiency of a project, it is necessary to provide effective notations, techniques, and methods for the developer. As the primary goal of every software development process is the executable and correctly implemented product system, UML should not only serve for documentation of drafts. Instead, the automated transformation into code through *code generators*, the definition of *test cases* with UML/P for quality management purposes, and the evolution of UML models with *refactoring* techniques are essential.

The combination of code generation, test case modeling, and refactoring presents considerable synergetic effects. Therefore, these techniques are described based on UML/P in the second book "Agile Modeling with UML" published by Springer. Both books complement each other.

Agile Modeling: Some essential foundational elements of agile software engineering methods are elaborated, and an agile model-based developing method is outlined. The core of agile developing methods is the usage of models for a representation and discussion, but also especially for programming purposes and the definition of test cases through code generation and for the planning of evolution through model-based refactoring.

Code Generation: A well-parameterized code generation based on abstract models is crucial for efficient development of a system. The discussed form of code generation allows the compact and mostly technology-independent development of application-specific models. Only during generation are technology-dependent aspects such as database connections, communication, or graphical user interface (GUI)-mapping added. As a result, UML/P can be used as a programming language and there is no conceptual breach between modeling and programming language. However, it is important to explicitly distinguish executable and abstract models in the software engineering process and to use them adequately.

Modeling Automated Tests: Systematic and efficient testing is an essential part of the quality management of a system. The goal is that tests can run automatically after their generation. Code generation is not only used for developing production systems but also especially for test cases in order to check whether specification and implementation are consistent. Thus, the usage of UML/P in test case modeling is a fundamental element of an agile methodology. For this purpose, mainly object diagrams, OCL, and sequence diagrams are used.

Evolution by Using Refactoring: The discussed flexibility to react quickly to changing requirements or technology requires a technique for systematic evolution of the already existing model and its implementation. The evolution of a system because of new requirements or a new field of application as well as the correction of structural deficits of the software architecture ideally happen through refactoring techniques. A further focus is on the foundation and embedding of refactoring techniques into the more general methods of model transformation and the discussion of which refactoring rules can be developed for UML/P or carried over from other approaches. There, especially class diagrams, Statecharts, and OCL are taken into account.

In terms of test case modeling as well as refactoring techniques, insights originating from some theoretical approaches are outlined and transferred to UML/P. This book explains these concepts by means of numerous practical examples and prepares them in the form of test patterns and refactoring techniques for UML diagrams.

2

Class Diagrams

A fact is conceivable, means
we can picture it.
Ludwig Wittgenstein

Class diagrams form the architectural backbone of many system modeling processes. Hence, this chapter introduces class diagrams defined in UML/P with the core elements *class, attribute, method, association,* and *composition.* The section about *views* and *representations* discusses forms of use for class diagrams. Furthermore, it is shown how modeling concepts are adapted for project-specific demands using *stereotypes* and *tags.*

© Springer International Publishing Switzerland 2016
B. Rumpe, *Modeling with UML*, DOI 10.1007/978-3-319-33933-7_2

Class diagrams still represent by far the most important and widely used modeling technique of UML. Historically, class diagrams originated from the ideas of entity/relationship modeling [Che76] and the graphical representation of modules, which themselves were influenced by data flow diagrams [DeM79]. Class diagrams describe the structure of a software system and thus form the first discussed core notation for object-oriented modeling.

Appendix C.2 additionally compares the kind of class diagrams introduced here with the UML standard and specifies the syntax of class diagrams.

2.1 Relevance of Class Diagrams

Object-oriented systems are highly dynamic. This makes the modeling of a system's structures a complex task in object-oriented software development. Class diagrams describe this structure, or architecture, of a system, forming the basis for nearly all other description techniques. However, class diagrams and the modeled classes fulfill various tasks.

Structure Modeling

In any object-oriented implementation, the code is organized into classes. Therefore, a class diagram constitutes an overview of the code structure and its internal relations. As programmers are familiar with the concept of *class* from programming, class diagrams used in modeling can be understood and communicated rather easily. Class diagrams are used for showing structural relations of a system and for that reason form the skeleton for almost all other notations and types of diagrams, as these rely on the classes and methods defined in class diagrams. Therefore, they also represent an essential—although not the only—form of description for modeling of software architectures and frameworks.

Classes During Analysis, Design, and Implementation

In analysis, class diagrams are used in order to structure real-world concepts. In contrast, in design and implementation documents, class diagrams are especially used to depict a structural view of the software system. The classes presented in the implementation view can actually be found in implemented systems too. But classes from analysis are often significantly modified, supplemented by technical aspects, or fully omitted when they only belong to the system context.

One of the deficits of UML arises from the less-than-ideal option to explicitly ascribe diagrams a purpose. Assuming that a class diagram reflects an implementation, the semantics of a class diagram can be explained relatively easily and understandably. A number of introductory textbooks about class modeling or UML take this position [Mey97, Fow00]. Besides, this point of view is often implied by tools. Fusion [CAB⁺94], however, clearly distinguishes between classes belonging to the system and external classes and, thus, demonstrates that modeling of non-software-engineering concepts with class diagrams is feasible and reasonable.

The language profile UML/P is implementation oriented. This is why the following semantics of class diagrams based on the Java code modeled thereby is perfect for this purpose.

Variety of Tasks for a Class

In object-oriented programming and even more so in modeling, classes have numerous tasks. Primarily, they serve to *group* and *encapsulate* attributes and associated methods to create a conceptual unity. By assigning a *class name*, *instances* of the class can be created, saved, and passed on at arbitrary places in the code. Hence, class definitions at the same time act as *type system* and *implementation description*. They can (in general) be instantiated any number of times in the form of *objects*.

In modeling, a class is also understood as the *extension*, i.e., the number of all objects existing at a certain point in time. Due to the explicit availability of this extension in modeling, invariants for each existing object of a class can, for example, be described.

The potential unlimitedness of the number of objects in a system makes cataloging these objects into a finite number of classes necessary. Only this makes a finite definition of an object-oriented system possible. For this reason classes present a *characterization of all possible structures* of a system. This characterization at the same time also describes necessary structural constraints without determining a concrete object structure. As a result, there are usually an unlimited number of different object structures that conform to a class diagram. In fact, each correctly running system can be regarded as an evolving sequence of object structures where at each point in time the current object structure conforms to the class diagram.

In contrast to objects, classes, however, in many programming languages have no directly manipulable representation during the runtime of a system. One exception is, for example, Smalltalk, which represents classes as objects and therefore allows for unrestricted reflective programming.[1] Java is more restrictive, as it allows read-only access to the class code. Generally, reflective programming should be used only very reluctantly because maintenance of such a system gets far more complex due to reduced understandability. This is why reflective programming is ignored in the rest of the book.

---

[1] In Smalltalk, a class manifests as a normal object during runtime being manipulable like any other object. However, the content of such an object is a description of the structure and behavior of the instances assigned to this class object. See [Gol84].

Classes fulfill the following tasks:

- Encapsulation of attributes and methods in order to create a conceptual unity
- Manifestation of instances as objects
- Typing of objects
- Description of the implementation
- Class code (translated, executable form of the implementation)
- Extension (set of all objects existing at a certain time)
- Characterization of all possible structures of a system

Figure 2.1. Task variety of a class

Metamodeling

Due to the two-dimensional form of model representations, *metamodeling* [CEK+00, RA01, CEK01, Béz05, GPHS08, JJM09, AK03] has prevailed as a form of description of a diagrammatic language and thus replaced the grammars commonly used for text. A *metamodel* defines the abstract syntax of a graphical notation. At least since UML standardization, it is customary to use a simplified form of class diagrams as the metamodel language. This approach has the advantage that only one language needs to be learnt. We discuss metamodeling in Appendix A and use a variant of the class diagrams in order to represent the graphical parts of UML/P.

Further Concepts for Class Diagrams

UML offers further concepts that should be mentioned here for the sake of completeness. Association classes, for example, are classes that are attached to the associations that are subsequently introduced to store information that cannot be assigned to any of the classes participating in the association but only to the relation itself. But there are standard processes for modeling such data without association classes.

Modern programming languages such as C++ and Java [GJSB05] as well as UML since version 2.3 [OMG10a] now offer generic types first introduced by functional languages such as Haskell [Hut07]. In Java, this introduction has been integrated nicely [Bra04]. In UML, this has to be done carefully, because types appear in nearly all kinds of diagrams. As generics do not play such an important role in modeling but are applied for reuse of generic components especially in implementation, UML/P waives the full generality of generic classes with wildcards, bound typecasts, etc., and only the most important container classes are offered in a generically realized form, i.e., with type parameters. Thus, UML/P class diagrams do not provide mechanisms for defining generics. OCL/P, however, as well as the code generation allow us to use generics.

2.2 Classes and Inheritance

When introducing classes, attributes, methods, and inheritance, an implementation view—as already discussed—is taken as a basis in this section. Figure 2.2 contains a classification of the most important terms for class diagrams.

Class A class consists of a collection of attributes and methods that determine the state and the behavior of its *instances* (*objects*). Classes are connected to each other by associations and inheritance relations. The *class name* identifies the class.

Attribute State components of a class are called attributes. An attribute is described by its *name* and *type*.

Method. The functionality of a class is stored in methods. A method consists of a *signature* and a *body* describing the implementation. In case of an *abstract* method, the body is missing.

Modifier. For the determination of visibility, instantiatability, and changeability of the modified elements, the modifiers `public`, `protected`, `private`, `readonly`, `abstract`, `static`, and `final` can be applied to classes, methods, roles, and attributes. UML/P offers the following iconic variants for the first four modifiers of these: "+", "#", "−" and "?".

Constants are defined as special attributes with the modifiers `static` and `final`.

Inheritance. If two classes are in an inheritance relation to each other, the *subclass* inherits its attributes and methods from the *superclass*. The subclass can add further attributes and methods and *redefine* methods—as far as the modifiers allow. The subclass forms a *subtype* of the superclass that, according to the *substitution principle*, allows use of instances of the subclass where instances of the superclass are required.

Interface. An interface describes the signatures of a collection of methods. In contrast to a class, no attributes (only constants) and no method bodies are specified. Interfaces are related to abstract classes and can also be in an inheritance relation to each other.

Type is a basis data type such as `int`, a class or an interface.

Interface implementation is a relation between an interface and a class, similar to inheritance. A class can implement any number of interfaces.

Association is a binary relation between classes that is used for the realization of structural information. An association is described by an *association name*, a *role name* for each end, a *cardinality*, and information about the *directions of navigation*.

Cardinality. The cardinality (also called multiplicity) is given for each end of the association. It has the form "0..1", "1" or "*" and describes whether an association in this direction is optional or mandatory, or allows for multiple bindings.

Figure 2.2. Definitions for class diagrams

Figure 2.3 shows a simple class diagram that consists of a class and a comment attached. The explanation in italics and the curved arrows do not belong to the diagram itself. They serve to describe the elements of the diagram.

Usually, the representation of a class is divided into three compartments. In the first compartment, the class name is given.

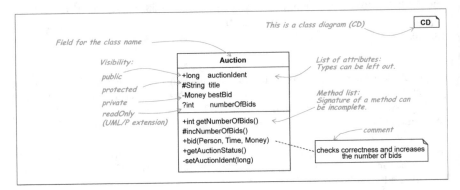

Figure 2.3. Class Auction in the class diagram

2.2.1 Attributes

The middle compartment of a class definition describes the list of attributes that are defined in this class. The information on attributes can be incomplete in many respects. First, an attribute can be indicated with or without its type. In the example in Fig. 2.3, the data types of all four attributes are shown. As we use Java as target language, the default notation for the UML "attribute: Type" has been replaced by the Java-compliant version "Type attribute".

A number of *modifiers* are available for attributes, defining the attribute's properties more precisely. As compact forms, UML provides "+" for public, "#" for protected, and "−" for private in order to describe the visibility of the attribute to foreign classes. "+" allows for general access, "#" for subclasses, and "−" allows access only within the defining class. The UML standard does not contain a fourth visibility declaration "?", which is only offered by UML/P to mark an attribute as *readonly*. An attribute marked in this way is generally readable but can only be modified in subclasses and the class itself. This visibility thus has the same effect as public while reading and protected while modifying. It proves helpful in modeling in order to define access rights even more precisely.

Further modifiers offered by the programming language Java such as static and final for the description of static and nonmodifiable attributes can also be used in the class diagram. In combination, these modifiers serve for defining constants. However, constants are often omitted in class diagrams. An attribute marked static is also called a *class attribute* and can be marked alternatively by an underscore (see Fig. 2.4).

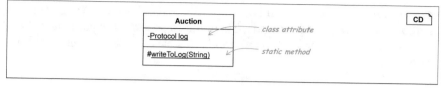

Figure 2.4. Class attribute and static method

UML provides *derived attributes* that are marked with "/" (see Fig. 2.5). In case of a derived attribute, its value can be calculated ("derived") from other attributes of the same or other objects and associations. Usually, the calculation formula is defined in the form of a constraint `attr==`.... UML/P provides OCL that is introduced in Chap. 3 for this purpose.

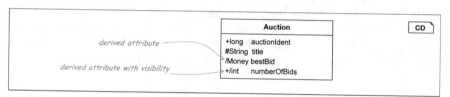

Figure 2.5. Derived attributes

2.2.2 Methods

In the third compartment of a class representation, methods are shown with names, signatures, and if any, modifiers for methods. Here, also the notation in line with Java `Type method (Parameter)` is used instead of the official UML notation `method (Parameter): Type`. While attributes store the state of an object, methods serve for the execution of tasks and data calculation. For this purpose, they use data stored in attributes and call other methods of the same or other objects. Like Java, UML/P also provides methods with variable arity that, e.g., are given in the form `Type method(Type variable ...)`. The access rights for methods can be defined analogously to the visibilities for attributes with "+", "#", and "−".
    Further modifiers for methods are:

- `static` in order to make the method accessible even without an instantiated object
- `final` in order to make the method unchangeable for subclasses
- `abstract` in order to indicate that the method is not implemented in this class

Just like class attributes, UML prefers to outline static methods alternatively by underlining. Constructors are shown like static methods in the form `class(arguments)` and are underlined. If a class contains an abstract method, the class itself is abstract. Then, the class cannot instantiate objects. In subclasses, however, abstract methods of a class can be implemented appropriately.

2.2.3 Inheritance

In order to structure classes into hierarchies, the inheritance relation can be used. If multiple classes with partly corresponding attributes or methods exist, these can be factorized in a common superclass. Figure 2.6 demonstrates this by means of similarities of several messages occurring in the auction system.

If two classes are in an inheritance relation, the *subclass* inherits its attributes and methods from the *superclass*. The subclass can extend the list of attributes and methods as well as *redefine* methods—as far as the modifiers of the superclass permit. At the same time, the subclass forms a *subtype* of the superclass that, according to the *substitution principle*, allows for the use of instances of the subclass where instances of the superclass are required.

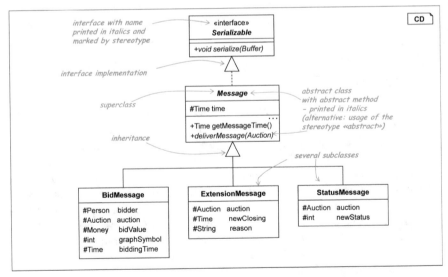

Figure 2.6. Inheritance and interface implementation

In Java, each class (except `Object`) inherits from exactly one superclass. However, a superclass can have many subclasses that in turn can have further subclasses. By using inheritance as a means of structuring, we define an *inheritance hierarchy*. A superclass can be regarded as a generalization of its subclasses, as its attributes and method signatures determine the similarities of all subclasses. If in an inheritance hierarchy the code inheritance is less important than structuring, we speak of a *generalization hierarchy*. Especially for requirements elicitation and the architectural design, generalization plays a vital role to structure the system.

In object-oriented modeling, inheritance is an essential structuring mechanism, but deep inheritance hierarchies should be avoided as inheritance couples the classes and, thus, the code contained. To fully comprehend a subclass, its direct as well as all other superclasses have to be understood.

2.2.4 Interfaces

Java offers a special form of class, the *interface*. An interface consists of a collection of method signatures and constants and is applied especially for defining the usable interface between parts of the system, respectively its components. In Fig. 2.6, the interface `Serializable` is used in order to enforce a certain functionality from all classes that implement this interface.

An interface, like a class, is depicted by a rectangle but marked with the *stereotype* «interface». Objects can be instantiated neither directly from an interface nor from an abstract class. Instead, the given method signatures have to be realized in classes which implement the interface. Furthermore, interfaces can only contain constants but no attributes.

While in Java a class is only allowed to inherit from one superclass, it can implement any number of interfaces. An interface can extend other interfaces and, hence, have a *subtype relation* to these interfaces. In this case, the *subinterface* includes the method signatures defined by the *superinterface* in its own definition and extends these by additional methods. Figure 2.7 shows this by means of an extract of the Java class library.

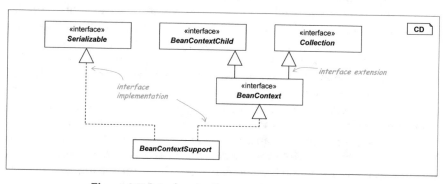

Figure 2.7. Interface implementation and extension

Technically, interfaces and classes as well as inheritance and interface implementation are similar concepts. That is why hereinafter, for the sake of simplification, the term *class* is often used as a generic term for classes and interfaces as well as *inheritance* for the inheritance between classes, the implementation relation between interfaces and classes, and for the subtype relation between interfaces. This simplification is reasonable especially with regard to analysis and early design if the decision of whether a class can be instantiated, is abstract, or becomes an interface as not yet been made.

2.3 Associations

An association has the purpose of relating objects of two classes. Using associations, complex data structures can be formed and methods of neighboring objects can be called. Figure 2.8 describes a part of the auction system with three classes, two interfaces, and five associations in different forms.

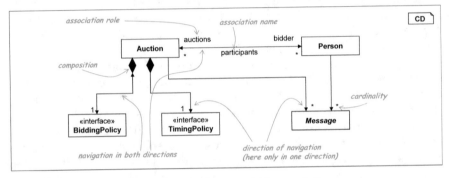

Figure 2.8. Class diagram with associations

Usually, an association has an *association name* and an *association role* for each of the two ends as well as information about the *cardinality* and a description of possible *navigation directions*. Details can also be omitted from the model if they are not important for the representation of the desired facts and if no ambiguity occurs. Association names, e.g., often serve only to distinguish associations, especially between the same classes. In case of a lack of the association or role name, there are standard rules for obtaining a surrogate name as outlined in the next section and further discussed in Sect. 3.3.8.

Just like a class, an association is a modeling concept in the class diagram. During the system's runtime, an association manifests through *links* between the connected objects. The number of links is limited by the association's cardinality. If an association is navigable in one direction, the implementation provides mechanisms to efficiently realize this navigability.

2.3.1 Roles

A role name is used to navigate to objects that are connected through an association or its links. In this way, one can access the auctions from an object of the class `Person` by using the role name `auctions`. If no explicit role name is given, we use the name of the association or that of the target class as role name, provided that these unambiguously describe the intended navigation. In the example in Fig. 2.8, one can access the respective objects from an object of the class `Auction` with the names `biddingPolicy` and `messages`. According to the programming language used for the implementation and the cardinalities given in the class diagram, schematic conversions of the first letter in the name are made. Role names in UML/P always begin with a lower-case letter while class names begin with an upper-case letter.

If both ends of the association are connected to the same class, it is called a *reflexive association*. Reflexive associations enable the realization of a number of design patterns [GHJV94, BMR⁺96] such as a part–whole relationship. In a reflexive association, it is necessary to furnish at least one end with role names. By doing so, a distinction of the participating objects by their roles is possible.

Figure 2.10 shows a reflexive association *fellow* in which each observer is assigned to the bidder he can "observe." Although that leads to a reflexive structure, the recursion depth is limited to 1 because bidders themselves are not observers and observers have direct connection to the bidders. This can be expressed through appropriate OCL conditions (see Chap. 3).

2.3.2 Navigation

During design and implementation activities, the navigation arrows of an association play an important role in a class diagram. The example in Fig. 2.8 describes the access of a `Person` object to its linked `Message` objects. Vice versa, (direct) access from a `Message` object to the `Person`s to which the object is linked is not possible. Therefore, the model allows the distribution of a message, e.g., using broadcasting, to several persons without duplication.

Basically, associations can be uni- or bidirectional. If no explicit arrow direction is given, a bidirectional association is assumed. Formally, the navigation possibilities are regarded as unspecified, and thus, no restriction is given in this situation.

If the fundamental navigability is modeled by the arrow, the role name determines how the association or the linked objects can be addressed. The modifiers `public`, `protected`, and `private` can be used for roles in order to correspondingly restrict the visibility of this navigation.

2.3.3 Cardinality

A cardinality can be indicated at each end of an association; For example, the association `participants` enables a person to participate in multiple auctions and allows various persons to place bids in the same auction, but only exactly one `TimingPolicy` is linked to each auction. The three cardinality specifications "`*`", "`1`", and "`0..1`" permit linking *any number of* objects, *exactly one*, and *at most one* object respectively (see Fig. 2.8). More general cardinalities are of the form m..n or m..*, and they could even be combined in the earlier UML 1.x versions (example 3..7, 9, 11..*). However, especially the three forms mentioned first can be directly implemented. Because of this, we abstain from discussing the general forms of cardinalities here. OCL invariants introduced in Chap. 3 allow for the description and methodical use of generalized cardinalities.

In the UML literature, a distinction is sometimes made between *cardinality* and *multiplicity*. In this case, cardinality designates the number of actual links of an association while multiplicity indicates the scope of potential cardinalities. The entity/relationship models do not make this distinction and consistently use the term cardinality.

2.3.4 Composition

Composition is a special form of association. It is indicated by a filled diamond at one end of the association. In a composition, the subobjects are strongly dependent on the *whole*. In the example in Fig. 2.8, `BiddingPolicy` and `TimingPolicy` are dependent on the `Auction` object in their lifecycle. This means that objects of these types are instantiated together with the `Auction` object and become obsolete at the end of the auction's lifecycle. As `BiddingPolicy` and `TimingPolicy` are interfaces, suitable objects which implement these interfaces are used instead.

An alternative form of representation expresses the nature of the composition of an association better by using graphic containedness instead of a diamond. Figure 2.9 shows two alternatives differing only in details. In class diagram (a), the association character of the composition is highlighted. It also describes navigation possibilities. In class diagram (b), navigation directions are not directly shown but both classes have a role name that describes how to access the components from the containing `Auction` object. The cardinality is indicated in the upper-right corner of the class. Representation (b) seems on the one hand more intuitive but is on the other hand less expressive. It is possible neither to clarify the backwards direction of the navigation nor to add further tags to the composition associations. The cardinality on the composition side is "1" by default but can be adjusted to "0..1", i.e., one object is assigned to at most one composite.

There are a number of interpretation variants regarding the possibility to exchange objects and for the lifecycle of dependent objects in a composite.[2] Thus, a precise definition of a composite's semantics should always be determined project specifically. This can, for instance, be done by stereotypes introduced in Sect. 2.5, which accompany supplementary project- or company-specific, informal explanations or by self-defined stereotypes.

---

[2] A detailed discussion on this topic is, e.g., provided by [HSB99] and [Bre01].

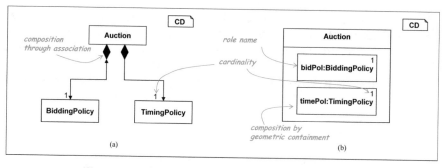

Figure 2.9. Alternative representations of composition

2.3.5 Derived Associations

Besides derived attributes, there are also derived associations in UML/P. They are also marked by a "/" in front of the association's name. An association is considered derived if the set of its links can be calculated ("derived") from other state elements. Other attributes and associations can be used for the calculation. In the example in Fig. 2.10, two associations are given, describing which persons are allowed to place bids in an auction and which persons can observe the behavior of a bidding colleague ("fellow"). The derived association /observers is calculated from these two associations. For this purpose, e.g., the OCL characterization given in Fig. 2.10 (see Chap. 3) can be used.

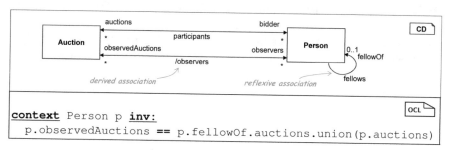

Figure 2.10. Derived association

2.3.6 Tags for Associations

The UML standard offers a variety of additional tags for associations that concretize the properties of associations more precisely. Figure 2.11 contains three tags that are interesting in this context. {ordered} indicates that an association with cardinality "*" allows ordered access. In the case shown, the order of the messages of an auction is relevant. {frozen} indicates that the two associations to the policy objects can no longer be changed after the initialization of an Auction object is completed. In this way, the same policies are available throughout the whole lifetime of an Auction object. {addOnly} models that objects can only be added to the association and that removing them is prohibited. Thus, the model in Fig. 2.11 expresses that messages that have been sent in an auction cannot be withdrawn.

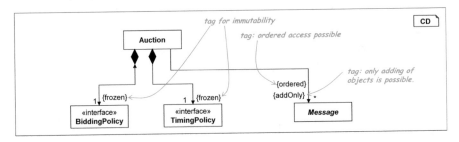

Figure 2.11. Tags for associations

An association that is tagged with {ordered} on one end certainly has to provide a mechanism that allows access according to this order. Associations with the tag {ordered} present a special case of qualified associations.

2.3.7 Qualified Associations

In their most general form, qualified associations provide an opportunity to select a single object from a set of assigned objects by means of a *qualifier*. Figure 2.12 shows several associations qualified in different ways. In addition, it is possible to qualify a composition or to use qualification at both ends of an association.

In the auction system, an object of the class AllData is used in order to store all currently loaded auctions and their participants. The qualified access via the auction identifier auctionIdent is understood as a mapping, and thus, the functionality of the interface Map<long, Auction> is provided, but this does not determine the form in which the qualified association is implemented. During code generation, a transformation into an alternative data structure can be applied or further functionality, e.g., from the NavigableMap, can be added.

As the key for the mapping, the auction identifiers already existing in the auction are used in the example. Analogously, persons can be selected via their name, which is of the type String. However, there is a significant difference between the cases where the qualifier is a type (in the example: String) or an attribute name of the associated class. While in the first case any object or value of the given type can be used as a key, only the actual

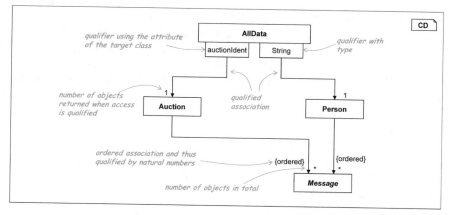

Figure 2.12. Qualified associations

attribute content is legitimate as a qualifier in the second case. This property can be formulated with OCL, which we will introduce in Chapter 3, as follows:

```
context AllData ad inv:
    forall k in long:
        auction.containsKey(k) implies
            auction.get(k).auctionIdent == k
```

While in explicitly qualified associations the type of qualifier can be freely chosen, ordered associations use integer intervals starting with 0.[3]

Wherever an explicit qualifier is used, only one object is reached by the qualified access even if another cardinality is given. Usually, the target object is uniquely identified only in terms of the source object and the qualifier; For example, each auction can store a different message at index 0. The qualifier allIdent is only unique system-wide as it presents at the same time an unambiguous key of the target object. In case the qualifier is not set, access requests have to react appropriately, e.g., with a null pointer as in Java maps or an exception. In an ordered association (tag {ordered}), the qualifier remains implicit and is not indicated in a respective box at the end of the association.

2.4 View and Representation

A class diagram is mainly used to describe the structure and the relations necessary for a certain task. A complete list of all methods and attributes is often obstructive in this case. Instead, only those methods and attributes that are helpful for presenting a "story" should be illustrated. "Story" is a

---

[3] As common in Java, indexing starts with 0.

metaphor that is deliberately used to indicate that a diagram has a focus highlighting significant and omitting unimportant information. Diagrams can, e.g., model different parts of the system or particular system functions.

Hence, a class diagram often represents an incomplete *view* of the whole system. Some classes or associations can be missing. Within classes, attributes and methods can be omitted or presented incompletely. For example, the argument list and the return type of a method can be omitted.

Unfortunately, in general it is not evident from a UML diagram whether the information contained therein is complete or not. Therefore, "©" has been taken over from [FPR01] for the display of complete information. It supplements the representation indicator ". . ."already offered by UML to mark incomplete information.

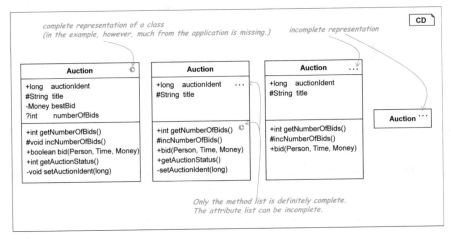

Figure 2.13. Complete class representation

Figure 2.13 shows how the two indicators ". . ." and "©" can be used. The indicators "©" and ". . ." do not have any effect on the class itself but on their representation within the class diagram. A "©" in the class name shows that the attribute as well as the method list is complete. In contrast, the incompleteness indicator ". . ." means that the presentation *can* be incomplete. Due to the dualism between associations and attributes later discussed, it is implied that all associations that can be navigated from this class are also modeled when the attribute list is marked as incomplete.

Both indicators can also be applied to the list of attributes and methods individually. The incompleteness indicator ". . ." acts as default when no indicators are given. This corresponds to the usual assumption that a diagram presents an abstraction of the system.

To explain the use of these indicators precisely, the three model levels illustrated in Fig. 2.14 are to be distinguished: the system itself, the complete

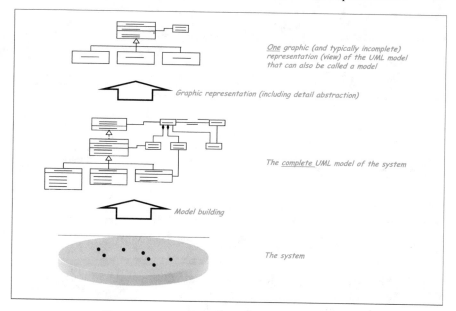

Figure 2.14. Illustration of the three model levels

UML model of the system, and a graphic, incomplete *representation* of the model, e.g., on screen. In most cases, the representation is also called a *view* but is itself a model. Both indicators "©" and "..." describe a relation between the view and the incomplete UML model on which the view is based. As Fig. 2.13 shows, there are a number of different views for the same class. The two marks are thus called *representation indicators*.

If a software system reaches a certain size, a complete class diagram can seem quite overloaded. Due to the many details, the story is concealed rather than presented. Because of this, in software development it is reasonable to work with multiple smaller class diagrams. Necessarily, class diagrams that each show an extract of the system have overlaps. Through these overlaps, the correlation between the individual models is established. Figure 2.15 shows two extracts of the auction system in which the class Auction is represented in different forms. Here, the indicator "..." allows one to explicitly describe that only the information necessary for the respective story is illustrated.

Through *fusion*, a complete class diagram can be obtained from a collection of single class diagrams. As discussed in Sect. 1.4.4, some tools always use a complete class diagram internally as their model and the user gets extracts in the form of views. A fusion of class diagrams is basically a unification of all the class, association, and inheritance relations, whereas in the case of a repeatedly occurring class, attribute and method lists are also consolidated. There are of course a number of consistency conditions to be fol-

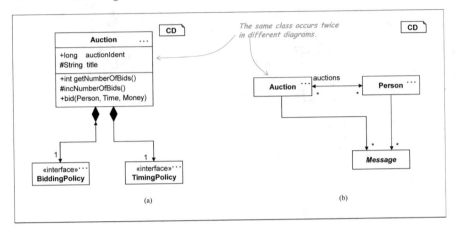

Figure 2.15. Overlapping of class diagrams

lowed. These include conforming types for attributes and methods, compatible navigation roles and multiplicity specifications for associations, as well as prevention of cyclical inheritance relations.

2.5 Stereotypes and Tags

Although UML is designed as a graphic language for the implementation, it has a lot in common with natural languages. UML has a core structure that corresponds to a grammar, and its sentences are built in the form of diagrams. Similar to natural languages, there are mechanisms to extend and adjust the language vocabulary according to the respective necessary requirements. These mechanisms form the basis for project- and company-specific dialects or profiles of UML.

However, the introduction of a new class already extends the available vocabulary, as we can then use this class in other places. From this perspective, programming is a steady expansion of the vocabulary at hand in the system. But while in a programming language the introduction of a new control structure is not possible, UML allows, in a restricted form, the introduction of new kinds of model elements by offering *stereotypes* and *tags* by means of which existing model elements can be specialized and adjusted (see Fig. 2.16).

Without providing an explicit mechanism, UML allows on the one hand for modification of the syntactic appearance through restriction or expansion, but on the other hand also to change the semantics of the language. As UML is designed as a "universal" language, its forms of use can impose a certain bandwidth for its semantics. This so-called *semantic variability* [Grö10] enables project-specific adjustment of the semantics and tools. "Semantic variation points" cannot be described in standard UML itself. This is why, in [GRR10, CGR09], an independent mechanism on the basis of feature diagrams is defined and can be used for profile creation. The generally possible adaptations go far beyond the concept of stereotypes and tags introduced here.

Stereotype. A stereotype classifies model elements such as classes or attributes. Through a stereotype, the meaning of the model element is specialized and can thus, e.g., be treated more specifically in code generation. A stereotype can have a set of tags.

Tag. A tag describes a property of a model element. A tag is denoted as a pair consisting of a *keyword* and *value*. Several such pairs can be combined in a comma-separated list.

Model elements are the (fundamental) parts of UML diagrams. For instance, the class diagram has classes, interfaces, attributes, methods, inheritance relations, and associations as model elements. Tags and stereotypes can be applied to model elements, but they themselves are not model elements.

Figure 2.16. Definition: tag and stereotype

In the previous examples in this chapter, *stereotypes, tags*,[4] and related mechanisms have already been used occasionally. In the class shown in Fig. 2.3, the visibility markers "+", "#", "?", and "−" were introduced. Figure 2.13 shows the two representation indicators "©" and "..." referring to the representation of a view of the model. Figure 2.6 shows the stereotype «interface» that marks a "special" class, namely an interface. The tags {ordered}, {frozen}, and {addOnly} exclusively serve to mark the ends of associations, as shown in the example in Fig. 2.11.

2.5.1 Stereotypes

Figure 2.17 exhibits three kinds of stereotypes. While the stereotype «interface» is provided by default by UML, the two stereotypes on the right «JavaBean» and «Message» are to be defined in the project, tool or framework itself.

Stereotypes are normally indicated in French quotation marks (guillemots) with reversed tips. In principle, each UML model element can be equipped with one or several stereotypes. However, stereotypes are often used in order to assign special properties to classes.

The stereotype «interface» tags an interface, which is regarded as a special form of class. The stereotype «JavaBean» acts as an indicator for the fact that the class tagged provides the functionality required by JavaBeans. The stereotype «Message» is used in the auction project in order to record in

---

[4] In the UML definition, the terms *tagged values* and *properties* are used, being summarized, among others, as *tags* in [Bal99].

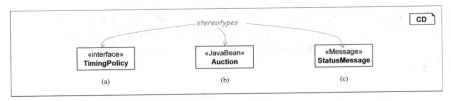

Figure 2.17. Types of stereotypes for classes

compact form that the class tagged is a subclass of `Message` and thus serves for the transfer of information.

Hence, there are a multitude of application possibilities for stereotypes. They can classify model elements, e.g., in order to specify additional properties or functionalities or to impose restrictions. The UML standard offers a metamodel-based and a tabular approach for informal definition of stereotypes. Depending on the stereotype's intention, restrictive conditions can also be formulated more precisely, or mechanisms for a specific code generation can be indicated. The following list shows some application possibilities for stereotypes:

- A stereotype describes syntactic properties of a model element by demanding additional properties or specializing already existing properties.
- A stereotype can describe the representation of a model provided to the user. The indicator "©" can be considered such a special form.
- A stereotype can describe application-specific requirements. The «persistent» stereotype, for example, can specify that objects of this class are persistently stored, although it is not explained how this storage is to happen.
- A stereotype can describe a methodical relation between model elements. For instance, the stereotype «refine» in the UML standard is designed for this purpose.
- A stereotype can reflect the modeler's intention describing how a programmer should use a certain model element. A class can, e.g., be tagged as «adaptive» in order to imply that this class is well suited to extension. Such stereotypes are especially suited for frameworks (see [FPR01]). With stereotypes of the form «Wrapper», the role of a class in a design pattern can be documented.

Of course, there are a number of overlaps between the mentioned and further application options for stereotypes.

To allow the developer to specify properties in a more detailed form, a stereotype can be equipped with a variety of tags. Then, the application of a stereotype in a model element implies that its assigned tags are also defined on the model element.

2.5.2 Tags

Figure 2.18 shows a test class of the auction system marked by a corresponding stereotype. Information on the indicated test and its execution is stored in the form of tags.

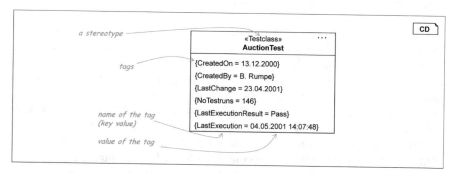

Figure 2.18. Tags applied on a test class

Tags can be attached to basically each model element. In addition, tags, as shown in Fig. 2.18, can be bound to a stereotype and thus applied together with the stereotype to model elements. In the example, the existence of the last three tags is demanded by the use of the stereotype «Testclass», as in the auction project these three tags are assigned to the stereotype.

A tag is usually denoted in the form {name = value}. Principally, strings and numbers are accepted as values. An explicit typing of the tag values would be desirable, but up to now it is supported by neither the UML language standard nor the tools. If the value is not relevant or it is the Boolean value `true`, it can also be omitted; For example, {are_Tests_OK = true} and {are_Tests_OK} are alternative representations. The UML standard [OMG10a] by default offers tags for associations such as {ordered} but also allows one to define new, situation-specific tags.

Even if a tag is added to a class, it considerably differs from an attribute. A tag assigns a property to the model element, while an attribute has an independent value in each instance of the class. Attributes appear at the runtime of a system while tags do not exist there. Tags, however, can have effects on the system if they influence the properties of the model element with regard to its implementation. Among others, tags qualify for the presentation of the following properties:

- The initial value of an attribute can be specified.
- Figure 2.18 shows how project information is presented in the form of tags. This includes the name of the author of a class, the date of the most recent change, the current version number, and suchlike.
- Informal comments can be indicated by tags.

- Designated techniques for data storage or transfer via a network can be filed, e.g., in the model.
- For graphic representation in a tool, a suitable graphic symbol can be assigned to a model element whose file name is stored in the tag.

2.5.3 Introduction of New Elements

The variety of application options for stereotypes and tags makes it nearly impossible to describe the meaning of such elements directly within UML. Hence, when defining a tag or stereotype, usually an informal description is given. By doing so, not only the concrete appearance but especially the intention and the application domains are described.

The most important reason for the introduction of a stereotype is the methodical, tool-supported handling during software development. As there are many different application possibilities for stereotypes, ranging from controlling code generation to documentation of unfinished pieces in the model, one can in general say little about the meaning of stereotypes. Therefore, Table 2.19 only gives a general notation proposal for the definition of stereotypes that can be adjusted and extended by appropriate tools for concrete tasks.

Stereotype «Name»	
Model element	To which element is the stereotype applied? If applicable, pictures can illustrate the concrete form of presentation.
Motivation	What is the purpose of the stereotype? Why is it necessary? How does it support the developer?
Glossary	Concept formation—as far as necessary.
Usage condition	When can the stereotype be applied?
Effect	What is the effect?
Example(s)	Illustrations through application examples, mostly underpinned with diagrams.
Pitfalls	Which special problems can occur?
See also	What other model elements are similar or supplement the stereotype defined here?
Tags	Which tags (name and type) are associated with the stereotype? Which ones are optional? Are there default values? What is the meaning of a tag (unless defined in a separate table)?

(continued on the next page)

(continues Table 2.19.: Stereotype ≪Name≫)

Extendable to	The stereotype can often be applied to a superior model element or a whole diagram in order to be applied element-wise on all subelements.

Table 2.19. Stereotype ≪Name≫

The definition of a stereotype follows the general form of design patterns [GHJV94], recipes [FPR01], and process patterns [Amb98] by discussing motivation, requirements, application form, and effects on an informal basis. However, the template should not be regarded as rigid but, as needed, should be extended as appropriate or shortened by removing unnecessary sections. In principle, the same template can be used for tags.

Tags, however, are basically more easily structured and easier to understand, so that such a detailed template often seems unnecessary.

UML offers a third form of adaptations for model elements. *Constraints* are an instrument for the detailed specification of properties. As constraint languages, OCL introduced in Chap. 3 or informal text is suggested. A constraint is generally given in the form {constraint}. The UML standard by default provides some constraints. These include the already known constraint {ordered} for associations that, however, can also be defined as a tag with Boolean type. This example illustrates in particular that the differences between constraints, tags, and stereotypes cannot always be clarified precisely. It also makes little sense to introduce a stereotype consisting of exactly one tag, as this tag could also be attached directly to a model element. When introducing new stereotypes, tags or constraints, certain creative freedom is given that can be used by the modeler in order to design a suitable model.

3

Object Constraint Language

> Mathematics is a condition
> of all exact insight.
>
> Immanuel Kant

The Object Constraint Language (OCL) is a property-orientated modeling language that is used to model invariants as well as pre- and postconditions of methods. In this book, an extended variant of OCL called OCL/P, which is adjusted to Java, is introduced. After giving an overview of OCL, the logic used and the concepts for modeling container data structures and functions in OCL are described. Considerations regarding the expressiveness of OCL conclude this chapter.

© Springer International Publishing Switzerland 2016
B. Rumpe, *Modeling with UML*, DOI 10.1007/978-3-319-33933-7_3

Graphic notations are especially suited for giving the reader a quick overview of the modeled system. However, in order to achieve lucidity, it is necessary to abstract from details. That is why, e.g., class diagrams are not able to depict many structural and behavioral constraints.

In general, due to their two-dimensional nature, graphic notations are only partly suited for the representation of any kind of constraints for a system. Pure visual programming languages such as VISTA [Sch98a] attempt this, thus revealing an interesting approach but are not widespread. Hence, it can be expected that programming languages in the near future will continue to be text-based or contain tight interlocking of graphic and textual elements.

A textual notation that conceptually leans on known mathematics is reasonable, particularly for constraints. Graphic abbreviations can, of course, be defined for certain kinds of properties that occur frequently. For example, UML provides cardinalities for associations as shortcuts for constraints. Also the type system of a language such as Java can be understood as a restriction regarding a system's properties. [GHK99] introduces visual concepts for further kinds of constraints.

Textual modeling of constraints allows one to model system properties that cannot be described with a graphic notation or often clumsily only. The compactness of a textual notation in contrast to a graphic description technique has the effect that the former is generally regarded as less comprehensible. Therefore, good modeling consists of comprehensible as well as compact and, thus, concisely formulated constraints. Furthermore, it is important to use the formulated constraints constructively in the software engineering process. Therefore, tools such as a parser or a checker for type correctness are helpful. In addition, the executability and, hence, the automated verifiability of a constraint is an essential prerequisite for the use of a constraint language for test definition.

The *Object Constraint Language* (OCL) is defined by the UML standard and provides a textual notation that can be used for the definition of *constraints* in the form of invariants as well as for pre- and postconditions of methods. Furthermore, [OMG10b] gives the precise definition of its syntax and meaning. [WK98] presents an introduction to OCL.

The history of the definition of programming and specification languages shows that it is very difficult to design a generally satisfying and sufficiently well-defined language on the first attempt. OCL offered in the UML standard is not derived from a widespread programming language. For this very reason, it has a rather unusual syntactic appearance that exacerbates the difficult access to OCL for many developers. Hence, a syntactic form of OCL that is derived from Java was proposed in [Rum02b] . This chapter contains an extension of that proposal, which in the following is called OCL/P or short OCL.

Apart from the adaption of the syntactic form of OCL, a number of conceptual improvements have been integrated in the form of OCL/P as presented here. Some of these improvements have already been described in [CKM+02], and some have been taken over from functional programming languages.

After introducing the reader to OCL/P in the next section, technical details of OCL are informally discussed in the following sections. This includes the presentation of a reasonable logic for OCL, the introduction of containers, and a demonstration of how operations are modeled in OCL. Finally, the expressiveness of OCL is studied, and OCL is compared with the complete algebraic specification language Spectrum [BFG+93]. Appendix C.3 presents the context-free syntax of OCL. The essential differences between the OCL standard and OCL/P are introduced here as well as their motivations are summarized in Appendix C.3.2.

3.1 Overview of OCL/P

Figure 3.1 explains the most important expressions in OCL.

Constraint. A constraint is a Boolean statement about a system. It describes a property that a system or a result shall have. Its interpretation always yields one of the logical values `true` or `false`.

Context. A constraint is embedded in a context. Thus, a constraint includes statements about this context. The context is defined by a set of *names* used in the constraint and their signatures. That includes names of classes, methods, and attributes of the model and especially variables explicitly introduced in the context of a constraint.

Interpretation of a constraint is carried out based on a concrete object structure. The variables introduced in the context are assigned values or objects.

Invariant describes a property which must hold in a system at each (observed) point in time. The points in time of observation can be restricted in order to allow time-limited violations, e.g., during the execution of a method.

Precondition of a method characterizes the properties that need to be valid to ensure that the method produces a defined and correct result. If the precondition does not hold, nothing is known about the result.

Postcondition of a method describes which properties hold after the execution of the method has finished. Here, it is possible to refer to objects in the state which was valid directly before the method call (at the "time" of the interpretation of the precondition). Postconditions are interpreted by means of two object structures showing the situations before and after the method call.

Method specification is a pair of pre- and postconditions.

Query is a method offered by the implementation whose call does not affect the system's state. New objects may be created as a result of the call. However, these must not be connected to the state of the system by links. So, queries do not have side-effects and can be used in OCL constraints.

Figure 3.1. Term definitions for OCL

The abilities of OCL for describing constraints are demonstrated in this section by means of examples from the auction system. These and further OCL constructs are explained in detail in the following sections. The complete OCL grammar can be found in Appendix C.3.

3.1.1 The Context of a Constraint

One of the prominent properties of OCL constraints is their embedding in a context consisting of UML models. Usually, this context is given by a class diagram. The class diagram in Fig. 3.2 provides such a context in the form of two classes and a number of attributes partly dependent on each other, modeling a part of the auction system. These attribute dependencies can be defined by means of OCL/P constraints.

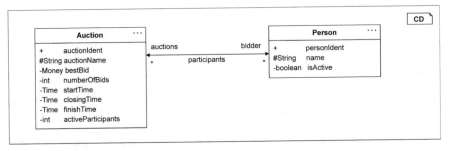

Figure 3.2. Part of the auction system

A simple constraint, for example, is the following: an auction always starts before it is completed. This constraint is described by explicitly including an `Auction` object in the context. The explicitly stated context of an OCL constraint consists of one or more objects whose name is declared by referencing them in the context of the constraint. The constraint uses a method of the Java class `Time` for comparison:

```
context Auction a inv:
  a.startTime.lessThan(a.closingTime)
```
`OCL`

This constraint requires that the signature of class `Auction` is provided in the context. The variable name `a` is locally introduced by the `context` statement and acts like a variable definition. An alternative is to explicitly *import* variables, for example, if they have already been defined in another constraint or diagram. Using this *importing* form of the context, OCL constraints are combined and connected to object diagrams in Chap. 4. By doing so, the objects named in the object diagrams can be used explicitly in the OCL constraints. Thus, the contexts defined by `import` are discussed in more detail in Chap. 4. The following context, for instance, characterizes a property of the `Auction` object `a` that might come from an object diagram:

```
import Auction a inv:                                    OCL
    a.startTime.lessThan(a.closingTime)
```

Objects connected in associations can be included by using navigation expressions. The expression `a.bidder` provides a set of persons, i.e., a value of the type `Set<Person>`, whose size can be determined with the attribute `size`. To ensure that the number of active participants is not larger than the number of persons actually participating in an auction, the following constraint is formulated:

```
context Auction a inv Bidders1:                          OCL
    a.activeParticipants <= a.bidder.size
```

As this example shows, a constraint can be given its own name (like `Bidders1`) so that it is possible to refer to it at another point. Navigation expressions can be chained. To navigate along an association, the role names opposite to the initial object are used. If the association `participants` is implemented properly, the following constraint is correct:

```
context Auction a inv:                                   OCL
    a in a.bidder.auctions
```

Refining the second last constraint `Bidders1`, it is now required that the number of active participants of an auction be the same as the number of its assigned persons whose attribute `isActive` is set:

```
context Auction a inv Bidders2:                          OCL
    a.activeParticipants == { p in a.bidder | p.isActive }.size
```

The *set comprehension* used here is a convenient extension not present in the OCL standard. It is further discussed in several forms later. If in a context only the class is defined instead of an explicit name, the name `this` is used by default. In this case, there is direct access also to attributes. This is shown by the following condition in which logic conjunctions are used as well:[1]

```
context Auction inv:                                     OCL
    startTime.greaterThan(Time.now()) implies
        numberOfBids == 0
```

This constraint is equivalent to the version with explicit use of the name `this`:

```
context Auction inv:                                     OCL
    this.startTime.greaterThan(Time.now()) implies
        this.numberOfBids == 0
```

---

[1] Auctions can already exist but may not be open yet in the described auction system.

The context of *closed constraints*, such as the following, is empty. A context can always be replaced by quantifiers that are defined from the context over all existing objects of the class. The following constraint with empty context is, thus, equivalent to the previous one:

```
inv:
    forall a in Auction:
        a.startTime.greaterThan(Time.now()) implies
            a.numberOfBids == 0
```

3.1.2 The `let` Construct

Intermediate results can be assigned to an auxiliary variable using the `let` construct in order to reuse them in the body of the construct, possibly several times. The subsequent constraint demands that the initial and final time of each auction obey the right relation. Here, the if-then-else known from Java is used in the compact form `. ? . : .` as shown here:

```
context Auction a inv Time1:
    let min = startTime.lessThan(closingTime)
                    ? startTime : closingTime
    in
        min == startTime
```

The `let` construct introduces locally usable variables and operations which are only visible within the expression. The type of such a variable is inferred by the given expression on the right but can also be defined explicitly.

In a `let` clause, several local variables and operations can be defined. A definition can use all variables defined before.[2]

To ensure that, in the auction system, the latest possible auction end obeys the right relation with the initial time, the following can be formulated:

```
context Auction a inv Time2:
    let min1 = a.startTime.lessThan(a.closingTime)
                    ? a.startTime : a.closingTime;
        min2 = min1.lessThan(a.finishTime) ? min1 : a.finishTime
    in
        min2 == a.startTime
```

---

[2] As described in [CK01], the simultaneous (recursive) use of a previously defined element increases the complexity of the typing in the body of the definition (compare Gofer [Jon96] and SML [MTHM97]). Furthermore, a recursive equation in general has multiple solutions in a specification language such as OCL (compare Sect. 3.5). As recursive definitions also become possible through the basic object system, the possibility of a recursive definition is relinquished.

Here, two intermediate results with the same structure but different parameters are defined. To simplify this, the `let` construct can also be used to define auxiliary functions. The following example illustrates the usage of an auxiliary function for calculating the minimum of timestamps and is, thus, equivalent to the constraint `Time2`:

```
context Auction a inv Time3:
   let min(Time x, Time y) = x.lessThan(y) ? x : y
   in
      min(a.startTime, min(a.closingTime, a.finishTime))
            == a.startTime
```

When defining an auxiliary function, arguments have to be specified together with their types, as in usual Java methods. Operations are given in functional style that, at the same time, corresponds to object-oriented style for methods of the same object, as known from Java.

If an auxiliary function is required more often, it is expedient to place it in a class of the underlying model or in a library specially provided for this purpose. Such a library is discussed in Sect. 3.4.4.

Intermediate variables and auxiliary functions can also be regarded as attributes or methods, respectively, of an anonymous class that, in case of a `let` construction, is implicitly included into the context. This is further explained in Sect. 3.4.3 by means of an example after having introduced the method specifications. A special case, which is further discussed in the next section, is, however, the handling of undefined results. The `let` construct allows undefined intermediate results and can provide a defined overall result if intermediate results do not occur there.[3] For instance, the following holds:

```
inv:
      5 == (let x = 1/0 in 5)
```

3.1.3 Conditional Expression

In contrast to an imperative programming language, a specification language has no control structures for steering the control flow. However, some operations oriented towards imperative constructs are offered. This, e.g., includes the conditional expression `if-then-else` or the equivalent form `.?.:.` already used in condition `Time1`. On the basis of the first argument, it is determined which of the two other arguments is evaluated and accepted as the result of the conditional expression. Contrary to imperative conditional expression, the `then` and the `else` path always need to be included. Both paths contain expressions of the same data type. A conditional expression then has the data type of the first expression; i.e., the second expression has to be a subtype of the first expression's type.

---

[3] If the OCL condition is evaluated, the demand-oriented ("lazy") evaluation of the expressions in `let` constructs is to be used.

A special form of conditional expression allows the treatment of type conversions such as those occasionally occurring in case of subtype hierarchies. For this, OCL/P offers a type-safe construction using a combination of a type conversion and a conditional expression regarding its convertibility. According to Fig. 2.6, the bidder can be extracted from the bids as follows:

```
context Message m inv:
    let Person p =
            typeif m instanceof BidMessage then m.bidder else null
    in ...
```

Equivalently, a more compact form of the case differentiation can be chosen, as follows:

```
context Message m inv:
    let Person p = m instanceof BidMessage ? m.bidder : null
    in ...
```

In both forms, the type of the variable m is, in addition to a normal conditional expression, cast to BidMessage in the then path of the case distinction. Variable m temporarily switches to this type and thus allows for the selection m.bidder. In contrast to the type conversion with (BidMessage) common in Java, type safety is guaranteed with this construction; i.e., a conversion error leading to an exception in Java and to an undefined value in OCL cannot arise.

3.1.4 Basic Data Types

The basic data types are those known from Java: boolean, char, int, long, float, byte, short, and double. Also, operators known from Java such as + or − are used in OCL/P. Table 3.3 contains a list of the infix and prefix operators available in OCL/P, including their priorities.[4] This list also contains the subset of the operators of Table B.7 which may be used in OCL as they have no side-effects. Therefore, the increment operators ++ and −− as well as all assignments are excluded. Newly introduced are the Boolean operators implies and <=>, which denote implications and equivalence, and the postfix operators @pre and **.

Like in Java the data type String is not a primitive data type but as a class available by default. From the Java class libraries and packages java.util and java.lang, a number of such classes are available.

Among the primitive data types, the type of logical values boolean has a special role because it is also used for interpreting OCL conditions. As in

---

[4] The priorities are taken over from Java, thus the new operators implies and <=> contain a decimal point in priorities.

Priority	Operator	Associativity	Operand(s), meaning
14	@pre	Left	Value of the expression in the precondition
	**	Left	Transitive closure of an association
13	+, -, ~	Right	Numbers
	!	Right	Boolean: negation
	(type)	Right	Type conversion (cast)
12	*, /, %	Left	Numbers
11	+, -	Left	Numbers, String (only +)
10	<<, >>, >>>	Left	Shifts
9	<, <=, >, >=	Left	Comparisons
	instanceof	Left	Type comparison
	in	Left	Element of
8	==, !=	Left	Comparison
7	&	Left	Numbers, Boolean: strict and
6	^	Left	Numbers, Boolean: xor
5			Left	Numbers, Boolean: strict or
4	&&	Left	Boolean logic: and
3	||	Left	Boolean logic: or
2.7	implies	Left	Boolean logic: implies
2.3	<=>	Left	Boolean logic: equivalence
2	? :	Right	Conditional expression (if-then-else)

Table 3.3. Priorities of the OCL Operators

(classic) logic, only two logical values are used, and as the treatment of non-terminating or interrupting interpretations causes some problems, the correlation between the data type `boolean` and the logic which is to be used in OCL is studied in detail in Sect. 3.2.

3.2 The OCL Logic

For practical usage of a constraint language, it is important to define the underlying logic correctly. Therefore, in this section we first introduce potential variants by means of an example and then define the OCL logic.

3.2.1 The Boolean Conjunction

In Java, an expression of the type `boolean` can have three different "values": it can evaluate towards the defined values `true` or `false` or have an *undefined pseudovalue*. This pseudovalue models that an exception is thrown or the calculation does not terminate. There are several possibilities to handle this third value. This can be discussed very well on the basis of possible semantics of the Boolean conjunction (`&&`). Figure 3.4 shows five distinct possibilities to define the conjunction. In this figure, it is assumed that the pseudovalue is indicated by undef. The five given interpretations for the conjunction each differ in their handling of this pseudovalue.

a ∧ b	true	false
true	true	false
false	false	false

(a) Classical two-valued logic

a & b	true	false	undef
true	true	false	undef
false	false	false	undef
undef	undef	undef	undef

(b) strict evaluation, like Java &

a and b	true	false	undef
true	true	false	undef
false	false	false	false
undef	undef	false	undef

(c) parallel evaluation, Kleene logic

a && b	true	false	undef
true	true	false	undef
false	false	false	false
undef	undef	undef	undef

(d) sequential, like Java &&

a ∧ b	true	false	undef
true	true	false	false
false	false	false	false
undef	false	false	false

(e) lifting: undef is used in the same way as false

Figure 3.4. Interpretations of the OCL Conjunction

If the classic two-valued case 3.4(a) should be taken, the logical values of the logic and the Boolean data type need to be strictly separated from each other. The CIP [BBB+85] example shows that this leads to a duplication of the logic operators and, hence, becomes unwieldy in practice. Beside this approach, there are four sensible possibilities to extend the && operator to handle the undefined value.

For the logic, mapping the undefined value onto the logical value false is the easiest, as this de facto leads to the two-valued logic again (case 3.4(e)). Specifications as well as reasoning become particularly easy as a third case does not exist and, thus, need not be taken into consideration in conditional expressions. This is, at least, a remarkable reduction from nine to four cases that need to be taken into consideration. This semantics for the conjunction is quite comfortable for the specification but, unfortunately, cannot be fully implemented because one needs to determine whether a calculation does not terminate and then assign false as the output.[5]

In contrast, all other semantics in 3.4(b,c,d) can be implemented and also find practical utilization. The *strict* implementation (b) already provides an undefined value when one of the arguments is undefined. This corresponds to the Java operator &, always evaluating both arguments. However, this operator is slow as well as inappropriate for many conditions, as in Java the first expression often serves as a guard for the second one, which is to be evaluated only when the first one results true. This order of evaluation manifests

---

[5] The termination problem, however, is undecidable.

itself in the asymmetric sequential conjunction that can be used with the Java operator `&&` while programming. For example, for an `Auction` object a,

```
a.bestBid != null && a.bestBid.value > 0
```
OCL ⬛

is a Java expression that can always be evaluated. For programming purposes, the sequential conjunction is a good compromise between evaluation efficiency and expressiveness. Its severe disadvantage, however, is that

```
x && y   <=>   y && x
```
OCL ⬛

is not always valid and, thus, refactoring (i.e., a transformation meeting the laws of logic) is considerably aggravated.

In the UML standard, the Kleene logic is suggested for the conjunction's semantics (case (c)) and formalized in HOL in, e.g., [BW02a, BW02b]. There it is assumed that, if one argument evaluates to `false`, then the whole expression evaluates to `false`. Kleene logic has the very pleasing advantage that fundamental laws of Boolean logic such as the commutativity and associativity of the conjunction remain valid.[6] But the conjunction can only be implemented with great effort in this logic, by evaluating both arguments in parallel. If an evaluation terminates with `false`, the other evaluation needs to be stopped. Unfortunately, this form of implementation is computationally intensive for programming languages such as Java.

3.2.2 Two-Valued Semantics and Lifting

Due to the considerations in the previous section, the following questions arise for the semantics of the expressions of a specification language:

1. Which semantics is chosen for the logic operators?
2. Which Boolean laws hold or are violated?
3. Does the official (denotational) semantics correspond to the evaluation strategy implemented in a tool? What effects do differences have?

For the abstract specification of functionality, the two-valued logic seems to be the best. It alone does not force the modeler to perpetually consider the third, undefined case. This is why *lifting* is introduced for the semantics of OCL constraints when it comes to handling undefined subexpressions.

Lifting means that an OCL expression is interpreted as not fulfilled also when it evaluates the pseudovalue `undef`. As a consequence, the OCL operator `&&` cannot be implemented and correct code generation from OCL expressions is not possible. This poses a problem for test procedures and simulations, but it shows that in practice this problem is only rarely of significance as there are only two kinds of situations in the programming language Java

---

[6] The OCL standard [OMG10b] describes only in the noncommittal, informative appendix that the Kleene logic should apply.

where the pseudovalue `undef` manifests itself. On the one hand, exceptions are thrown, on the other hand it can be a nonterminating calculation.

In the first case, this exception can be caught and evaluated as `false`. The constraint a&&b, for example, can be implemented with the following piece of code:

```Java
boolean res;
try {
  res = a;                       // Evaluation of expression a
} catch(Exception e) {
  res = false;
}
if(res) {                        // Efficiency: only evaluate b if a is true
  try {
    res = b;                     // Evaluation of expression b
  } catch(Exception e) {
    res = false
  }
}
```

Nonterminating calculations occur relatively rarely in object-oriented practice. Apparently, nonterminating calculations such as infinite while-loops can be avoided quite easily. Due to the restrictedness of the resources in Java, less apparent situations such as nonterminating recursions usually also lead to exceptions (e.g., stack overflow). Thus, all in all, it can be observed that there exists an evaluation strategy for OCL expressions that is sufficient for pragmatic purposes and nearly identical to the two-valued semantics. This is why, after this digression into the evaluability of OCL expressions, the semantics for Boolean operators will be determined according to the truth tables in Fig. 3.5. In accordance with [HHB02], we demand use of a two-valued logic for OCL.

!a	
!true	false
!false	true
!undef	true

a ^ b	true	false	undef
true	false	true	true
false	true	false	false
undef	true	false	false

a && b	true	false	undef
true	true	false	false
false	false	false	false
undef	false	false	false

a || b	true	false	undef
true	true	true	true
false	true	false	false
undef	true	false	false

a implies b	true	false	undef
true	true	false	false
false	true	true	true
undef	true	true	true

a <=> b	true	false	undef
true	true	false	false
false	false	true	true
undef	false	true	true

Figure 3.5. The Boolean operators

For this semantics definition, there is an alternative explanatory approach, namely the usage of a *lifting operator* ↑ that is applied to each argument of a Boolean operator.

This operator ↑ has the interesting property to lift ↑undef==false while the normal Boolean values ↑true==true and ↑false==false remain unchanged.

Thus, a&&b corresponds to the expression (↑a) && (↑b), and the Boolean operators remain two-valued. The lifting operator ↑ must not be provided explicitly in OCL as it can be added implicitly by a parser. However, the lifting operator cannot be implemented completely. A workaround uses catch exceptions as described above.

3.2.3 Control Structures and Comparisons

Some of the operators provided by OCL/P describe comparisons between objects or values. Like the data type boolean, all data types contain an undefined pseudovalue. Therefore, comparison operators are extended by this undefined value. For reasons of convenience, it is determined that all OCL constructs on undefined values—despite the already described logic operators, the two case distinctions and the let construct—are always strict, i.e., always yield undefined if they receive an undefined argument. In particular, a==b is undefined when a or b are undefined. This also means that, even if both expressions a and b are undefined, they are not equal. Figure 3.6 shows the definition of the conditional expression.

if then else		
if true	then a else b	a
if false	then a else b	b
if undef	then a else b	b

? :		
true	? a : b	a
false	? a : b	b
undef	? a : b	b

Figure 3.6. Conditional expression in two syntactical forms

Each of the two arguments of the then-else expression can have undefined values that, however, have no effects if the other expression is chosen and evaluated. Also, the Boolean condition of the case differentiation may be undefined. In this case, the else expression is evaluated.

The comparison == used in OCL is, with the above-described convention, identical to the comparison == available in Java. On primitive data types it compares values, and on object classes it compares the objects's identity. Furthermore, the comparison equals() offered by the data model is provided as a normal query in OCL. The usage of comparisons on containers is discussed in the following section.

The strictness of the comparison == on all data types has a consequence that is not so convenient for the logic but which improves the handling of the undefined pseudovalue. In general, it does not hold that

$$(a \ == \ b) \ \ || \ \ (a \ != \ b), \qquad\qquad \boxed{\text{OCL}}$$

as if one of the two expressions is undefined, both sides of the disjunction evaluate to false. But in this way, undefined values can be recognized in the OCL logic because ! (a==a) is exactly true when a is undefined. This effect is used as a characterizing property for the defined operator introduced in Sect. 3.3.11.

3.3 Container Data Structures

In OCL, navigation via associations is an essential concept for the compact description of constraints. Starting from a single object, a *set* or a *list* of reachable objects can be described by a navigation expression, and certain properties can be attached to its elements.

These two data structures serve for the management of collections of objects and are therefore summarized under the expression *collection* in OCL. Quite similar to the generic types from Java, OCL/P offers three *type constructors* for containers, which are summarized in Fig. 3.7. However, OCL does not provide the full genericity of Java [Bra04].

Set<X> describes sets over a data type X. On these sets, the usual operators such as unification or addition are provided. For the type X, each primitive data type, class, and container type can be used. For checking equality, value comparison for primitive data types and object identity for classes are used, although objects of selected classes such as String can use and overwrite the comparison equals() and, thus, also provide a value comparison via their attributes.

List<X> describes ordered lists and their viable operations. List<X> allows the administration of its objects in linear order, starting with the index 0.

Collection<X> is a supertype for both above-mentioned types Set<X> and List<X>. It provides their common functionality.

Figure 3.7. Type constructors of OCL

Comparison of containers requires a binary operation executing an equality test on the elements. If the elements are primitive data types or again containers, the comparison == is used for the elements. But if the elements are objects, the comparison equals() is used. This is equivalent to a value comparison for basic data types and containers[7] as well as to a comparison

---

[7] In OCL, containers have no object identity. The OCL comparison ==, thus, corresponds to the Java operation equals() on containers.

of object identity on objects in most cases. For special types—Strings, for instance—equals(), however, is overwritten so that a value comparison is offered.[8]

The subtype relation of Set<X> and List<X> towards Collection<X> allows for use of values of types Set<X> or List<X> instead of values of type Collection<X> for any type X. Containers can be nested in more complex type structures. So the following data types are, for instance, allowed in OCL/P:

```
inv:
  let Set<int>           si  = { 1, 3, 5 };
       Set<Set<int>>     ssi = { {}, {1}, {1,2}, si };
       List<Set<int>> lsp = List{ {1}, {} }
  in ...
```

The type constructor Set<X> allows to use an arbitrary data type for the element type X. However, experience shows that nested data structures strongly increase the complexity of a model and should, hence, be used only to a very limited extent. This complexity can be isolated, e.g., by embedding complex data structures in classes specifically designed for this purpose. In OCL/P, nested container structures are avoided as navigation along associations only has flattened container structures as results. For details, see Sect. 3.3.8.

Regarding containers, OCL/P shows some differences compared with the OCL standard. Instead of the original Sequence from OCL, the type constructor List was taken over from Java. Furthermore, a type constructor for multisets (also called bags) was waived. This was done for mere pragmatic reasons as practice has shown that multisets are a rarely used concept that rather contributes to the increase of complexity.

3.3.1 Representation of Sets and Lists

In OCL, a class (or an interface) can be used as a type and, at the same time, as extension, i.e., the set of all currently existing objects; For example,

```
inv:
  Auction.size < 1700
```

describes the maximum number of simultaneous auctions in a system. So, the expression Auction indicates the set of all currently existing objects of the type Auction. This set has the type Set<Auction>. It contains all objects belonging to the class Auction or its subclass. Only object-valued

---

[8] The redefinition of equals() must be used by the modeler only with great precaution as it has considerable effects on the OCL logic. However, practice has proven that responsible handling leads to specification and implementation advantages.

classes and interfaces may be used for building an extension; Neither primitive data types nor container types constitute extensions.

A second possibility for the description of sets is direct enumeration in the form `Set{...}` with a list of object expressions separated by commas. `Set{}`, e.g., is the empty set, `Set{8,5,6,8}` a set of three integers, and `Set{"text",(Auction)a}` consists of a string and an `Auction` object. Optionally, the indicator `Set` can also be left out, as `{}`, `{8,5,6,8}`, and `{"text",(Auction)a}` describe the same sets.

As the last example shows, type correctness has to be guaranteed when enumerating sets with heterogeneous (i.e., differently typed) arguments. In explicitly enumerated sets, the type of the first argument `X` determines the type of the whole expression `Set<X>`. All other arguments of the list have to be subtypes of `X`. If the explicit enumeration is heterogeneous, the desired result type can be enforced by explicitly adding the of the element type in the set comprehension: `Set<Object>{"text",(auction)a}` is typed with `Set<Object>`.

The empty set can also be typed, e.g., as `Set<Person>{}`. If no type is indicated, the elementary type is left open, i.e., an anonymous type variable is assumed.

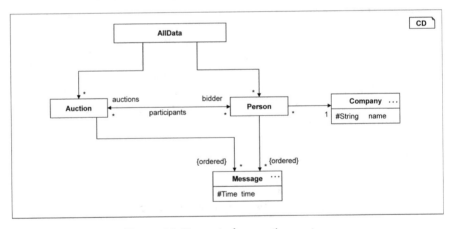

Figure 3.8. Excerpt of an auction system

The extract of the auction system in Fig. 3.8 serves as a basis for further OCL examples. Using the extensions of the class `AllData` and a one-element set, the following condition describes that the class `AllData` instantiates exactly one object, i.e., represents a *Singleton* [GHJV94]:

```
context AllData ad inv AllDataIsSingleton:
  AllData == {ad}
```

3.3.2 Set and List Comprehensions

In contrast to the OCL standard, OCL/P offers a comprehensive number of possibilities for property-oriented and enumerating description of sets and lists. These were taken over from the functional programming language Haskell [Hut07]. They allow compact handling of containers and have a precise and elegant semantics. As for sets generally, the following transformation for a correct body *"characterization"* applies (the description is explained for lists):[9]

```
Set{ characterization } == List{ characterization }.asSet        OCL
```

Enumerations of lists of integers and characters can be described by means of List{n..m}. Examples are:

inv:
```
                                                                 OCL
List{-3..3}       == List{-3,-2,-1,0,1,2,3};
List{1..1}        == List{1};
List{9..5}        == List{};
List{1,3..9}      == List{1,3,5,7,9};
List{9,8..5}      == List{9,8,7,6,5};
List{'a'..'c'}    == List{'a','b','c'};
List{3..5,7..9}   == List{3,4,5,7,8,9};
List{3..(2+5)}    == List{3,4,5,6,7};
```

In an enumeration, the first as well as the last element in the list are included. Lists can use increments. Enumerations and single elements can be used in a mixed way. The given limits do not necessarily have to be constants.

While enumerations are only suited for the enumeration types numbers and characters, list comprehensions can be used more generally. The common syntax of a list comprehension is in the form

```
List{ expression | characterization }                            OCL
```

Here, new variables are defined in the characterization (right) that can be used in the expression (left). For this purpose, the characterization consists of multiple, comma separated variable definitions and filter conditions. The expressiveness of such list comprehension lies precisely in the combination of the three mechanisms introduced below: the *generator*, the *filter*, and the *local variable definition*.

A *generator* v in list lets a new variable v vary over a list list. In this way, e.g., square numbers can be described:

inv:
```
                                                                 OCL
List{ x*x | x in List{1..5} } == List{1,4,9,16,25}
```

---

[9] *characterization* is a scheme variable (a place holder) for an OCL subexpression. Scheme variables are usually written in natural language.

The type of variable x equals the element type of the list over which the variation takes place. It can, however, explicitly be defined, as in the case of other local variable definitions. In the following example, messages are converted into milliseconds:

```
context Auction a inv:
  let List<long> tlist =
         List{ m.time.asMsec() | Message m in a.message }
  in ...
```

The *filter* describes a restriction on a list of elements. Such a filter evaluates to a truth value which decides whether an element is included in a list. In its pure form, without combination with a generator, its characterization is as follows:

```
List{ expr | condition } ==
         if condition then List{ expr } else List{}
```

In combination with a generator, filters can be described to select sublists; For example, a list with odd square numbers can be described with:[10]

```
inv:
  List{ x*x | x in List{1..8}, !even(x) } == List{1,9,25,49}
```

Analogously, a list of messages can be filtered by timeframes:

```
context Auction a inv MessageTimes:
  let List<long> tlist = List{ m.time.asMsec()
         | m in a.message, m.time.lessThan(a.startTime) }
  in ...
```

For further convenience of the description, intermediate results can be calculated and assigned to local variables. The definition of a new variable has the form v=expression and is considered the same as the introduction of a new variable by means of the let construct. The type of the variable can be defined explicitly, or it is inferred from the type of the expression as in case of the let construct. The set of all odd square numbers can therewith also be described as follows:

```
inv:
  List{ y | x in List{1..8}, int y = x*x, !even(y) } ==
         List{1,9,25,49}
```

The definition MessageTimes can, thus, be modified to

```
context Auction a inv MessageTimes2:
  let List<long> tlist = List{ t | m in a.message,
              t = m.time.asMsec(), t < a.startTime.asMsec() }
  in ...
```

---

[10] The method even comes from the OCL library introduced in Sect. 3.4.4.

This example also shows how helpful the combination of filters, generators, and variable definitions is. Multiple generators can also be used for example for the generation of concatenated strings:

```
inv:
  List{ z+"?" | x in List{"school","team","play"},
                y in List{"mate","grounds"},
                String z = x+y,
                z != "teamgrounds" }
  ==
  List{ "schoolmate?", "schoolgrounds?",
        "teammate?",
        "playmate?",    "playgrounds?" }
```

Here, the order of the emerging list is precisely determined. The generators are varied from the right to the left. Thus, all elements of the right generators are iterated first. In addition, the characterizations being further to the right, typically constraints, are allowed to access the variables of the characterizations on the left, i.e., generators and local definitions.

Up to now, only list-valued data types have been discussed for generators, but a generator can also be set-valued and yet used in a list comprehension. The chronology of the list, however, is not uniquely defined for the user:

```
inv:
  let la = List{ a | a in Set{1,2} }
  in la == List{1,2} || la  == List{2,1}
```

The ambiguity of this description has the advantage that certain degrees of freedom remain for a realization. But it is essential that, despite the ambiguity of the description of the result, the result is determined, i.e., the same OCL expression always has the same value in the same context. According to this convention the following applies:

```
inv:
  let la = List{ a | a in Set{1,2} };
      lb = List{ a | a in Set{1,2} }
  in la == lb
```

When using a set as a generator of a list comprehension, a conversion by means of asList is implicitly conducted. As a consequence, the following property can be regarded as characterizing:

```
inv:
  List{ a | a in Set{1,2} } ==
    Set{ a | a in Set{1,2} }.asList
```

In the opposite case, list generators are converted to sets. This conversion, however, is unambiguous. As each class represents its extension at the same time in OCL, access to all objects of a class is particularly easy. So, the set of all running or completed auctions can be described by

```
inv:                                                          OCL
   let Set<Auction> sa =
      Set{ a | a in Auction, Time.now().lessThan(a.startTime) }
   in ...
```

As the combination of a generator `a in Auction` with a filter occurs particularly often, a shortcut applies where the first generator can already be defined on the left side:

```
inv:                                                          OCL
   let Set<Auction> sa =
         Set{ a in Auction | Time.now().lessThan(a.startTime) }
   in ...
```

3.3.3 Set Operations

The operations available for sets are listed in Fig. 3.9. This signature outlines an integration of sets known from the Java realization and the functionality offered by the OCL standard, and is defined as a collection of method signatures. When operator names with the same functionality were contradictory, Java names were chosen. In OCL, the operators `size`, `isEmpty`, and `asList` can, like attributes, be written without brackets because a query without arguments can be treated as an attribute. Notation as a query with brackets is also possible due to the compatibility with Java.

```
Set<X>   add(X o);                                   Signature
Set<X>   addAll(Collection<X> c);
boolean  contains(X o);
boolean  containsAll(Collection<X> c);
int      count(X o);
boolean  isEmpty;
Set<X>   remove(X o);
Set<X>   removeAll(Collection<X> c);
Set<X>   retainAll(Collection<X> c);
Set<X>   symmetricDifference(Set<X> s);
int      size;
X        flatten;                    // only for Collection type X
List<X>  asList;
```

Figure 3.9. Signature of type `Set<X>`

All set operators, other than the `flatten` operator discussed in Sect. 3.3.6, are analogous to Java and need no detailed description. This is why only some points are highlighted here.

In contrast to a Java implementation, there is no concept of exceptions for OCL expressions. Instead, all OCL operators are *robust* in the sense

that their interpretation always yields reasonable results. The expression
`Set{e}.add(e)`, for instance, has `Set{e}` as the result.

Equality on Sets and Elements

In Java, there is the equality on identifiers `==` and the equality on content
`equals()` individually definable for each class. The latter is used within
Java containers for comparing elements and thus allows a flexibilization of
the element comparison in the implementation. This distinction also exists in
some specification languages [BFG+93] which allow a freely definable equality besides the built-in equality. As in OCL containers have no object identity,
both operators `==` and `equals` are identical on containers:

```
context Set<X> sa, Set<X> sb inv:
    sa.equals(sb) <=> sa==sb
```
`OCL`

By definition, the equality of two sets exactly applies when both have
pairwise the same elements. When comparing the elements, `equals` is used
for objects and `==` for primitive data types. So, if X is a primitive data type or
a container, the following applies:

```
context Set<X> sa, Set<X> sb inv:
    sa==sb <=> (forall a in sa: exists b in sb: a==b) &&
               (forall b in sb: exists a in sa: a==b)
```
`OCL`

For object types X, the following holds:

```
context Set<X> sa, Set<X> sb inv:
    sa==sb <=> (forall a in sa: exists b in sb: a.equals(b))
            && (forall b in sb: exists a in sa: a.equals(b))
```
`OCL`

Hence, in OCL, `==` for containers is dependent on the freely definable
equality `equals` on elements and differs from the comparison in Java.

Type Inference in Heterogeneous Sets

A comfortable feature of OCL is automatic type conversion of arguments of
set operators. If `Guest` is a subclass of `Person`, Fig. 3.10 shows a part of the
induced subtype hierarchy for containers. Here, OCL differs from the type
system in Java [GJSB05], which cannot provide a subtype relation between
`Set<Guest>` and `Set<Person>`. This is restricted in Java, because `Set`s are
implemented as modifiable, identity-aware objects. One could, otherwise,
add `Person` objects to `Set<Guest>` sets. In OCL, containers basically do
not have an identity. In the strict sense, they are not modified either; rather
when, for example, objects are added, new containers are always created.
Therefore, the subtype relation can be established here.

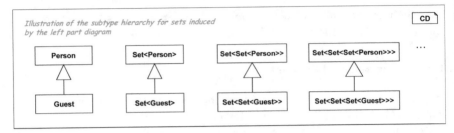

Figure 3.10. Type conformity of container types

This means in particular that merging of a set of persons with a list of guests is possible, as the latter can implicitly be converted to the type `Collection<Person>`. According to Fig. 3.9, the result of this merge (with the function `addAll`) is again a set of persons:

```
let Set<Person> pset = ...;
    List<Guest> glist= ...
in
    pset.addAll(glist)    // has the type Set<Person>
```

So, for heterogeneous usage of set operators, the types of arguments are converted, if necessary. The set on which the operator is applied is not converted, though. Thus, the last line in the following condition is not type-correct:

```
let Set<Person> pset = ...;
    Set<Guest>   gset = ...
in
    gset.addAll(pset)    // not type-correct
```

The authors of [Sch02] point out that the typing rules can be generalized for OCL in order to assign a correct type to the last expression. In principle, even further type information could be gained from the knowledge about the result of operation. So, the following intersection of two sets:

```
let Set<Person> pset = ...;
    Set<Guest>   gset = ...
in
    pset.retainAll(gset)
```

contains only objects of the class `Guest` and could, hence, not only have the type `Set<Person>` calculated by the type system but even the subtype `Set<Guest>`.

An unambiguous assignment of a type as in Java, however, is not always possible in the presence of multiple inheritance or multiple instantiation of interfaces. The restrictive typing for the first argument can also be understood here as protection, forcing the modeler to carry out an explicit type conversion of the first argument, if applicable.

3.3.4 List Operations

There are a number of operations for selecting, combining, and modifying lists as well. As in the case of sets, the interpretation of container expressions is free from side-effects and, thus, differs from lists offered in Java.

The list operations are given in Fig. 3.11. As in the case of sets (see Fig. 3.9), an integration of the functionality known from the Java realization of lists and offered by the OCL standard has been carried out here as well.

```
List<X>  add(X o);                                           Signature
List<X>  add(int index, X o);
List<X>  prepend(X o);
List<X>  addAll(Collection<X> c);
List<X>  addAll(int index, Collection<X> c);
boolean  contains(X o);
boolean  containsAll(Collection<X> c);
X        get(int index);
X        first;
X        last;
List<X>  rest;
int      indexOf(X o);
int      lastIndexOf(X o);
boolean  isEmpty;
int      count(X o);
List<X>  remove(X o);
List<X>  removeAtIndex(int index);
List<X>  removeAll(Collection<X> c);
List<X>  retainAll(Collection<X> c);
List<X>  set(int index, X o);
int      size;
List<X>  subList(int fromIndex, int toIndex);
List<Y>  flatten;                    // X has the form Collection<Y>
Set<X>   asSet;
```

Figure 3.11. Signature of lists of the type `List<X>`

Regarding practical issues, it is convenient, i.e., more systematic, to start the indexing of the list elements with 0 as known from Java and to exclude the upper border at `subList`. The properties of lists can be demonstrated by means of some valid statements:

```
List{0,1}                     != List{1,0};          OCL
List{0,1,1}                   != List{0,1};
List{0,1,2}.add(3)            == List{0,1,2,3};
List{'a','b','c'}.add(1,'d')  == List{'a','d','b','c'};
List{0,1,2}.prepend(3)        == List{3,0,1,2};
List{0,1}.addAll(List{2,3})   == List{0,1,2,3};
```

```
List{0,1,2}.set(1,3)                  == List{0,3,2};
List{0,1,2}.get(1)                    == 1;
List{0,1,2}.first                     == 0;
List{0,1,2}.last                      == 2;
List{0,1,2}.rest                      == List{1,2};
List{0,1,2,1}.remove(1)               == List{0,2};
List{0,1,2,3}.removeAtIndex(1)        == List{0,2,3};
List{0,1,2,3,2,1}.removeAll(List{1,2}) == List{0,3};
List{0..4}.subList(1,3)               == List{1,2};
List{0..4}.subList(3,3)               == List{};
```

Adding elements of a container to a list with the aid of addAll has an unambiguous result only when this container is itself a list. Otherwise, the order of newly added elements is not fixed. By convention, however, it is guaranteed that an OCL expression is deterministic, i.e., the same OCL expression always describes the same values in the same context. In particular, the following applies:

inv: OCL

```
  forall s1 in Set<X>, s2 in Set<X>:
    s1 == s2  implies  s1.asList == s2.asList
```

The operations remove and removeAll each eliminate all appearances of their arguments from the list on which they operate. For comparison, the equality equals is used for objects and == for primitive data types. Different than in Java, the removal of an element at a certain index cannot also be called remove, as lists can directly be occupied with elements of primitive data types, i.e., also with int. This is why removeAtIndex has been introduced.

3.3.5 Container Operations

A container is either a set or a list. Thus, the signature assigned to containers consists of all operations common to sets and lists. Figure 3.12 summarizes the signature for containers.

The conversion functions asSet and asList allow for transformation of arbitrary containers into sets and lists, respectively. When applying one of these operations, a real transformation takes place. On the contrary, type conversions using (Set<X>), (List<X>), and (Collection<X>) have the purpose of changing type information without modifying the fundamental data structure. For a list l, a transformation into a set l.asSet is, therefore, reasonable but the type conversion (Set<X>)l is forbidden. The interaction of the conversions can be illustrated by the following example:

```
  let Collection<int> ci = List{1,2,1};                                OCL
  in
    ci.asSet  == {1,2} &&
    ci.asList == List{1,2,1} &&
    ci.asSet.asList.size == 2 &&
```

```
Collection<X> add(X o);
Collection<X> addAll(Collection<X> c);                    ┌──────────┐
boolean       contains(X o);                              │Signature │
boolean       containsAll(Collection<X> c);               └──────────┘
boolean       isEmpty;
int           count(X o);
Collection<X> remove(X o);
Collection<X> removeAll(Collection<X> c);
Collection<X> retainAll(Collection<X> c);
int           size;
Collection<Y> flatten;   // X has the form Collection<Y> or Set<Y>
List<Y>       flatten;   // X has the form List<Y>
Set<X>        asSet;
List<X>       asList;
```

Figure 3.12. Signature of containers of the type `Collection<X>`

```
(List<int>) ci == List{1,2,1} &&
!( (Set<int>) ci == {1,2} )    // as left side is undefined
```

To prevent an undefined conversion, the operator `instanceof` can be used to check whether an object or value has a certain type.

```
let Collection<int> ci = List{1,2,1};                     ┌──────┐
in                                                        │OCL   │
                                                          └──────┘
    (ci instanceof Set<int>          <=> false) &&
    (ci instanceof List<int>         <=> true ) &&
    (ci instanceof Collection<int> <=> true )
```

In combination with the `typeif` operator, this enables safe type conversion that prohibits explicit type conversion and possible emerging failures and makes the specifier explicitly think about the case of erroneous type conversion. If, e.g., the second element from the above-mentioned list c_i is to be selected with the type `Collection<int>`, this can be done as follows (-42 is a chosen replacement value):

```
let Collection<int> ci = List{1,2,1};                     ┌──────┐
in result ==                                              │OCL   │
    typeif ci instanceof List<int> then ci.get(0) else -42└──────┘
```

The above expression represents a shortcut for

```
let Collection<int> ci = List{1,2,1};                     ┌──────┐
in result ==                                              │OCL   │
  if ci instanceof List<int> then                         └──────┘
     let List<int> cinew = (List<int>) ci
     in   cinew.get(0)
  else -42
```

The auxiliary variable `cinew` is required in order to assign another type to the value stored in `ci` that allows access as a list element.

3.3.6 Flattening of Containers

Deeply nested container structures contain certain structuring information that, in some cases, is helpful for specifying systems. Thus, a grouping of persons can be described with the type `Set<Set<Person>>`, e.g.,

```
let Set<Set<Person>> ssp = { a.bidder | a in Auction }
in ...
```

describes the groups of persons each participating in an auction.

However, such deep structuring is often not desired and a simple set or list is already sufficient. Therefore, the operator `flatten` is used to flatten nested container structures.

The constraints for this operator given in Figs. 3.9, 3.11, and 3.12 show that it can only be applied on nested container structures. Depending on the type of the container, either a set or a list emerges when flattening. But if only the type `Collection` is known from the argument, the type `Collection` may be the only information about the result. The different variants of the `flatten` operator have the signatures indicated in Fig. 3.13, with the result given on the left and the type of the argument given in front of the dot.

```
Set<X>              Set<Set<X>>.flatten;
List<X>             Set<List<X>>.flatten;
Collection<X>       Set<Collection<X>>.flatten;
List<X>             List<Set<X>>.flatten;
List<X>             List<List<X>>.flatten;
List<X>             List<Collection<X>>.flatten;
Collection<X>       Collection<Set<X>>.flatten;
List<X>             Collection<List<X>>.flatten;
Collection<X>       Collection<Collection<X>>.flatten;
```

Figure 3.13. Flattening of containers in OCL/P

The `flatten` operator merges only the two "upper" container levels without taking into consideration the internal structure of the element type X contained therein. This is also referred to as *shallow* flattening. Complete flattening to a set or a list of simple objects can be achieved through repeated use.

When flattening containers, generally the tenet was followed that a list is created if a list is involved (i.e., lists *dominate*). If no list but a container is involved, a container results. Only nested sets become sets again.[11]

---

[11] This flattening rule can be comprehended more easily than the one used in the OCL standard, where a less intuitive typing emerges due to the usage of multisets.

Figure 3.14 shows some applications of the `flatten` operator.

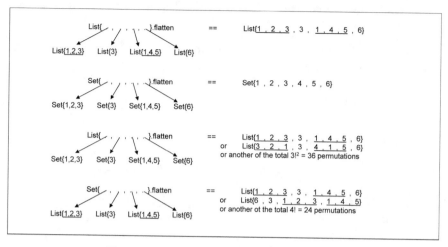

Figure 3.14. Flattening of nested sets and lists

The use of nested containers partly leads to conditions formulated more complicatedly than the problem requires. Hence, the `flatten` operator is implicitly used in navigation chains so that the result of such a chain never represents a container structure which is nested more deeply than the initial structure. The only exception is the navigation chain starting from a single object, which can result in a set or sequence.

3.3.7 Typing of Containers

In the previous sections, the problem of correct typing of OCL expressions has already been discussed occasionally. This section now gives an overview, in which the already discussed aspects are briefly repeated:

- There is a collection of primitive data types known from Java. Subtypes only exist between numbers in the familiar form.
- Each class and each interface of the model underlying OCL is a type. This includes in particular classes of the Java library and all type instantiations of generic classes. The inheritance relations from the class diagram are taken over. The special type `Object` is the common superclass of all these types (primitive data types and containers excluded).
- By using type constructors, set- and list-valued types as well as types for collections are built. For all types X, the generic terms `Set<X>`, `List<X>`, and `Collection<X>` again denote types.

- For operations with several arguments with the same type and a container as the result, usually the first argument is used to determine the element type of the container. This also includes enumerations. If necessary, the first argument can be typed, e.g. `Set{(Object)"Text", person}`.

Figure 3.10 shows the effect of the subtype hierarchy of classes on the corresponding container types. As container types can be nested arbitrarily, further types and subtype relations are induced, as illustrated in Fig. 3.15.

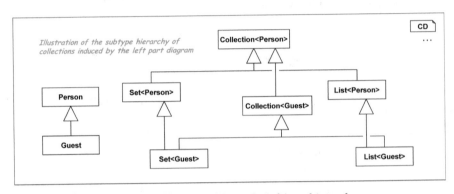

Figure 3.15. Excerpt of the induced type hierarchy

In Java, the class `Object` is, just like in OCL/P, the most general superclass which *contains* all other classes and interfaces. This means that the extension of `Object` contains all objects of the system. In contrast to Java, containers are not classes in OCL. This is why an inheritance relation between `Set<Person>` and `Object` does not exist. By strictly separating the type hierarchy for objects and sets of objects, some semantically unpleasant implications are prohibited. `Set<Object>`, for example, is not a subtype of `Object` and the typing ensures that a set cannot contain itself as an element.[12] This separation continues on further levels; for instance, `Set<Set<Object>>` is not a subtype of `Set<Object>`, and `List<Object>` is not a subtype of `Object`.

Therefore, the creation of the following set illustrating the anomaly in set theory is not type-correct:[13]

---

[12] The problem of a set that contains itself is well studied in mathematics and leads to some surprising anomalies of the previously used logic theory. Among others, the hierarchical type theory of B. Russell, that has, concerning typing, finally been taken over into programming languages, offers a solution.

[13] The question of whether x contains itself would cause contradictions, but it cannot be asked, as either the conversion or the `instanceof` inquiry is not type-correct.

```
let Set<Object> x =
    { Object y | y instanceof Set<Object>
                 && !(y in (Set<Object>)y) }
in ...
```

Set$\{3, \text{Set}\{1, 2\}\}$ is not type-correct either.

3.3.8 Set- and List-Valued Navigation

Navigation along a chain of associations attracts particular attention in OCL as, with this construct, states of a whole object group can be described even if the explicitly indicated context only consists of one object. The extract of the auction system in Fig. 3.8 serves as a basis for explaining the navigation possibilities of OCL/P. To make sure that employees of the company "BAD" do not participate in auctions, the following constraint can be imposed:

```
context Auction a inv:
    !("BAD" in a.bidder.company.name)
```

In doing so, a navigation chain with three steps is applied, according to Fig. 3.8. While a represents a single object of the type Auction, the navigation over a.bidder provides a number of objects of the type Set<Person>, as the association participants in this navigation direction has the cardinality *. Beginning with the set of persons, the set of companies assigned to these persons can be described with .company. The result is still a set in which the company of each person previously detected is contained. Finally, the whole navigation expression a.bidder.company.name provides a set of company names belonging to the type Set<String>.

In the following example, the association between persons and companies is passed through against the given navigation direction. In a specification, this is allowed without further ado even if the implementation would not facilitate it:

```
context Company co inv:
    co.name == "BAD" implies co.person.auctions == {}
```

The navigation along an association can be formulated in three ways. Starting from the object a of the class Auction, the navigation towards the persons usually takes place with the *role name* bidder opposite the initial class in the class diagram in Fig. 3.8. However, it is also possible to use the association name (a.participants) if it is given and, e.g., the role name is lacking. If there is only one association between the two classes and if the role name is missing, the opposite *class name* can be used in *decapitalized form*: p.message.

A specification language such as OCL is used in several activities of the software development process. Especially regarding the specification and the design of a system, it is thus of interest to access encapsulated attributes of a class, even if the constraint was not defined in the class context. Therefore, the modifiers `protected` and `private` are ignored when defining OCL constraints, so that attributes and methods with these modifiers can be used in OCL constraints as well. This is quite convenient.

If an association has a cardinality other than 1 or 0..1, the navigation result based on an object is set-valued. If the end of an association, furthermore, has the tag {ordered}, the result is a list. If the navigation already starts using a set, the navigation is applied pointwise and the result is a union of the pointwise results. In the class diagram in Fig. 3.8, it can, e.g., be specified that a person does not participate in more than 20 auctions using the set-valued navigation expression `ad.auction.bidder`:

```
context AllData ad inv:                              OCL
   forall p in ad.auction.bidder:
      p.auctions <= 20
```

For pragmatic reasons, nested sets are not used in the OCL standard [OMG10b] while navigating.[14] In case of set-valued navigation chains, flattening leads to clearer and easier data structures, but it has the disadvantage that structural information gets lost.

So, in case of a navigation chain along multivalued associations, flattening happens according to given rules using the `flatten` operator. These rules are explained by means of the following examples, which are formulated depending on the class diagram in Fig. 3.8:

```
context AllData ad, Person p inv:                    OCL
let
   Company         c    = p.company;    // 1: simple type
   Set<Auction>    sa   = p.auctions;   // 2: set-valued
   Set<Person>     competitors = p.auctions.bidder;
                                        // 3: chain remains set-valued
   List<Message> lpm   = p.message;     // 4: due to tag {ordered}
   List<Message> lam   = p.auctions.messages;   // 5
   List<Auction> lma   = p.messages.auctions;   // 6
in ...
```

Examples 1, 2, and 4 show how, through a navigation chain, a set or a list emerges from a one-element origin. In example 3, a chain of two set-valued navigations is conducted, where the result is again a set. In example 5, an ordered navigation from auctions to messages is performed, starting from the set `p.auctions`. The result of this operation is a list of messages whose order, however, is partly unspecified. The characterization

```
context Person p inv:                                OCL
   p.auctions.messages == p.auctions.asList.messages;
```

---

[14] The OCL standard has no mechanism for representation of nested containers, sets of sets, for example. Through "flattening," navigation results instead become again a simple set, or at most a multiset.

acts as definition for this navigation expression and shows that the unspecified order emerges from the transformation of the set into a list. In a navigation chain in which first a list emerges and then a set-valued navigation is conducted, the result also is a partly underspecified list (Example 6).

The expression `ad.auction.message` should represent a set of lists, but it results in a data structure of type `List<Message>`. Here, one may assess, for example, how often a message occurs in total but not if it would have occurred in the first place in each list, as the information about the beginning of the single lists was lost during flattening. To ensure that the welcome message is sent in all auctions in the same form, a nesting of quantifiers can be used, where each single list becomes accessible, instead of a chain of navigations:

```
context AllData ad inv WelcomeMessage1:
  forall a in ad.auction:
    let List<Message> lmsg = a.message
    in
        lmsg.isEmpty || lmsg.get(0) == WelcomeMessage
```

As nested sets are available in OCL, the following expression shows how the structure information can be retained during the navigation:

```
context AllData ad inv:
  let Set<List<Message>> slm = {a.message | a in ad.auction}
  in
      ad.auction.message == slm.flatten
```

The typing of a navigation along an association can be characterized by the following specification based on the situation shown in Fig. 3.16. Starting from a single object, the result depends on the association's cardinality:

```
let Auction        a  = ...;
    Policy         po = a.policy;
    Set<Person>    spe = a.person;
    List<Message>  lm = a.message
  in ...
```

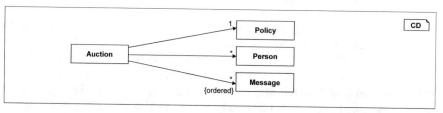

Figure 3.16. Abstract model for explaining navigation results

When starting from a set of objects, the `flatten` operator is used for keeping the nesting depth. As the association towards `Policy` is not set-valued itself, the `flatten` operator is not necessary here. All three subsequent statements compare sets:

```
let Set<Auction> sa = ...;                                    OCL
in
  sa.policy  == { a.policy  | a in sa } &&
  sa.person  == { a.person  | a in sa }.flatten &&
  sa.message == { a.message | a in sa }.flatten
```

More deeply nested structures keep the nesting depth. This means in particular that flattening is not applied completely down to the lowest level. The following equations compare sets of sets `Set<Set<X>>`:

```
let Set<Set<Auction>> ssa = ...;                             OCL
in
  ssa.policy  == { elem.policy  | elem in ssa } &&
  ssa.person  == { elem.person  | elem in ssa } &&
  ssa.message == { elem.message | elem in ssa }
```

The `flatten` operator is already contained implicitly in the expressions `elem.person` and `elem.message`, but is not necessary in `elem.policy` due to the cardinality 1. The next example shows a list where the inner flattening is once again explicitly depicted:

```
let List<Set<Auction>>  lsa = ...;                          OCL
    List<Set<Person>>   lsp = lsa.person
in
  lsp == List{ {a.person | a in sa}.flatten  | sa in lsa }
```

As the example of Fig. 3.17 illustrates, the difference between an application of the `flatten` operator inside and outside is only relevant at nesting depth of at least three.

This example also demonstrates the sometimes subtle problems leading to complexities during specification that a modeler should only take on in exceptional cases. Thus, we suggest to avoid nested container structures.

3.3.9 Qualified Association

In Sect. 2.3.6, qualifiers were introduced to facilitate access to single objects via a set-valued association. An example in analogy to the class diagram shown in Fig. 3.8 is shown in Fig. 3.18 using qualifiers.

Starting from the `AllData` object `ad`, the set of auctions can be reached by normal (unqualified) navigation in the form `ad.auction`. The result is of the type `Set<Auction>`. A qualified navigation allows the use of a selector to describe a specific auction. If `acIdent` denotes an auction identifier, the

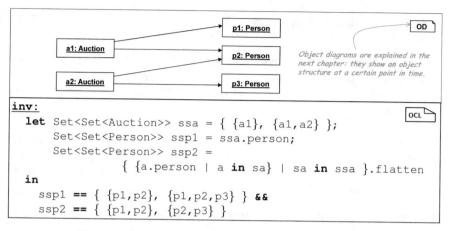

Figure 3.17. Example for flattening versus flat navigation

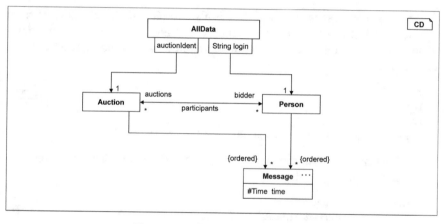

Figure 3.18. Qualified associations

corresponding auction is selected with `ad.auction[acIdent]`.[15] This expression evaluates to an object of the type `Auction`. If the auction does not exist, the expression has the value `null`. For further processing of a qualified association, methods of the type `Map` are available, for example, to allow determination of the set of used qualifier values.

The constraint below describes that, based on the singleton `ad` of the class `AllData` (cf. constraint `AllDataIsSingleton`), each `Auction` object is registered under the correct auction identifier:[16]

---

[15] `auction[acIdent]` is identical to `auction.get(acIdent)` also offered in Java, which is provided by the interface `Map`.

[16] As the attribute name `auctionIdent` is given as a qualifier in Fig. 3.18, this constraint is redundant due to Sect. 2.3.7.

```
context AllData ad, Auction a inv:                    OCL
    ad.auction[a.auctionIdent] == a;
```

The result of a qualified navigation has an element type (here: `Auction`) because the initial expression (here: `ad`) had an element type, and qualified associations in the navigation direction are distinctly marked with a cardinality 1 or `0..1`.

The tag `{ordered}` describes that both associations marked by it can also be used as qualified associations. Then, an integer from the interval `0..message.size-1` is used as qualifier. The result of a qualified access has an element type, as shown by the following statement equivalent to `WelcomeMessage1`:

```
context AllData ad inv WelcomeMessage2:               OCL
    forall a in ad.auction:
        a.message.size > 0 implies a.message[0] == WelcomeMessage
```

Qualified access via an association is also possible if already starting from a container. In this case, the selection by the qualifier is carried out element-wise. The following example characterizes how such a navigation is to be understood:

```
inv:                                                  OCL
    let Set<Auction> sa = ...;
    in
        sa.message[n] == { a.message[n] | a in sa }
```

For the qualified navigation starting from the container structures *container*, the following holds:

$$container.role[qualifier] ==$$
$$\{ elem.role[qualifier] \mid elem \ in \ container \}$$
OCL

3.3.10 Quantifiers

The two quantifiers `forall` and `exists` allow the description of properties that have to be valid for all or at least one element from a given set, respectively.

Universal Quantifier `forall`

Quantifiers can be combined over multiple variables. Several universal quantifiers can, e.g., be summarized into one:[17]

---

[17] The OCL standard uses the form *set*.`forall`(*body*) and is, thus, not suited for summarizing quantifiers. Furthermore, the quantified variable remains optionally undesignated, and as default, the variable `self` is assumed.

```
inv Message1:
    forall a in Auction, p in Person, m in a.message:
      p in a.bidder implies m in p.message
```

In doing so, one can refer to previously introduced variables in subsequent indications of sets, as formally the above invariant Message1 is equivalent to:

```
inv Message2:
    forall a in Auction:
      forall p in Person:
        forall m in a.message:
          p in a.bidder implies m in p.message
```

The third quantifier of this example also shows that the initial set, which is quantified, will be not only the extension of a class but also an arbitrary set- or list-valued expression. The body of the quantification is a Boolean expression. According to the chosen logic, the interpretation of this expression may return undefined values that are interpreted as `false`. The constraint

```
inv:
    forall a in Auction: even(1/0)
```

is thus a syntactically correct OCL formula. At first sight, this formula seems unfulfillable, as it is semantically equivalent to

```
inv:
    forall a in Auction: false
```

However, this constraint can be fulfilled by object structures which do not contain any object of the type Auction. In general, the following applies for empty sets:

```
inv:
    (forall x in Set{}: false)   <=>   true
```

The universal quantifier introduces one or more new variables whose values vary over a set or list. Hence, it allows statements to be made about these values or objects. In complex expressions, an explicit typing should be added to such a variable, because the expression `var in class` is formally not a typing, although it almost seems like one. The constraint Message1 can, thus, also be formulated as

```
inv Message3:
    forall Auction a:
      forall p in Person:
        forall Message m in a.message:
          p in a.bidder implies m in p.message
```

In the first quantifier, only the type was given, at the same time acting as an extension. In the second quantifier, an explicit typing was left out, and in the third quantifier, both were used. This condition makes it apparent that the universal quantifier is an alternative notation for the formulation of a constraint's context. The above constraint `Message3` can, therefore, also be formulated using context as:

```
context Auction a, Person p inv Message4:
    forall m in a.message:
        p in a.bidder implies m in p.message
```

Here, the difference between a context definition with `context` versus `import` becomes very clear. The condition

```
import Auction a, Person p inv Message5:
    forall m in a.message:
        p in a.bidder implies m in p.message
```

needs to be valid only for the *external* objects a and p; i.e., it is dependent on the context of its use. On the contrary, the body of `Message4` holds for all `Auction` objects a and for all person objects p.

It is always possible to express contexts introduced with the keyword `context` by universal quantifiers. The inversion for universal quantifiers, however, does not always hold, as the basic set of a quantifier can be described by a real expression instead of only an extension. The following invariant demands the existence of a test auction where all auction participants can practice:

```
inv TestAuction:
    exists Auction testauction:
        testauction.startTime.lessThan(Time.now()) &&
        Time.now().lessThan(testauction.closingTime) &&
        (forall Person p: !p.auctions.isEmpty
                        implies p in testauction.bidder)
```

Note that this is an interesting constraint regarding its implications with regards to time, as the invariant requires that such a test auction be open at any time. Since auctions close at a certain time, new test auctions have to be set up regularly to fulfill the above-mentioned condition.

Existential Quantifier `exists`

The existential quantifier is dual to the universal quantifier. It demands that a property be fulfilled by at least one element. The invariant `TestAuction` has already demonstrated the application of the existential quantifier. These quantifiers can also be nested. The existential quantifier can be characterized using the universal quantifier as follows:

```
inv:
    (exists var in setExpr: expr)        <=>
        !(forall var in setExpr:  !expr)
```

An existential quantification over an empty set has the expected effect:

```
inv:
    (exists x in Set{}: expr)    <=>    false
```

Finite and Infinite Quantifiers

Up to now, both quantifiers have only been applied to finite container structures. In fact, OCL is defined to work with finite sets and lists. This has several consequences that need to be taken into consideration when using quantifiers. The finiteness of the quantified set has the advantage of (at least theoretical) computability by assigning all values or objects to the quantified variable and, thus, interpreting the body. It is essential for the quantified set that the extension in the form of all currently existing objects assigned to classes such as `Person` is unrestricted but finite. If, instead, the set of all potential objects were assigned, a quantifier would not be testable. Thus, a side-effect is that a quantified variable quantifies neither over the pseudovalue `undef` for undefined expressions nor over the replacement value `null` but only over actually existing objects. It holds that:

```
inv:
    forall A a: a!=null
```

From the logic's point of view, OCL is no more powerful than without these finite quantifiers. In principal, a finite universal quantifier can also be expressed by a conjunction. However, besides the explicitly used quantifiers and the context definition, which also acts as a universal quantifier, there is another, implicit universal quantification: An invariant is equally valid for *all* occurring object structures of *all* system runs. This is illustrated in Fig. 3.19. The quantification over all potential object structures remains implicit. However, it is exactly this quantifier that is infinite and leads to the fact that an invariant cannot be completely verified by tests but new system runs with new object structures can always arise. The correctness of an invariant over this quantification had, therefore, to be verified.

Besides finite sets of objects, OCL/P also allows use of quantifiers over primitive data types; For example, a quantification over the data type `int` is

```
inv:
    exists int x: x*x > 5
```

An implementation, e.g., with exhaustive search will usually be slow and cannot terminate in case of a nonexisting suitable value. This is why the quantification over primitive data types and set- or list-valued data types is rejected in the OCL standard [OMG10b]. A constraint of the form

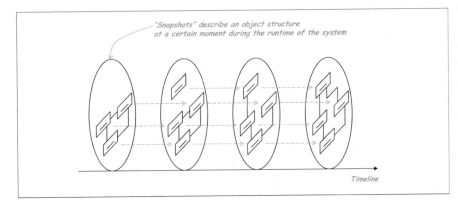

Figure 3.19. The system as a sequence of object structures

inv: `OCL`
   forall int x: x **!=** 5

can have two meanings. If `int` is the set of all integers existing at a certain
time in a system, the above constraint only means that 5 must not be used in
the system. This semantics, however, is far less intuitive for a quantifier over
integers and contradicts the mathematical usage of a quantifier. In the usual
mathematical interpretation, instead, the above invariant is not satisfiable.

For specification purposes, OCL/P allows quantification over infinite
sets. However, these cannot be used for a direct mapping to code or tests
without adaptation. The same holds for the processing of infinite sets in set
comprehensions.

inv: `OCL`
  let Set<int> squares =
        { int x | **exists** y **in** int: y*y = x **&&** x **<=** 400 }
  in ...

As an alternative, finite generators processing a finite extract are suitable:

inv: `OCL`
  let Set<int> squares = { y*y | y **in** Set{1..20} }
  in ...

The use of a quantification over sets of objects requires special attention.
The example

inv ListQuantor: `OCL`
  forall List<Person> lp: lp.size **!=** 5

allows multiple interpretations for the variable `lp`:

1. All *potential* lists of *potentially* existing `Person` objects. This is the mathematical interpretation that has already been rejected for objects.

2. All lists actually existing in a system at a certain time. Similar to the quantification over classes, this can lead to surprises if the system is extended and lists of this type are also used in a new location.
3. All *potential* lists about all objects actually existing at a certain time.

As containers show strong characteristics of primitive data types (such as value orientation and no object identity), the interpretation over all potential sets, i.e., variant 3, is also used for set-valued quantifiers. So, a quantification over Set<Person> represents a combination of the interpretation of an infinite quantifier on a primitive data type and finite quantifier over a reference type. Accordingly, quantifiers over lists are infinite and, hence, can be used only for specification. As the power set of a finite set is also finite, the quantification, e.g., over Set<Person> is finite and can, thus, be implemented, but an exhaustive search is not recommendable.

3.3.11 Special Operators

The Operator one

Many constraints can be conveniently formulated with the operations described so far. Therefore, OCL/P waives an operator for the description of the unambiguity of a set-valued expression and, instead, shows how these can be defined by given constructs. The following constraint describes that the login of each person is unambiguous:

```
context AllData ad inv:
   forall String lg in Person.login:
      { Person p | p.login == lg }.size == 1
```

OCL

Operator any

For selecting an element from a container structure, we use the special operator any. This operator is not clearly determined for sets, as the following defining equations show:

```
(any listExpr)  == listExpr.get(0);
(any setExpr)   == any setExpr.asList;
(any var in collection: expr)  == any { var in collection | expr }
```

OCL

Operator iterate

An element-wise processing of sets and lists can be described very easily by the existing forms of comprehension. A multiplication of a given set of numbers m with 2 can, e.g., be formulated easily with {2*x | x in m}. For more general cases, OCL offers the iterate operator which mimics a loop with state storage from functional as well as from imperative programming. The iterate operator can, e.g., be used for calculating the sum of a set of numbers as follows:

```
inv Sum:                                                        OCL
   let int total =
      iterate { elem in Auction;
                int acc = 0 :
                acc = acc+elem.numberOfBids
              }
   in ...
```

The locally defined variable `elem` iterates over the given set `Auction`. The also locally introduced variable `acc` acts as an "intermediate" storage for the accumulation of the results. It is initialized with 0. The expression `acc+elem.numberOfBids` is executed iteratively for all elements and the current stored value respectively. The general structure of the `iterate` operator can be characterized by

```
iterate { elementVar in setExpr;                               OCL
          Type accumulatorVar = initExpr :
          accumulatorVar = expr
        }
```

An iteration's result over a set can be ambiguous, as it, like a conversion into a list, depends on the order of processing. Implicitly, in case of sets, again a transformation into a list is applied. Therefore, the following holds:

```
inv:                                                           OCL
   iterate { elementVar in setExpr;
             Type accumulatorVar = initExpr :
             accumulatorVar = expr
           }

==

   iterate { elementVar in setExpr.asList;
             Type accumulatorVar = initExpr :
             accumulatorVar = expr
           }
```

However, in the case where the accumulation is commutative and associative, the result is determined unambiguously anyway. In the example `Sum`, addition was used, which also fulfills these properties.

The `iterate` operator is a relatively powerful but also implementation-related and less intuitive operator.[18] It is recommended not to use this operator, if possible.

Operator `defined`

Dealing with undefined values leads to additional effort in both a programming and a specification language and should, thus, be avoided to a large

---

[18] Due to its implementation-specific character, this operator is not part of the usual functional or specification-oriented flavor of OCL. This is why a syntax similar to the assignment was explicitly chosen.

extent, but at some points it is helpful or even necessary to handle undefined values. For this purpose, the particular operator `defined` is introduced, evaluating to `true` exactly when its argument is a defined value. For undefined arguments, this operator evaluates to `false`.

As an example, the existence of an object specified with a `let` construct can be checked therewith as follows:

```
context Auction a inv:
    let Message mess = a.person.message[0]
    in
        defined(mess) implies ...
```

The `defined` operator can decide whether an expression is defined. For this reason, this specification operator cannot be (fully) implemented. Due to the approach regarding handling of undefined values discussed in Sect. 3.2.2, however, a good approximation for this operator can be realized by using `try-catch` statements from Java. So, this operator is suited as an alternative to `typeif` in order to, for example, recognize elements from subclasses:

```
context Auction a inv:
    let BidMessage bm =(BidMessage) a.person.message[2]
    in
        defined(bm) implies ...
```

In some cases, the evaluation of the right side of the `let` assignment throws an exception that is stored in the variable `bm` and constitutes a representation for an undefined value. `defined(bm)` allows us to react to this undefined value.[19]

3.4 Functions in OCL

So far, only OCL invariants have been defined, which characterize a property over a system state consisting of a collection of objects. In doing so, predefined methods of OCL for processing of container data structures were used. While OCL, on the one hand, cannot define its own functions or methods outside the `let` construct, it is, on the other hand, perfectly suited for specification of effects of methods of the underlying models by means of pairs of pre- and postcondition. Vice versa, the model can also provide methods for specification of OCL conditions.[20]

---

[19] An extension of OCL could allow one to access exceptions also in the logical language and, hence, to handle different "undefined values." For the Statecharts in Chap. 5, for instance, exception stimuli are discussed.

[20] OCL/P offers methods in libraries which have been defined within the language in the OCL standard. Thus, OCL/P is on the one hand leaner and shows on the other hand how other functions of this kind can be defined by modelers themselves.

Such specification of methods by using pre/postcondition pairs corresponds to the specification of behaviors with *contracts* propagated by [Mey97]. This approach is refined in [PH97] on the basis of an independent core language called "Aicken," where also a theory including side-effects is designed. [MMPH99, MPH00] transfer parts of these results onto Java. The "observer" functions used are consistent with the subsequently introduced queries but do not allow creation of new objects.

3.4.1 Queries

In the hitherto formulated constraints, we have mostly used functions offered by OCL itself. However, in many places, it is helpful to access the methods provided by the implementation in order to compactly formulate a condition. Such a method is called a *query* and is characterized by the stereotype «query». As an extension of the class diagram in Fig. 3.8, a detailed description of the message structure is given in Fig. 3.20. Among others, it contains two query methods.

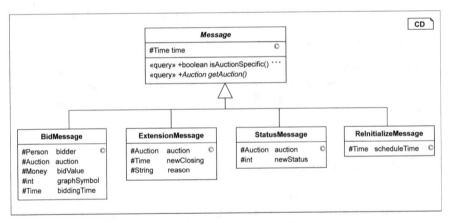

Figure 3.20. Query methods

These queries allow selection of a set of messages assigned to a specific auction. These can, thus, be compared with the messages contained in an auction to ensure that messages for distinctive auctions are forwarded correctly and in the right order to their participants.

```
context Auction a inv:
   forall p in a.bidder:
      a.message == { m in p.message |
            m.isAuctionSpecific() && m.getAuction() == a }
```

Due to the chosen two-valued logic, however, it is possible to formulate this in a shorter form if one assumes that the call `getAuction()` provides an undefined value or `null` in case the message is not auction specific:

```
context Auction a inv:
   forall p in a.bidder:
     a.message == { m in p.message | m.getAuction()==a }
```

OCL

Stereotype «query»	
Model element	Abstract and implemented methods; method signatures 
Motivation	Conditions are not allowed to cause side-effects if they are evaluated during a system run, e.g., for test purposes. This is why methods of the underlying model cannot be called arbitrarily in constraints. «query» marks methods that are free of side-effects and, thus, applicable in constraints.
Glossary	A method marked with «query» is called a *query*.
Usage condition	A query computes a result without changing the state of the system. Neither foreign nor object-local attributes can be manipulated. However, the result can consist of newly created objects if these are not accessible from the original system (see Fig. 3.22). «query» is inherited and carries over from interfaces to their implementations. A query can be overwritten, but a new implementation also has to avoid state changes.
Effect	Methods marked with «query» can be used for formulating constraints in OCL.
Example(s)	According to coding standards common for Java, queries mostly begin with a prefix in the form `get`, `is`, `has`, or `give`. Example: see Fig. 3.20.
Pitfalls	Queries may call other methods. However, it is only ensured that there are no side-effects if these methods are also queries. The creation of new objects requires calling a constructor. If a constructor has side-effects on other objects, it cannot be used in a query (but according to the coding standards, this should not be the case).
See also	«OCL» for queries that are not implemented in the production system.

(continued on the next page)

(continues Table 3.21.: Stereotype «query»)

Extendable to	Classes and interfaces if each method defined therein or inherited by a subtype relation is a query. «query» then distributes to all methods of the class or interface.
	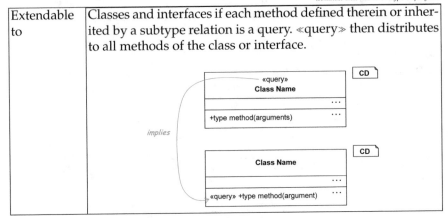

Table 3.21. Stereotype «query»

As the description of the stereotype «query» in Table 3.21 explains, it is an essential property of queries that they do not modify the underlying object structure. This means that neither attributes are modified nor associations changed in existing objects. Only in this way can it be ensured that an evaluation of a condition at runtime does not change the system itself. The allocation of the stereotype «query» to a method, thus, means an obligation of the programmer to not make any modifications of object states. The stereotype «query» is inherited to the methods of the subclasses. Queries can be overwritten, but in subclasses they must also be implemented as queries. Nowadays, it is good programming style and advised by coding standards to let query methods begin with the prefixes get, is, has, or give.

However, a query may create new objects and return these to the caller as long as new objects are not accessible from the previous data structure. In an implementation, these "temporary" objects are automatically removed by the Java runtime system. These new objects can be connected to each other and can have links into the original object structure (see Fig. 3.22).

Unfortunately, the creation of objects is not completely free of side-effects, as the set of all objects of a class (the extension) changes. If a query generates new objects, it is called *impure*.

If an impure query is applied in a specification, the generated objects are not included in the extension.[21]

If a query were not allowed to modify these objects after their creation, queries would be recognizable by static program analysis. The Java implementation of a query would then only be allowed to assign values to local variables, perform computations, and call other queries. However, a tech-

---

[21] Impure queries have been allowed for pragmatic reasons. Potential problems can be recognized by suitable data and control flow analysis techniques.

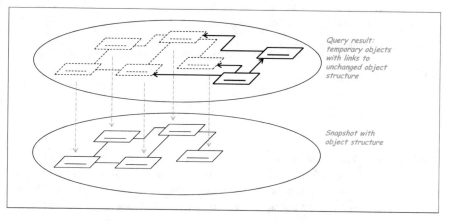

Figure 3.22. Query method may create objects

nique based on data and control flow analysis, which can statically check method bodies for being queries, is also conceivable here. Such an algorithm cannot recognize all cases as correct, but it is already sufficient if it conservatively rejects all implementations that are doubtful without excluding too many query implementations.

A query is an ordinary method of a class of the UML class diagram. Like other methods, a query is usually designed for use in an implementation. The result of a query, for example, can be integrated into the existing object structure by a calling method.

3.4.2 «OCL» Methods

For modeling more complex properties, it is often reasonable or even necessary to define additional queries. However, such queries are usually not designed for implementation but exclusively for specification. Therefore, they are not available in a product installation. In order to tag pure specification queries, the stereotype «OCL» is introduced in Table 3.23. In its meaning, it differs from «query» only by the fact that an implementation is not designated in the production system.[22] Figure 3.24 shows two such methods that have been added to the class `Person`.

---

[22] The OCL standard [OMG10b] does not store these methods in a class diagram but offers a definition clause similar to an OCL constraint.

Stereotype «OCL»	
Model element	Abstract and implemented methods; method signatures.
Motivation	The same as in «query»: the use of the method is allowed in constraints. However, these methods are available only in specifications and are not realized in the production system.
Glossary	A method marked with «OCL» is called a *specification query*.
Usage condition	Specification queries have the same restrictions as queries. Furthermore, they must not be used in the implementation code.
Effect	Methods marked with «OCL» can be used in OCL.
Example(s)	Like queries, these mostly begin with a prefix in the form `get`, `is`, `has`, or `give`. Example: see Fig. 3.24.
Pitfalls	The same as in «query» methods.
Also see	Stereotype «query».
Expandable to	Can be used on classes and interfaces if each method defined therein or inherited by a subtype relation is a specification query. «OCL» then spreads onto all methods. Usually, such classes belong to a specification library and are not included in a product installation.

Table 3.23. Stereotype «OCL»

Like the properties of queries or ordinary methods, these functions can be defined by a method specification or by a direct implementation in Java. However, a direct implementation in Java can only be realized if the signature does not contain OCL data types.

3.4.3 Method Specification

The goal of a software system is especially the adequacy of the behavior visible to the user. This behavior is mostly realized by complex interaction of methods. The data structure on which these methods work is, thus, actually only a means to an end. Correspondingly, it is interesting not only to characterize invariants with OCL but particularly to specify the behavior of

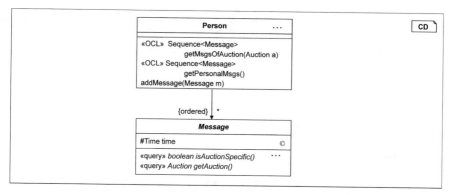

Figure 3.24. OCL-specific queries

methods. Hence, we introduce the pre/postcondition style particularly suitable for *method specifications*. The context of a method specification is determined by the method, which is usually qualified with the containing class as well as by its parameters. Two constraints, the *precondition* and the *postcondition*, which can both be decorated with names, characterize the method's effect. The method isAuctionSpecific from Fig. 3.24 can be specified in the subclass BidMessage as follows:

```
context boolean BidMessage.isAuctionSpecific()
pre   IAS1: true
post  IAS2: result == true
```

The precondition with the name IAS1 states that the method can be called at any time. The postcondition IAS2, in the variable result, characterizes the result of the method call. It states that each message of the type BidMessage is auction specific. As the next constraint shows, the auction concerned can be queried by messages of this type:

```
context Auction Message.getAuction()
pre:  isAuctionSpecific()
post: exists p in result.bidder: this in p.message
```

The postcondition describes that a person p that has received this message participates in the auction delivered as the result (result).

The restriction in the precondition of a method describes that, in case the precondition is fulfilled, the postcondition is guaranteed. It especially ensures that the method does not terminate with an exception. This *contract* in the sense of [Mey97], however, makes no statement about what can happen if the precondition is not fulfilled. A robust implementation should, also in this case, respond with a defined reaction. [HHB02] describes four different interpretations for method specifications for which the *total correctness* used here also enforces termination in case of a fulfilled precondition.

In the above condition, the keyword `this` is used in order to make a reference to the object on which the method is applied. The keyword is only available if the specified method is to be applied to an object, i.e., if it does not have the tag `static`. The static methods for creating message objects (compare Fig. 3.20) can, thus, be described as follows:

```
context «static» StatusMessage
    MessageFactory.createStatusMessage(Time time,
                        Auction auction, int newStatus)
pre:   true
post:  result.time == time &&
       result.auction == auction &&
       result.newStatus == newStatus
```

If the class `MessageFactory`, which this static method belongs to, is of subordinate significance or if this is not yet determined, the class can also be omitted. This is of interest particularly for the specification queries introduced in the last section, as these are usually not implemented and, thus, not assigned to a class.

The above and the following specification show that, besides the result variable `result`, also parameters of the method can be used in pre- and postconditions:

```
context List<Message> Person.getMsgOfAuction(Auction a)
pre:   true
post:  result == List{ m in p.message |
         m.isAuctionSpecific() && m.getAuction()== a }
```

The used list comprehension selects all messages that are assigned to an auction a. This example also shows that the specification queries attributed with the stereotype «OCL» are characterized with the presented specification technique without the need to indicate an implementation.

Figure 3.25. Excerpt of the `Person` class

Figure 3.25 contains a method `addMessage` that serves for adding another message to a person. The postcondition of the method specification contains an explicit reference to the state before the method call by using the postfix `@pre`:

```
context Person.addMessage(Message m)                          OCL
pre:  m.time >= messageList.last.time
post: messageList == messageList@pre.add(m)
```

Like in Java, it is possible to define methods with variable arity, as shown in the following example. The method `addMessages` can be called with many variable messages. Its parameter `ml` is, like in Java, of type `[Message]`:

```
context Person.addMessages(Message ml ...)                    OCL
pre:  forall t in ml.time: t >= messageList.last.time
      && ml.time.isSorted()
post: messageList == messageList@pre.addAll(ml)
```

@pre in Postconditions

The operator `@pre` can only be applied to single attributes or navigation elements. Already syntactically, an expression of the form `(a.b)@pre` is prohibited. However, the detailed meaning of `@pre` is to be defined precisely. Therefore, we show, using the example taken from [RG02, Ric02] and illustrated in Fig. 3.26, what effects the operator `@pre` has in dynamically changing object structures.

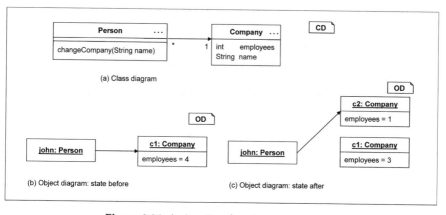

Figure 3.26. A situation for `changeCompany`

Figure 3.26(a) contains an extract of the auction model showing that persons can change their company. The object diagram[23] in Fig. 3.26(b) shows that `john` and three colleagues of his company are registered in the auction system. In the example, it is assumed that he is headhunted by a new company that so far has been undocumented in the auction system. The change

---

[23] Object diagrams are explained in detail in Chap. 4.

leads to the situation shown in Fig. 3.26(c) with the new object `c2`. In the postcondition, the operator `@pre` can be used in various ways when the expression is in the form `john.company.employees`:

`john.company.employees == 1`, as this expression is completely evaluated in the state after the method call. The navigation through `company` leads to the project `c2` with the corresponding attribute content.

`john@pre.company.employees == 1`, as the reference to object `john` has not changed during the method call. It holds that `john==john@pre`. Only through consideration of the attributes do the changes in object `john` become apparent.

`john.company@pre.employees == 3`; as with `company@pre`, one accesses the original state of the object `john`, and this subexpression evaluates to the object `c1`. But then, the current state of `c1` is reached by means of access via `employees`.

`john.company@pre.employees@pre == 4`, as, here, the evaluation accesses the original object `c1` in its original state.

`john.company.employees@pre` is undefined as `john.company` evaluates to `c2` and this object did not exist in the original state.

An alternative but equivalent approach for the comprehension of postconditions is possible by treating expressions in the form `company@pre` as additionally existing attributes in which old values of the attribute `company` are stored.

Characterization of Object Creation

Assuming that a person switches company, the method `changeCompany` introduced in Fig. 3.26 can be characterized as follows:

```
context Person.changeCompany(String name)                    OCL
pre  CC1pre:   !exists Company co: co.name == name
post CC1post:
     company.name          == name &&
     company.employees     == 1 &&
     company@pre.employees == company@pre.employees@pre -1 &&
     isnew(company)
```

The operator `isnew(.)` has been used in order to indicate that `company` is a new object. This operator is a shortcut for a comparison of object sets existing before and after a method call. The operator `isnew()` can, thus, be described in the following way:

```
context ...                                                  OCL
post: let X x = ...
        in
           isnew(x) <=> (x in X) && !(x in X@pre)
```

In OCL, the `isnew(.)` operator has only a descriptive function, while with the `new` construct known from Java new objects are created. So, it must be noted that the `isnew` operator checks within an OCL postcondition whether an object has been newly set up but does not create a new one. Hence, for example, `let X x = new X()` is not possible. The `let` construct, thus, is not suited for describing new objects but for storing intermediate results. The `isnew` operator has the signature

```
boolean isnew(Object o);
```

Signatur

and can be applied to objects only but not to primitive data types or containers.

Specification of a Constructor

A special case of a method is a `constructor`. This method form is distinguished by the fact that it generates its own object. Some corresponding peculiarities need to be considered when specifying a constructor. The keyword `this` and attributes of the object are only allowed to be used in the postcondition; i.e., the precondition can make statements only about the constructor's arguments. In the postcondition, it is furthermore prohibited to access the attributes of the generated object with `@pre`, as these did not yet exist in the prestate. The following specification shows an extract of the characterization for new `Auction` objects:

```
context new Auction(Policy p)
pre:   p != null
post:  policy == p &&
       status == INITIAL &&
       messages.isEmpty;
```

OCL

In the case of constructors, `result==this` always holds. Therefore, one can access the attributes of the result with `result.status` as well as with `this.status` or with `status` alone.

Integration of Multiple Constraints

The method `changeCompany` was characterized in the constraint denoted with `CC1pre/CC1post`, under the assumption that the new company does not yet exist. Figure 3.27 now illustrates a case in which the company already exists and the precondition `CC1pre` does not apply. In this case, the postcondition `CC1post` also need not be fulfilled. This means that the above specification is *incomplete*. It can, hence, be supplemented in the following way:

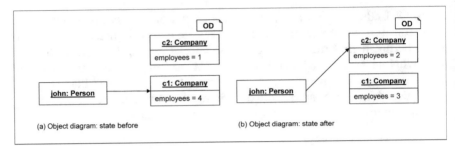

Figure 3.27. Further situation for `changeCompany`

```
context Person.changeCompany(String name)                    OCL
pre  CC2pre:   company.name != name &&
                 exists Company co: co.name == name
post CC2post:
     company.name          == name &&
     company.employees     == company.employees@pre      +1 &&
     company@pre.employees == company@pre.employees@pre  -1
```

This constraint describes another part of the behavior of the method
`changeCompany` by assuming that the company is already registered but
the person does not currently belong to the company. Such a case where two
method specifications exist for the same method can occur for several reasons. For example, different developers can make demands in parallel on a
method. It is also possible that demands on the same method can be inherited
from two different interfaces or superclasses. In both cases, an integration of
the constraint is necessary. The two method specifications can be understood
as implications of the form[24]

> $CC1pre'$ **implies** $CC1post$;
> $CC2pre'$ **implies** $CC2post$;

If both pairs are supposed to be valid, these combine to a new statement
of the form

> $(CC1pre'$ **implies** $CC1post)$ **&&** $(CC2pre'$ **implies** $CC2post)$

This means that, if both preconditions are fulfilled, both postconditions must
also be fulfilled. This causes inconsistencies if the two postconditions contradict each other. Thus, postconditions are often defined orthogonally to each
other by dealing with different aspects of the method or if, like in the case
mentioned above, the preconditions are disjunctive. The possibility to combine method specifications with overlapping preconditions can, e.g., be used
for separate modeling of different aspects of a method's behavior.

---

[24] $CC1pre'$ differs from $CC1pre$ in the fact that all occurring attributes, variables, etc.
are furnished with `@pre`. So, the interpretation of $CC1pre'$ can take place after the
method call and, however, the original value of $CC1pre$ can be determined.

In some cases, it is reasonable not only to place method specifications side by side to determine by tests or inspection whether they are consistent but to explicitly integrate them into a single characterization. This can happen, for example, according to the following scheme also introduced in [HHB02]:

```
context Person.changeCompany(String name)
pre:   CC1pre || CC2pre
post:  (CC1pre' implies CC1post) && (CC2pre' implies CC2post)
```

However, as different names were used for the method parameters, re-namings are necessary. Often, a constraint combined in this way can be simplified. Thus, in the example, we get the following specification:

```
context Person.changeCompany(String name)
pre:   company.name != name
post:  company.name == name &&
    company@pre.employees == company@pre.employees@pre -1 &&
    (company.employees    == company.employees@pre    +1
    || (isnew(company) && company.employees == 1))
```

Inheritance of Method Specifications

Usually, the specification of a method's behavior is inherited to subclasses; i.e., a subclass of Person is allowed to override the method changeCompany and, by doing so, change its behavior within the given method specification. Further method specifications for subclasses may also be given. Here, the described procedure for the integration of method specifications is used to combine the inherited and added method specifications.

In frameworks, it is common to provide default implementations for methods that are to be overwritten. Such a default implementation can be comprehended in much more detail by a method specification if this is only valid for the method of this class. Hence, in some situations, it is desirable not to inherit a method implementation. For this purpose, the stereotype «not-inherited» can be used, preventing the inheritance used as default.[25]

Figure 3.28 demonstrates the validity areas of inherited and non-inherited method specifications. The explicitly given specifications supplement each other and can be integrated by the already described procedure.

The stereotype «not-inherited» is introduced in Table 3.29. In the contrast to method specifications, the question concerning inheritance of invariants does not arise because the context can consist of several objects and the extension of a type given in the context contains the object of the subclasses.

---

[25] The negatively formulated stereotype «not-inherited» is supposed to explicitly indicate that this should rather be the exception.

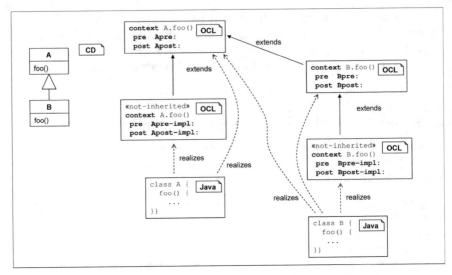

Figure 3.28. Specialization hierarchy for method specifications

Stereotype «not-inherited»	
Model element	OCL method specifications
Motivation	The inheritance of a method specification is prevented with «not-inherited».
Glossary	A method specification marked with «not-inherited» is called an *implementation description*.
Effect	An implementation description is valid for the implementation of this class but not for subclasses. Implementation descriptions are especially suited for tests on a default method that can be overridden.

Table 3.29. Stereotype «not-inherited»

Incomplete Characterizations

For constraint CC2post, there is an interesting implementation alternative at first sight. Instead of changing the link of the person to the new company, the implementation could also change the name of the old company object.

In general, a method specification does not provide a complete description of the favored behavior. This is because an implementation of the method can modify further system parts which are not explicitly mentioned at all. There are various approaches summarized by the expression *frame* concept to explicitly control potential changes [GHG+93, BMR95].

The direct approach is to explicitly give a list of unchangeable objects or attributes. In [MMPH99], e.g., the keyword `unchanged` is used for this purpose. This negative list, however, can become very large, and, furthermore, demands an overview of the whole system; i.e., it is not modular. A variant, thus, is to define a positive list of all changeable objects or attributes, as well as the potentially newly created objects. A third variant implicitly obtains this positive list from the set of objects and attributes mentioned in the specification.

However, the last approach has the disadvantage that, usually in the case of inherited methods, it is explicitly desired to alter new attributes that could not be anticipated in the specification of the method of the subclass.

For verification purposes, however, it is indispensable to exclude all potentially negative alterations in the specification. In a verification, we (implicitly) have to assume a *vicious* developer team and have to show that, for all potential implementations, the requested properties hold; i.e., the developers are forced to implement an innocuous system. In practice, this assumption is not sensible, as developers are usually *benevolent* people and each person in each phase of software development is able to make qualified decisions that determine further design and implementation details. The metaphor of the *benevolent developer*, in modeling, allows many details to be left open. In particular, it can be assumed that, in the implementation, the system state is modified to a minimum degree only in order to correctly realize the pre/postconditions.

Here, of course, tensions arise between the necessity of determining properties in the specification and the trust in the developer to correctly complete incomplete specifications with details. However, these tensions can be reduced, for example, by specifiers and developers belonging to the same group of people or by their closely intertwined cooperation.

The last case `company.name==name` for the method `changeCompany` can serve as an example here. In this case, the person already belongs to the company. This case is also specified separately and, if required, integrated into the whole specification:

```
context Person.changeCompany(String name)
pre  CC3pre:  company.name == name
post CC3post: company == company@pre &&
              company.employees == company.employees@pre
```

It is striking that the accomplishment of the postcondition demands no real activities but only ensures that activities taking place in the other cases are prevented. It is explicitly determined that the attributes changed in other cases are supposed to remain unchanged here. Further attributes are not mentioned, as we assume a benevolent developer. However, he can possibly make careless mistakes, which is why the third case modeled here can help with the development of code and tests.

Recursive Function Definition

If a method is described by a pre- and postcondition, this method can be used recursively already during its definition. The OCL standard [OMG10b] allows recursive definitions but does not precisely clarify their meaning. The specification

```
context foo(int a, int b)
post: result = if a <= 0 then b
               else foo(a-1,b*b)
```

uses `foo` recursively. Due to the particular structure, with `result` on the left-hand side of the equation, this specification can be read as a functional implementation and, thus, obtains a clear meaning. The precise meaning behind recursive functional definitions is relatively complex and shall not be explained in detail here. The essential issue is that, in case of a recursive equation, often many implementations are possible but, in case of special forms of the specification, a unique meaning is determined by fixed-point induction, exactly corresponding to the behavior of the implementation.

Let us give some examples that are correct in the sense of a specification and can even be reasonable for certain cases of application but also have very dangerous effects due to the recursive use of the defined function:

```
context A.foo(a,b)
post:   result = if a <= 0 then b
                 else foo(a,b)
```

would not necessarily terminate as an implementation. As a specification, for the case a <= 0, a statement is made, while for a > 0 simply no statement is made and, hence, every implementation is possible. A completely missing statement carries this to extremes:

```
context A.foo(a,b)
post:   result = foo(a,b)
```

In contrast,

```
context A.foo(a,b)
post:   result*a = foo(result,b)
```

definitely does constrain the method but has diverse implementations, even the rather simple foo(a,b)=0. However, none of the implementations is favored. Multiple implementation alternatives are also offered by

```
context A.foo(a,b)
post:   a = foo(result,b)
```

Because only queries can be used in constraints, recursive method definitions are possible only for queries. Thus, attribute manipulations disappear, and in case of a suitable definition structure in a functional body-like form, even a single and, hence, unique implementation can be described by using inductive data structures such as natural numbers. In Sect. 3.5.1, we use this in order to describe the transitive closure of a relation. As we generally apply OCL a as specification language, definitions with recursively used functions are allowed but remain property-oriented specifications.

Helper Variables and the `let` Construct

In complex method specifications, it is possible that a certain object, which is supposed to be modified and, therefore, checked in the postcondition, needs to be identified already in the precondition. In order to be able to introduce common variables for the pre- and postcondition, the `let` construct has been extended. It now allows the definition of variables which, then in both constraints, have the same assigned value. With this, the method specification `CC2pre/CC2post` can be converted to

```
context Person.changeCompany(String name)                    OCL
let oldCo  = company;
    newCos = { co in Company | co.name == name };
    newCo  = any newCos
pre:  oldCo.name != name && newCos.size == 1
post: newCo.employees == newCo.employees@pre +1 &&
      oldCo.employees == oldCo.employees@pre -1
```

This extension of the `let` construct can be regarded as a double application of the `let` construct:

```
context Person.changeCompany(String name)                    OCL
pre:  let oldCo  = company;
          newCos = { co in Company | co.name == name };
          newCo  = any newCos
      in oldCo.name != name && newCos.size == 1
post: let oldCo  = company@pre;
          newCos = { co in Company@pre | co.name@pre == name };
          newCo  = any newCos
      in newCo.employees == newCo.employees@pre +1 &&
         oldCo.employees == oldCo.employees@pre -1
```

The introduction of intermediate variables and helper functions by the `let` construct can, however, also be regarded as a definition of attributes or methods of an anonymous class that is implicitly integrated into the context. Figure 3.30 illustrates this by means of the two examples `Time2` and `Time3` from Sect. 3.1.2. For describing the new attributes and new operation, we also use OCL. As already discussed in [CK01], this form of illustration is, however, not equivalent to the definition with the `let` construct itself. The elements defined by `let` are only locally available and can, therefore, not be used outside the definition scope. Furthermore, there is a difference in handling defined results as the `let` construct allows undefined intermediate results and can yet deliver a whole result in a defined way.

As already mentioned in Sect. 3.1.2, the possibility of recursive definitions increases the complexity of the typing (compare [CK01], Gofer [Jon96], and SML [MTHM97]) within the `let` construct. It becomes less comprehensible, as shown by the many incorrect recursive definitions of an association's transitive closure, that can be found in literature. As OCL is a specification language, recursive definitions have to be regarded as equations and not as operational definitions. However, as already shown and further discussed in Sect. 3.5.1, equations are sometimes ambiguous. Recursive definitions are also possible using the underlying object system, so we omit the possibility of recursive definitions here.

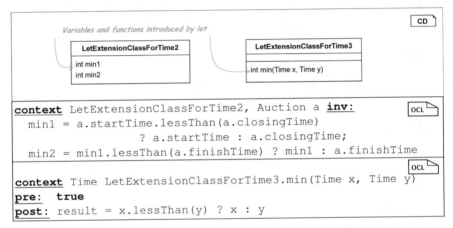

Figure 3.30. `let` construct as extension of the context

3.4.4 Libraries of Queries

OCL is designed as a constraint language that, with the exception of local definitions in `let` constructs, does not allow for the definition of its own data types, methods, or variables. Instead, data types and methods of the underlying model as well as the stereotypes «query» and «OCL» are used. Thus, the underlying model can offer predefined libraries of queries that enable a compact definition of OCL constraints. As examples, some of these functions are discussed in this section, and it is shown how libraries of this kind can be compiled.

Formally, the specification queries defined here are offered by a class that, for simplicity reasons, is called `OCLlib`. We assume that this class always implicitly exists in a constraint's context, so that its static queries can also be used, like `sum` instead of `OCLlib.sum`. Figure 3.31 contains the signature of an extract of this small library. The queries contained therein are declared static by underlining, so that they can be used without a reference to an object.

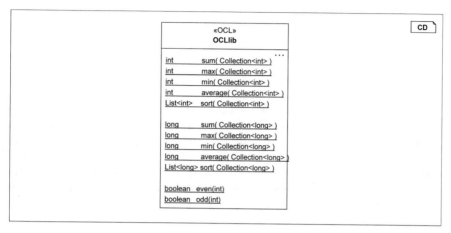

Figure 3.31. OCL example library with static queries

For containers with integers, mathematical operations such as sum or maximum are available:

```
inv:
   let Set<int> bids = { a.numberOfBids | a in Auction };
       int total   = sum(bids);
       int highest = max(bids)
   in ...
```

For sorting lists of integers in ascending order, the operator `sort` can be used.

```
inv:
   let Set<long> idents = { a.auctionIdent | a in Auction };
       List<int> sortedIdents  = sort(idents)
   in ...
```

A variety of further predefined and domain- or project-specific operations are conceivable and should, similar to in programming languages, be available for OCL.

3.5 Expressiveness of OCL

To use OCL successfully, it is reasonable to understand what OCL cannot describe or, at least, what it cannot describe adequately. Also, the nature of an invariant in object-oriented system runs and its field of application are to be explained further. The question of executability also belongs to the investigation of a language's expressiveness. A comparison with a complete specification language such as Spectrum [BFG⁺93] provides further information about the abilities of OCL.

3.5.1 Transitive Closure

A popular example for demonstrating OCL's abilities is the modeling of a transitive closure of a binary relation. For this, a self-referential association of the underlying model is used as the basis relation. The whole–part relation used in compositions is a typical example of this. A further example is the transitive closure of the inheritance relation used for modeling context constraints at metamodel level in the UML standard [OMG10b]. Figure 3.32 shows the class Person and friends can also be stored in the system. The derived association clique is now supposed to be specified in such a way that it depicts the transitive closure of the friend association and, thus, makes the set of all ancestors directly accessible.

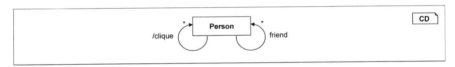

Figure 3.32. Reflexive association and transitive closure

In the aforementioned examples, the transitive closure is specified according to the following pattern:

```
context Person inv TransitiveWrong:
  clique = friend.addAll(friend.clique)
```

Unfortunately, this specification is incomplete. Indeed, it guarantees that the association clique is a superset of the association friend and that the association is transitive, but there are a variety of further realizations for the clique association. Figure 3.33(a) shows an object structure with three objects and the association friend for which multiple solutions for the invariant Transitive are given in Fig. 3.33(b–d).

In total, there are correct solutions for the object structure described in Fig. 3.33(a), but only one should be described. The desired solution has one vital characteristic in contrast to all other solutions: it is contained in all solutions; i.e., it is the *minimal solution*. If the constraint Transitive was regarded as a logical program, exactly the minimal solution would be calculated. The minimality of the requested solution, hence, corresponds to the interpretation of the constraint as a computation rule. However, OCL is not a

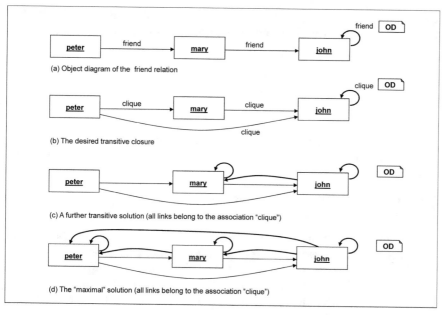

Figure 3.33. Solutions for the transitive closure

programming language but a property-oriented specification language. The problem in this characterization lies in the *recursion* embedded therein: it uses the association `clique` already for its own definition. In specifications, such a recursive situation should be avoided as far as possible, as it repeatedly causes problems. Also, a variant defining the transitive closure in method form has the same variety of implementation possibilities:

```
context Person.clique() inv Transitive2:
post:
    result = friend.addAll(friend.clique())
```

By relying on fixed-point theory, the minimality property of the transitive closure can be cleverly used for a unique characterization. OCL, however, is only a first-order logical language and does not (directly) offer such concepts. But there is a trick that can be used in OCL in order to describe second-order operations such as inductive or recursive structures, transitive closures, term generation, etc. by referring to nonnegative integers, which are a fixed part of OCL. For completeness reasons, it should be mentioned that nonnegative integers contain an inductive structure[26] in their characterization, which says that each integer can be described by a finite expression of the form $0+1+1+1\ldots$. Hence, the transitive closure can be characterized

---

[26] The fifth Peano axiom serves as the basis for the term generation of nonnegative integers.

by a method that takes a step towards calculating the transitive closure and
that keeps count of the steps over a nonnegative integer parameter:

```
context «query» Set<Person>                                    OCL
          Person.cliqueUpToN(int n):
post:
  result == if (n<=1) friend
            else friend.addAll(friend.cliqueUpToN(n-1))
```

Now, the association clique can be determined by characterizing a sufficient number of steps. The set of all participating objects is a suitable upper
limit.

```
context Person inv Transitive3:                               OCL
  clique = cliqueUpToN(Person.size)
```

Sequences also have an inductive structure and can, thus, also be used for
defining a transitive closure, but this is often rather laborious.[27]

However, as in particular handling of the transitive closure of reflexive
associations occurs rather often, OCL/P offers a special operator $**$, characterizing the transitive closure. This operator is applied in the following form:

```
context Person inv Transitive4:                              OCL
  this.clique = this.friend**
```

The expression friend** itself can be regarded as a derived association
and can be used in OCL in exactly this form, whereby the additional association clique becomes redundant.

The operator $**$ is only directly applied to a reflexive association.[28] It
cannot be applied on chains of associations of the form (a.b.c)$**$. In order
to still be able to talk about nested associations, a derived association that
consists of a chain of associations can be introduced.

The transitive closure of an association is also calculated if the association's source and target are not identical or even if they are not subclasses of
each other. In that case, the transitive closure is identical to the initial association. Figure 3.34 illustrates that, in all four occurring cases, the transitive
closure has the same source and target class as the initial association. However, the cardinality of the transitive closure is always "$*$" (not shown in the
figure).

Likewise, the transitive closure and a number of similar constructions can
be cleverly modeled by functions of higher order. Functions of higher order
are functions that have other functions as arguments. However, in object-
oriented programming and modeling and, thus, also in OCL, functions of

---

[27] [MC99, Ric02] use the procedural operator iterate and the data structure of the
sequences to describe the Warshall algorithm for calculating a transitive closure.

[28] An association is called *reflexive* if both ends belong to the same class and are subclasses of each other. Reflexivity of the depicted relation at link level is not demanded.

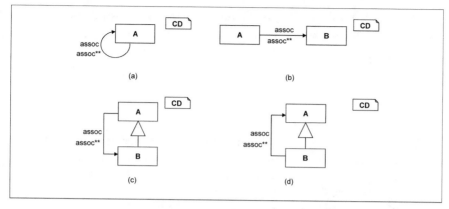

Figure 3.34. Typing of the transitive closure

higher order do not currently exist. Instead, functions are encapsulated as methods in objects and these objects are passed onto other objects as arguments, hence simulating functions of higher order. Several design patterns such as *Command* [GHJV94] are based on this principle. This principle can be used indirectly in OCL by defining suitable queries in the object system and applying them in OCL constraints.

3.5.2 The Nature of an Invariant

OCL constraints are usually applied as invariants, pre- or postconditions. Although there is an intuitive understanding that invariants hold at "each point in time of the system run," a detailed consideration of the actual validity of an invariant is necessary.

Invariants of the system are primarily formulated by OCL constraints. However, in Chap. 4, also object diagrams are used for defining invariants. As well, several modeling concepts of class diagrams can be understood as invariants. Extensions that cannot directly be expressed in class diagrams, such as cardinalities of associations, can also be expressed as invariants. Correspondingly, a cardinality of the form "3-7" can be depicted by

```
context Class object inv:
   let s = object.assoziation.size
   in  3 <= s && s <= 7
```
OCL

A typical example for an invariant is the characterization of a relation between two or more attributes. A standard example is the redundantly stored length of a list. Let us assume that a class A has two integer attributes x and y;

```
context A inv Equals:
   x == y
```
OCL

describes such a relation. If an attribute is changed, the second one must also be changed. This can, e.g., happen by

```Java
void incX() {
  x++;
  // (1)
  y++;
}
```

Due to the invariant `Equals`, developers may need to rely on the fact that the values of both attributes actually are the same. As Java does not have the possibility to atomically make a set of attribute modifications, the invariant, however, does not hold *at all times*. In the case where another code is executed in parallel and method `incX` is briefly interrupted at point (1), this violation, in fact, can have effects on the system behavior. Basically, there are two options where foreign code is executed: on the one hand, concurrent processes (threads) can interact with the code; on the other hand, method calls can be bound to other objects at point (1).

Although Java has no transaction concept, concurrent execution of code can be controlled by synchronization of methods. In the implementation, an invariant can then be violated "temporarily" without any effect because the critical location is blocked. If an invariant is more complex, this can theoretically lead to system runs where it is permanently violated, although the system works properly. The invariant could, for example, be alternately violated and restored by concurrent processes at different points.

In pure sequential systems without concurrency, control can be passed on only be a method call. Therefore, a method call should only be conducted very sparingly while an invariant is violated, as the called method may have been overridden and, thus, behave in a different way than expected. This is why method calls should be carried out before violation or after restoration of the invariants. The conclusion of this discussion is that an invariant's scope of validity does not stretch across the total runtime of the system.

Thus, a precise approach is to explicitly determine the validity of an OCL constraint in Java code. For example, the method `incX` can be formulated by using a Java extension with the keyword `ocl` for invariants as follows:

```Java
void synchronized incX() {
  ocl Equals;
  x++;
  ocl x==y+1;
  y++;
  ocl Equals;
}
```

The integration of OCL constraints with Java code bodies by using the `ocl` statement for assertions, as presented in Appendix B, can form a basis for the Hoare logic for the programming language Java. Articles [vO01,

RWH01] show that, especially for the language Java which is spread on the Internet and confronted with security problems, such a logical calculus can be reasonably implemented. Another helpful tool is the Extended Static Checker for Java (ESC/Java) [RLNS00] that allows, due to a number of annotations, for example, to formulate assertions and statically verify these. However, the explicit annotation of code with assertions in larger systems requires considerable effort as, at many places, invariants that only become relevant in called methods have to be "dragged along."

In development, invariants are practically used for the formulation of properties that still need to be realized, in tests, for assertions that need to be automatically verified, and for invariants in the code. Using assertions, however, is also of interest when advancing models in which, e.g., an old data structure is related to a new one.

3.6 Summary

In this section, OCL/P has been introduced as an integration of the OCL standard from [OMG10b] and the programming language Java. By doing so, semantic adjustments of the logic and syntactical modifications of the appearance of OCL have been carried out. In addition, elements of functional languages such as Gofer [Jon96] have been integrated to allow smart handling of sets and lists. The extended possibilities for the property-oriented definition of containers, in particular, provide considerably elegant options for the formulation of constraints.

The modified form of OCL provides a solid basis for the chapters to come. It can be applied for the generation of tests as well as for the description of functions and actions in Statecharts.

4

Object Diagrams

> Things only have the significance
> we assign to them.
>
> Molière

In UML/P, object diagrams take on the role of modeling structures on an exemplary basis. Thus, they are particularly suitable for depicting statically unchangeable structures in otherwise dynamic object-oriented systems or special situations that, e.g., are used as post- or preconditions in tests. In this
chapter, we introduce object diagrams and discuss their methodical use. The
integration with OCL results in a "logic for object diagrams."

© Springer International Publishing Switzerland 2016
B. Rumpe, *Modeling with UML*, DOI 10.1007/978-3-319-33933-7_4

Object diagrams are wellsuited for modeling the structure of a software system and, thus, complement class diagrams. An object diagram describes a collection of objects and their relations at a point in time in the lifecycle of a system. Therefore, object diagrams focus on instances and have exemplary character. Several object diagrams can describe differing situations at different points in time within the same part of the system.

An object diagram can, for instance, be used in order to characterize the situation during the startup of a system, describe an initial or a desired situation for a test, or illustrate an imperfect situation. Due to their exemplary nature, object diagrams lack expressiveness if the situation's context is not described. This is why we discuss in this chapter how to use object diagrams and, in addition, how to integrate them with the OCL logic. On the one hand, OCL constraints are used for characterizing additional properties of an object diagram; on the other hand, the OCL logic is used in order to combine object diagrams and use them as pre- and postconditions for method specifications.

In the UML standard [OMG10a], object diagrams are treated as standalone notation. This has led to the situation that this kind of diagram still receives too little attention and is only now escaping from its niche existence in form of better tool support and improved methodical use. Amongst other things, an object diagram is perfectly suited for describing the initial situation of a test. In the test framework JUnit [JUn16, BG98, BG99], special methods for the setup of object structures that can be generated from object diagrams are used.

By separating the notations for object diagrams and class diagrams, a stand-alone kind of diagram emerges that can be used in a methodically independent way. Still, object diagrams are less important than class diagrams, because class diagrams show and constrain the essential architectural description of a system. Object diagrams mainly have illustrative character and, due to their exemplary nature, are usually not able to completely describe a system. Nevertheless, object diagrams can be very important in several different phases of software development, starting from the definition of requirements up to the representation of erroneous situations in maintenance.

Apart from the UML standard [OMG10a], there is hardly any independent literature covering the use of object diagrams. But in [GHK99], for example, extensions that are especially interesting due to a number of notational constructs for particular situations are discussed. An extension of object diagrams for interface descriptions is introduced in [HRR98]. The question of how to model large object structures has been dealt with in [Ber97]. There, an interesting expansion is discussed, breaking down objects into subobjects along the inheritance hierarchy and, thus, being able to present object-internal call structures. This is particularly practical when using multiple inheritance, as in C++. Additionally, relatively rich component diagrams in which components can communicate via ports are introduced. Another form of handling object-diagram-like structures can be found in graph grammars

[Roz99, EEKR99, WKS10, AKRS06], where a grammar rule identifies a sub-graph in an object structure where it applies structural and attribute changes.

Section 4.1 offers an example-oriented introduction to the usage of object diagrams. The following section discusses the semantics of an object diagram and, thus, the statements that can be described with an object diagram. The integration of object diagrams with the OCL logic is carried out in Sect. 4.3, and the resulting methodical application possibilities are demonstrated in Sect. 4.4 by means of examples. Additionally, Appendix C.4 finally describes the complete abstract syntax of object diagrams and their logic extension.

Object in an object diagram. An object is the instance of a *class* and contains the *attributes* that the class defines. These attributes are initialized with a value (or not initialized, if applicable). In the object diagram, *prototypical objects* are used in order to illustrate exemplary situations. Usually, there is no 1:1 relation between the *prototypical objects* visible in the diagram and the real objects of the system (also see the discussion in Sect. 4.2).

Object name allows the unique identification of the object in the object diagram. As the object name, a descriptive name is chosen that, usually, cannot be retrieved in the real system, as system-specific object identifiers are used there.

Attribute describes a state component of an object. An attribute in the object diagram is characterized by its name, the type, and a concrete value. Further characteristics, such as visibility, can be attached to the attribute. In *abstract object diagrams*, variable names or expressions can be used instead of concrete values. For these variables the value remains "unspecified" in the diagram. The attribute type or value can be omitted as well.

Link is an instance of an association between two objects whose classes are connected through the association. The navigation directions and the names of associations and roles can also be depicted on the link.

Composition link is a special form of link where further dependencies of the sub-object from the whole exist beside the mere connection. A composition link is an instance of a composition.

Figure 4.1. Definitions for object diagrams

4.1 Introduction to Object Diagrams

Figure 4.1 contains a brief description of the most important concepts regarding object diagrams. Subsequently, these concepts are explained in greater detail.

Figure 4.2 shows a simple object diagram from the auction system that consists of one object only. This object describes a power auction.

Object diagrams have to *conform* to the structure predefined by class diagrams. As most of the object diagrams in this chapter are taken from the

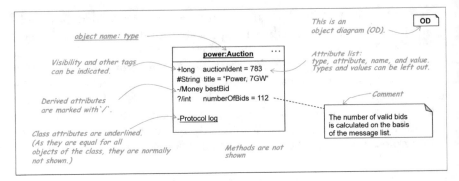

Figure 4.2. Single `Auction` object

auction system, the properties of the auction system that are essential for the object diagrams in this chapter are summarized in the class diagram shown in Fig. 4.3.

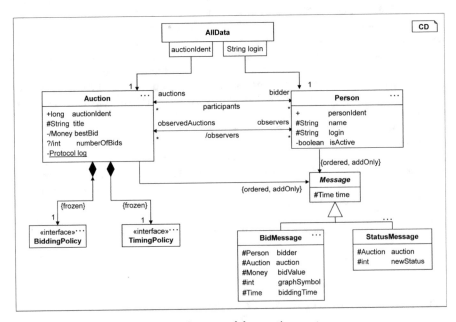

Figure 4.3. Excerpt of the auction system

4.1.1 Objects

Objects are the core elements of an object diagram. The object contained in Fig. 4.2 shows crucial elements for depicting such an object. The graphic representation of an object is very similar to that of a class. The first field includes the *object name* together with the *type* of the object. The object name is a freely chosen identifier for this object that is unambiguous within the diagram. It plays a role similar to that of the actual object identifier of objects in the real system, but these two must not be confused. The real object identifier is an anonymous entity that occurs explicitly neither in the model nor in the program code.

The top right marker `OD` for object diagrams serves for the precise distinction of class and object diagrams. Furthermore, object names are underlined in the form `name:Type`. The name begins with a lower-case letter. If the name of the object is of no further significance, it may be omitted. The colon, however, before the type declaration is preserved (see Fig. 4.4(b)). If, vice versa, the object type is already known from the context or if it can be deduced from the attribute list, we can omit the type instead (see Fig. 4.4(c)).[1]

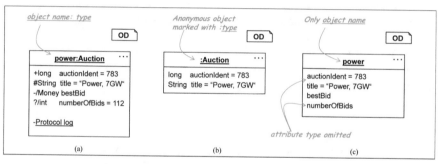

Figure 4.4. Forms of representation of the `Auction` object

This figure also shows that attributes obey the same rules for the usage of visibility modifiers and other tags as in class diagrams. The attribute list need not be complete. Accordingly, the two representation indicators "..." and "©" introduced in Fig. 2.4 are used.

Even if a type declaration exists, it does not necessarily describe the object's class. Instead, the object can also be an instance of a subclass. Hence, it is a real *type declaration*. Therefore, abstract classes and interfaces are also allowed as types for the objects of the object diagram.

4.1.2 Attributes

The second field in an object representation consists of a list of attributes. This field closely resembles that of class diagrams. Attributes can be omitted or visibilities, tags, and stereotypes attached to attributes. In contrast to the

---

[1] According to Java, `Type name` would be common. Then, however, the optional omission of the object name `name` or type `Type` would be ambiguous. Therefore, the notation from the UML standard is used.

attribute description of a class, concrete values for the attributes are usually also given. A completely described attribute without additional tags thus consists of the *attribute type*, the *attribute name* and the *attribute value* in the form `Type name = value`. A concrete value can be omitted if the content of the attribute is not relevant for depicting the desired facts or if it is described by another concept, e.g., an OCL constraint. The type of an attribute can be omitted as well, as it can be found in a class diagram.

If required by the representation, not only attributes directly assigned to the object can explicitly be listed in an object, but also class attributes, derived attributes and inherited attributes. If the value of a class attribute is given, it remains the same in all depicted objects of this class. Generally, derived attributes are related to other attributes of the object by an invariant. Such invariants need to be taken into consideration in an object diagram.

There is no representation of inheritance relations in an object diagram. Instead, the attributes inherited from the superclass are usually explicitly listed in the subclass. The inheritance structure between classes is thus "expanded" in an object diagram.

While classes in class diagrams have a third field for methods, no methods are shown in the object diagram. Therefore, a method list does not exist in the object diagram.

4.1.3 Links

A link brings two objects into relation. An object is an instance of a class, so a link is an instance of an association. This is why there may be multiple objects of the same type and multiple links of the same association in an object diagram. Figure 4.5 shows an object structure for an auction where, at least, the three given persons participate. One of them is permitted only as an observer.

Usually, links are marked with the association name and, optionally, with further tags of the association. Especially role names and the navigation direction are expedient when it comes to links and can be taken over from the association. Like associations, links can be bidirectional, unidirectional or depicted without explicitly defined direction.

If the association name is not given explicitly, role names can be used, as in the case of an association. If the association can be identified from the connected ends, the link does not need a name. In this case, however, the types of both objects participating in a link must be given.

Links of derived associations are depicted like those of ordinary ones. However, the invariant that characterizes a derived association must be taken into account in order to obtain a valid object diagram.

The association tag {frozen} that, for instance, was used for associations to message lists in Fig. 2.11, can, in object diagrams, be applied to links as well. It shows that the link is already created and that it must not be changed during the lifetime of the two objects.

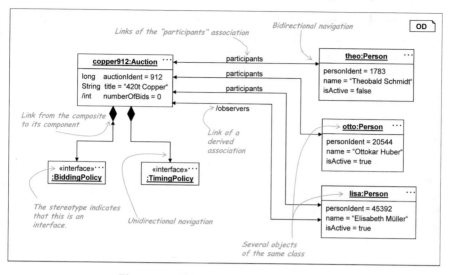

Figure 4.5. Object structure of an auction

Two prototypical objects depicted in a diagram represent two different objects in the system. This also applies when both objects have the same type and cannot be distinguished by their names or their attribute values. Figure 4.6 shows an object diagram with seven different anonymous Person objects, all participating in the auction copper913. This rule for distinction also applies for links.

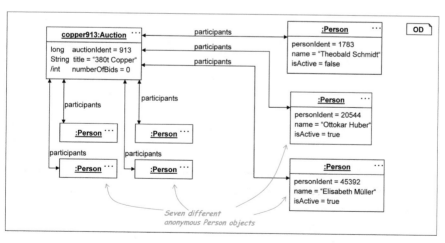

Figure 4.6. Several anonymous objects

The level of detail for presenting an object is left to the modeler. The example in Fig. 4.6 shows that even objects of the same type can be presented in distinctly detailed forms.

In analogy to the class diagram, it is, of course, possible to depict objects and links with some helpful icons. In object diagrams, the legibility can be increased through appropriate application of icons as well.

4.1.4 Qualified Links

An association can have a *qualifier* at one end that is used to select a unique target object from a number of objects. In an object diagram, the concrete qualifier value can be added to each link of such an association. Figure 4.7 contains an object diagram with multiple auctions that can be reached using a qualifier starting from the singleton of the class `AllData`.

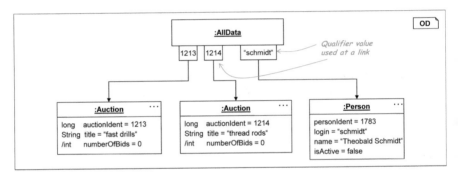

Figure 4.7. Qualified links

The qualifiers in this example are always identical to the attribute of the target object distinctly defining the target. If this attribute is defined in the object, the qualifier value is redundant information. In these cases, the qualifier can also be omitted, or the link can name the qualifying attribute instead of indicating a concrete qualifier value (see Fig. 4.8).

An association is regarded as qualified if it has the tag {ordered}. In this case, integers can be used as qualifier values. Figure 4.9 shows a collection of message objects that are assigned to an auction. The highest given qualifier is 14 so that, due to the completeness of the interval available as qualifier scope, at least 15 messages with the indexes 0 to 14 must be available. Here, the 12 bids are not shown.

4.1.5 Composition

A *composition* is shown by a filled diamond at one end of the association in the object diagram as well. This expresses a strong dependency of the subobjects from the whole. We have already seen in the example in Fig. 4.5 that, for

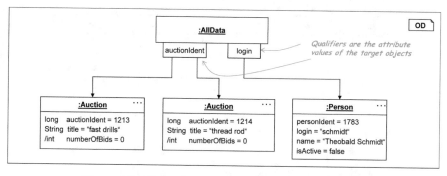

Figure 4.8. Alternative representation of qualified links

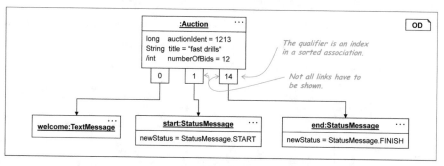

Figure 4.9. Links of an ordered association

links, these diamonds can be taken over in a similar manner. The anonymous objects shown with :BiddingPolicy and :TimingPolicy are in fact objects that implement respective interfaces. These are created together with the Auction object and become obsolete at the end of its lifecycle. When it comes to exchangeability and the lifecycle of dependent objects in a composite, there are, however, considerable differences in interpretation that have already been discussed in Sect. 2.3.4.

While in class diagrams a class may occur in several compositions, it is not allowed in the object diagram to assign a subobject to multiple composition links. This is demonstrated by the two valid diagrams (a) and (b) as well as the illegal diagrams (c) and (d) in Fig. 4.10. The only exception is a hierarchically nested composition in which a subobject belongs at the same time to the subordinate composite and, thus, indirectly to the superior one.

In order to underline more strongly the dependency of the subobject on the whole as well as the compositional character, there is, like in the case of classes, an alternative form of representation that makes use of graphic containedness as a form of expression. Figure 4.11 shows two object diagrams outlining an extract of the object diagram in Fig. 4.5 in two semantically equivalent forms.

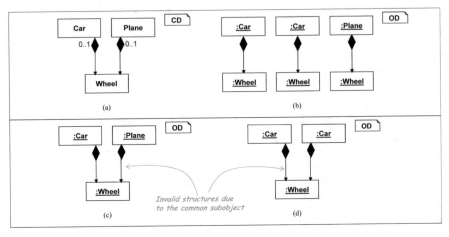

Figure 4.10. Subobjects in a composition

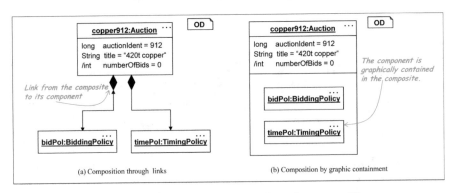

Figure 4.11. Alternative representation of a composition

In a composition, subobjects are often shown in anonymous form or given a name that is identical to the attribute name of the contained object. The object names `bidPol` and `timePol` were chosen in the object diagrams in Fig. 4.11 accordingly.

The subobjects of a composition can, for their part, contain attributes, have links to other objects (also to objects outside the composite), and themselves contain further subobjects. Thus, a complex composition structure can arise, although it should not be nested too deeply as, otherwise, the clarity of the representation is lost. Figure 4.12 shows an object composition with three composition levels.

4.1.6 Tags and Stereotypes

In a class diagram, tags and stereotypes are used to specialize the semantics of the marked element or to specify its usage. These tags and stereotypes can

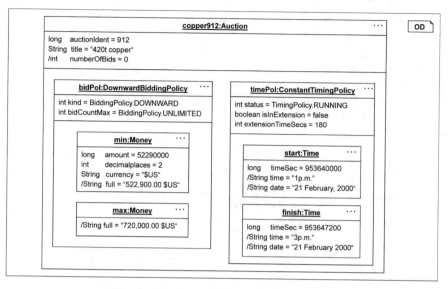

Figure 4.12. Composition with three levels

be transferred from the class to their objects and from associations to their links. Therefore, it is possible to point to special properties of the depicted objects or links, also outside the class diagram. This, for example, is helpful for {frozen} in order to indicate that the link does not change during the lifetime of both participating objects.

Figure 4.13 shows the repetition of the {frozen} tag for both policy objects.

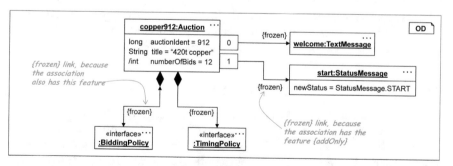

Figure 4.13. Tags in object diagrams

However, tags can also be directly assigned to elements of the object diagram without these being valid in the class diagram. The tag {addOnly} for associations also has the effect that links, once established, are not changed. Thus, the tag {frozen} can be assigned for their links without the association itself having this tag (compare the object diagram in Fig. 4.13 and the class diagram in Fig. 4.3).

Prototypical objects in an object diagram can also be marked with tags which, as described in Sect. 2.5.3, belong to the project management. This, e.g., includes tags for the creator and date of creation. Figure 4.14 shows a test object of the auction system that refers to at least three further objects used during the test execution.

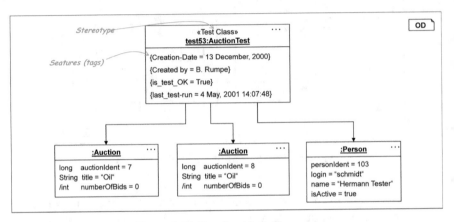

Figure 4.14. Tags in object diagrams

4.2 Meaning of an Object Diagram

In order to correctly assess the methodical use of object diagrams, the exemplary character and the relation between the prototypical objects of the object diagram and the real objects of the system need to be understood.

4.2.1 Incompleteness and Exemplaricity

Like class diagrams, object diagrams are also in general incomplete. Due to the dynamic instantiation and destruction of objects, the number of objects in a system is rapidly changing. In contrast to the number of classes, it is even unrestricted.[2] Moreover, links in object structures can change dynamically. As a result, there is no limit on the number of object structures that emerge. And these, of course, cannot be completely depicted.

Therefore, an object diagram models an excerpt of a system. This snippet is valid for a limited period of time that is, in extreme cases, reduced to a single point in time, a *snapshot*, for example, between two method calls. An

---

[2] Here, we ignore dynamic loading of classes.

object diagram illustrates this situation and contains all relevant data without being overloaded. It is at the modeler's discretion to find the correct level of abstraction. In doing so, attribute values or types, links, tags or whole objects can be omitted.

4.2.2 Prototypical Objects

The structures modeled with object diagrams have a *prototypical, pattern-like* character. They exemplarily show a situation that does not necessarily need to have a normative character. Because of this, the usage of object diagrams in descriptions of design and architecture patterns [GHJV94, BMR+96, FPR01] is popular.[3] The situation described by the object diagram need not occur in the actual system execution, but it can occur more than once, in a timely succession, or even at the same time. Different or (partly) the same objects can participate in each of the occurring situations. Thus, object diagrams can represent overlapping structures in a system. Therefore, it is necessary to clearly distinguish between the representation of an object in an object diagram and the real object in a system. Hence, objects depicted in object diagrams are called *prototypical*.

An object diagram, however, can be filled with concrete values such that, as derivable from the context, it can occur at maximally one point in the system. For example, the Auction objects of the previous figures always contain an explicit value for their identifier auctionIdent. On the other hand, the object diagram given in Fig. 4.15 can be applied to many of the auctions. Actually, this diagram represents a pattern for many purchasing auctions, as concrete values have been omitted at several places.

The attributes that are not specified in the object diagram can have arbitrary values in the system. In order to specify the potential scope of an attribute, we can use OCL to contain its values. In this way, it can be determined that, in this pattern, the minimal value is lower than the maximum value and that the auction takes two to three hours.

```
min.amount < max.amount;
start.timeSec + 2*60*60 <= finish.timeSec;
finish.timeSec <= start.timeSec + 3*60*60;
```

OCL

This constraint needs to be considered in the context of the object diagram in Fig. 4.15. Therefore, not only an object a of the type auction is nominally available but also the objects min, bidPol, start, etc. Object min, for instance, is identical to a.bidPol.min.

The integration of OCL constraints into object diagrams and the combination of object diagrams using the OCL logic is discussed in Sect. 4.3 more precisely.

---

[3] Occasionally, not only object diagrams (in the respective syntactic form) but also their expansion by call structures in the form of communication diagrams are utilized.

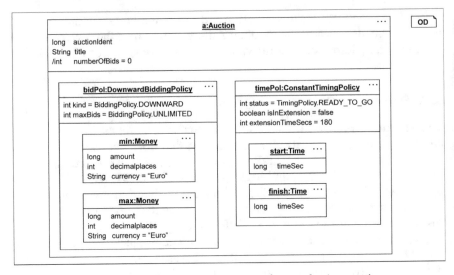

Figure 4.15. Object diagram as pattern for purchasing auctions

Based on the integration of the OCL logic into object diagrams (see Sect. 4.3), a powerful notation emerges which is used for modeling and the testing of systems. This notation also allows to describe under which conditions the situations defined by object diagrams arise, whether they have universal validity, whether they have a unique or pattern-like character, or for how long they are valid.

4.2.3 Instance Versus Model Instance

A prototypical object of an object diagram is an element of a model and not an element of the production system. There is, however, a kind of instance relation between the prototypical object and its class that is similar to the instance relation between a class and a system's real objects. Figure 4.16 aims to clarify this situation by distinguishing between system and model level. The model level is further divided into layers between which a model instantiation takes place. A class diagram is located one layer higher than the object diagram. Hence, a prototypical object is a *model instance* of the class assigned to it.

This triangular relationship can be extended if the manifestation of a class at runtime is considered as an entity on its own. In Smalltalk, classes at runtime are even separate objects that can be arbitrarily manipulated. Java also represents classes as objects but only with restricted possibilities for their access. Other programming languages, such as C++, also have structures that correspond to the representation of a class, but usually, these are not accessible by the programming code. We call the (accessible or inaccessible) man-

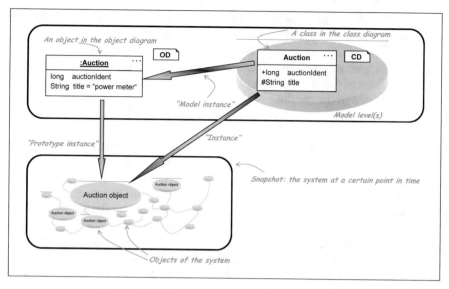

Figure 4.16. Class, prototypical object and object

ifestation of a class at runtime *class code*. The result is the relation illustrated in Fig. 4.17.

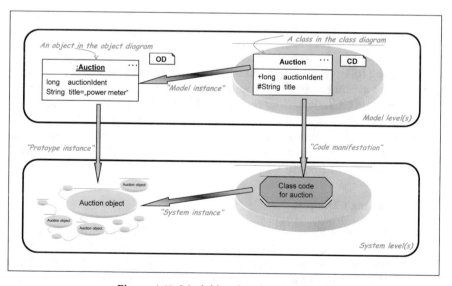

Figure 4.17. Model level and system level

In the system, there is exactly one *class code* for each class. In contrast, there can be several different representations of the same class in the model.

In each class diagram, a separate representation can be given with a slightly different focus that describes a part of the class code.

The number of prototypical objects of a class in a model is also unrestricted. Frequently, multiple objects of the same class occur within an object diagram. Each of these prototypical objects must conform to each of the class representations in the model.

The number of real objects is unrestricted as well. Their structure and functionality, however, are determined by the class code and, thus, also conform to all class representations of the model. As prototypical objects contain additional information in the form of concrete values and links, real objects can intermittently conform to prototypical objects. Basically, it would also be possible that the same real object takes over the roles of two prototypical objects in the same object diagram. This is only prevented by the corresponding rule saying that, for reasons of clarity, two different prototypical objects in the object diagram should be mapped to two individual objects in the system.

The distinction between objects, prototypical objects, classes, and class code might seem rather artificial for practical application, but it leads to a considerably clearer and, especially, simpler description than, e.g., meta-modeling with its four-layer model could·provide. There, model and system level mingle and a clear distinction between syntax and semantics is considerably aggravated. In practical use, however, these semantic details can often be neglected provided that the users of a language can recall these differences when necessary.

4.3 Logic of Object Diagrams

This and the following section introduce an essential expansion of object diagrams that facilitates their methodical application. For this purpose, we use operators from OCL that allow one to precisely define when object diagrams are valid and how they are interconnected. The integration of the object diagrams with the OCL operators results in a "logic of object diagrams." Thus, object diagrams can be integrated into OCL as statements but also combined with each other in different ways.

4.3.1 Name for a Diagram

In order to be able to include object diagrams in OCL constraints, the diagrams are named. Figure 4.18 shows the object diagram called `BidTime1`.

This diagram can be referred to in OCL as a statement of the form `OD.BidTime1`. This allows us to determine additional constraints that must hold in an object structure described by `BidTime1`:

```
OD.BidTime1 &&
timePol.start.lessThan(bid.biddingTime) &&
bid.biddingTime.lessThan(timePol.finish)
```

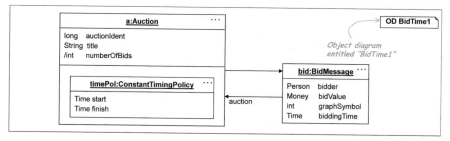

Figure 4.18. Object diagram `BidTime1`

However, in order to achieve the desired effect of the statement, one needs to pay special attention to the names used in object diagrams and OCL constraints.

The desired statement is of the form: "always when an object structure like the one in the object diagram `BidTime1` occurs, the constraints ...additionally hold." This statement is actually an invariant that, in part, is graphically specified by the object diagram. The above-mentioned OCL statement does not achieve the desired effect, as the quantification of the vacant variables is ambiguous.

4.3.2 Binding of Object Names

In object diagrams, usually several objects that can be referred to in the OCL constraint are introduced by name. The binding scope of the names `a`, `timePol`, and `bid` in the object diagram shown for `BidTime1` are, hence, to be determined outside the object diagram. The above OCL constraint can, therefore, be embedded in a completing context:

```
context Auction a, ConstantTimingPolicy timePol,
        BidMessage bid inv BidTime1A:
    OD.BidTime1 implies
      timePol.start.lessThan(bid.biddingTime) &&
      bid.biddingTime.lessThan(timePol.finish)
```

If an object diagram is used in an OCL constraint, one needs to pay attention to the fact that all names used in the object diagram are introduced in the OCL constraint; i.e., the constraint has no free variables anymore. Using the quantifier for binding object names allows flexible application of object diagrams. With the following statement, it can be demanded that, in each auction that has already started, a welcome message is sent. The two object diagrams from Fig. 4.19 are used, where `Welcome1A` is the precondition for the requirement `Welcome1B`.

Figure 4.19. Object diagrams for the welcome message

```
inv Welcome1:                                                    OCL
  forall Auction a, TimingPolicy timePol:
    OD.Welcome1A implies
      exists Message welcome: OD.Welcome1B
```

Compared with the first example BidTime1A, not all objects of the object diagrams are bound by a universal quantification here. Therefore, both diagrams are used in different forms. The statement is: "if objects a and timePol exist and fulfill the object diagram Welcome1A, then object welcome exists and all properties formulated in the object diagram Welcome1B hold." The details of the first subdiagram need not be repeated. Specifying the new relevant properties (i.e., the existence of the link with the qualifier 0) is sufficient.

As a precondition for formulating the constraint Welcome1, it was defined that the auction is already RUNNING. If the auction is closed, nothing is said about the existence of a welcome message.

We note that the statement using two object structures has no temporal implications but is interpreted on only one snapshot of the system. The used keyword implies results in a statement of the form: "if the state is RUNNING, then a welcome message exists in the auction with the index 0." A similar statement would be: "if the state is set to RUNNING, then a welcome message is to be sent." This, however, cannot be be specified as an invariant but, e.g., as a method specification (of a still unknown method to open auctions), because this second statement contains a temporal implication. The assertion Welcome1, in contrast, is truly weaker, as it allows implementation alternatives by, for example, creating the welcome message already together with the auction.

4.3.3 Integration of Object Diagram and OCL

Basically all structural properties of object diagrams and the attribute values contained therein can also be expressed directly by OCL, because all constructs of an object diagram can be implemented in OCL statements. Hence, the means for specifying properties can be chosen freely. As an example, the statement `Welcome1` can be specified as an OCL formula as follows:

```
inv Welcome2:
  forall Auction a, TimingPolicy timePol:
      (Object)a != timePol &&
      a.timePol == timePol &&
      timePol.status == TimingPolicy.RUNNING
    implies
      exists Message welcome:
        (Object)a != welcome &&
        a.messages[0] == welcome
```

In OCL, the pairwise distinction of objects of an object diagram must be defined explicitly using inequations. This can be achieved with inequations of the form `a != timePol`.[4,5]

Practice shows that comprehensive specifications of object structures using OCL quickly become unclear. On the other hand, object diagrams have restricted expressiveness. The synergy of both notations allows a powerful and compact representation of object structures.

4.3.4 Anonymous Objects

The usage of explicit object names in an object diagram enables access to these objects from outside the diagram. Anonymous objects show that such objects must exist but only allow indirect access via links. The implementation of an anonymous object can be explained by a transformation introducing an existential quantification. Actually, the implementation of anonymous objects is helpful as they reduce the dependence on the context of an object diagram. Figure 4.20 shows anonymized versions of the object diagrams in Fig. 4.19. As a result, two quantifications can be omitted in the following statement which is equivalent to `Welcome1`:[6]

```
inv Welcome3:
  forall Auction a:
      OD.Welcome3A implies OD.Welcome3B
```

---

[4] In order to obtain syntactic correctness of the comparison, the type of the first object needs to be converted, if applicable.

[5] As a is of the type `Auction` and `timePol` of the type `TimingPolicy`, both objects seem to be necessarily different anyway. But it may occur that, later in the project, a subclass of `Auction` is developed that directly implements the interface `TimingPolicy`. Then, the inequation is no longer redundant.

[6] In `Welcome1`, the object `timePol` is universally quantified, as it was moved outside the implication. It holds that $\forall a : (X \implies Y)$ is equivalent to $(\exists a : X) \implies Y$, as Y is independent of a.

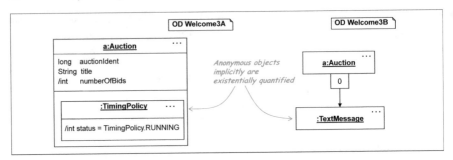

Figure 4.20. Anonymized object diagrams from `Welcome1`

To understand anonymous objects better, we examine the example in Fig. 4.21(a), which is equivalent to the conjunction of the object diagram in Fig. 4.21(b) and the OCL formula `InvA1214B` (which does not yet bind the variable `ac1214`).

```
inv InvA1214B:
    exists Person anon1, anon2: OD.A1214B
```

OCL

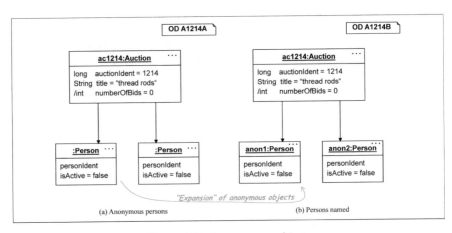

Figure 4.21. Anonymous objects

The only difference lies in the names not exported by `A1214A`, but by `A1214A`. The anonymous objects of `A1214A` have explicit labels in diagram `InvA1214B` (called `anon1` and `anon2`) and bound by an existential quantifier in the OCL part.

4.3.5 OCL Constraints in Object Diagrams

The previous examples have shown how object diagrams are embedded in OCL constraints. That, of course, is possible vice versa. Thereby, the context is defined by the object diagram and the OCL constraint can use the objects modeled therein for defining its statement. This does not restrict the binding scope of the object names. The names are still usable outside the object diagram and the OCL constraint. Therefore, the OCL constraint's context is defined by another keyword called `import`. As Fig. 4.22 shows, such OCL constraints are part of the object diagram or are assigned to the object diagram.

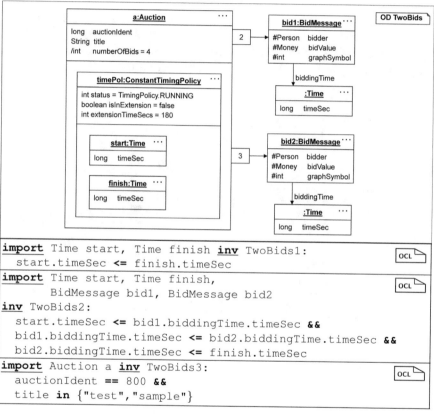

Figure 4.22. Auction with two bids and OCL conditions

The given OCL constraints are of rather different nature. `TwoBids1` is an invariant universally valid for `Auction` objects. It could be formulated in a class diagram as well. `TwoBids2` is an invariant over both bids that rank second and third in the message bar. This invariant could be generalized, as it analogously holds for other bids in the list of messages. `TwoBids3` is not an invariant but a more detailed description of the appearance of a concrete object structure. This is typical for the description of object structures for tests. However, the value for the attribute `auctionIdent` could have been entered directly into the object structure.

The example in Fig. 4.22, thus, already shows some application possibilities for OCL constraints in object diagrams. However, the descriptive convenience of object diagrams ist further enhanced in the following section by introducing *abstract values* and OCL expressions into the object diagram.

4.3.6 Abstract Object Diagrams

So far, modeling with object diagrams has been confined to either using a constant or leaving the attribute value unspecified. Now, this is generalized by the option of using free OCL expressions as attribute values. The object diagram NBids in Fig. 4.23 containing abstract values as qualifiers shows such an application.

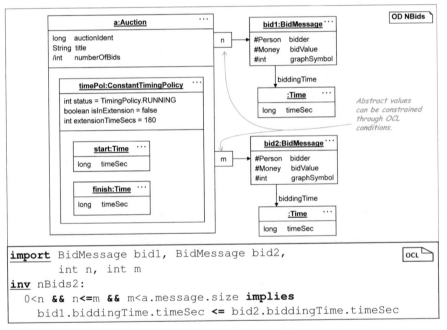

Figure 4.23. Auction with bids and generalized OCL conditions

The concrete qualifiers for selection in the list of messages used in the previous object diagram TwoBids have been replaced by abstract values in NBids. These abstract values can be imported into an OCL constraint and used for the specification of properties.

OCL expressions can describe constraints between single attributes and qualifiers more precisely. In order to set up a test auction, for example, with

100 persons, the simple object diagram NPersons in Fig. 4.24 can be used. Here, the abstract value x is used in order to determine the appearance of the individual person. The 100 persons in the test auction are determined by the OCL constraint Test32.

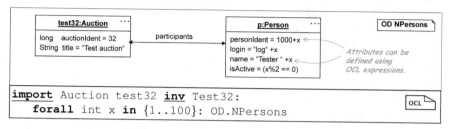

Figure 4.24. Auction with parameterized Person object

Because of the requirement that there is an incarnation of the object diagram for each x from the set 1..100 and that the attributes of the Person objects are set differently, there must be at least these 100 Person objects in the auction test32.

The use of OCL expressions in object diagrams is also especially suited for describing derived attributes. Therefore, OCL constraints for describing derived elements can often be replaced by a representation in the object diagram.

4.4 Methodical Use of Object Diagrams

The last section defined the basics for using object diagrams in different situations and for specifying them in combination with OCL constraints. In this section, default situations are outlined by means of examples in order to give better insight into the abilities and to illustrate the methodical use of object diagrams.

The expressiveness of the notation integrated with OCL and object diagrams is the same as in OCL. The reason for this is that each object diagram can be translated into an OCL formula, even though it is rather illegible. Correspondingly, the resulting integration provides a higher level of convenience when compactly and understandably describing situations. Vice versa, the expressiveness of object diagrams has increased as, for instance, alternatives, combinations, or generalizations can be used through abstract values.

The previous section showed how both notations, i.e., object diagrams and OCL expressions, can be integrated into the other notation. Adding OCL constraints to an object diagram has, e.g., been demonstrated in Fig. 4.22.

Conversely, it is possible to integrate object diagrams as short forms for expressions using OD.Name. The unassigned names of the object diagram, i.e., object names and variables for abstract values, can be referred to in the OCL constraint. These references and the embedding into the OCL logic enable flexible use of object diagrams. This is discussed for several methodical applications using examples.

Structural combinations of object diagrams, alternatives, or undesired situations can be modeled with the help of operators of the propositional logic &&, ||, and !.

4.4.1 Composition of Object Diagrams

The && operator can combine multiple object diagrams and, thus, describe a larger object structure. The elements where the object diagrams are combined are the objects with common names. With this technique a larger object structure can be decomposed into manageable pieces and illustrated by suitable object diagrams. Figure 4.25 shows several individual diagrams that are connected using a conjunction.

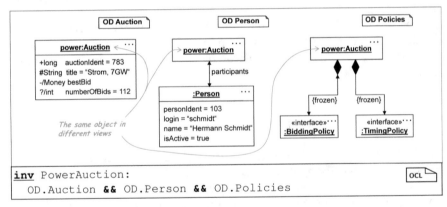

Figure 4.25. Combination of object diagrams

The resulting OCL constraint PowerAuction can be understood as composed object diagram. The Auction object named power serves as a connecting element because it occurs in all object diagrams.

A more complex decomposition of an object diagram with 100 similarly looking persons has already been shown by the OCL statement Test32 in Fig. 4.24. This example demonstrates how complex data structures can be modeled out of relatively simple representations by combining OCL quantifiers and parameterizing object diagrams. With this technique, complex object structures can be decomposed into modular parts and these parts can be reused in other combinations. For structuring tests, it is particularly With this technique, complex object structures can be decomposed into situations.

4.4.2 Negation

Apart from the conjunction, the other Boolean operators can also be used. For example, undesirable situations can be depicted with negation. However, an object diagram's negation is relatively weak in its expressiveness as it only states that the object diagram does not occur in exactly this form. This means that only one detail has to be different. Figure 4.26 shows the constraint that each message, except the first message (the "welcome"), belongs to at most one auction, using an object diagram.

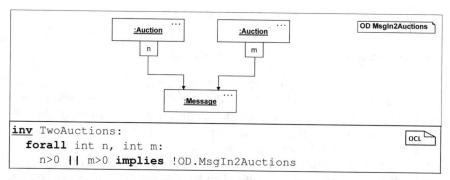

Figure 4.26. Negated object diagram

Here, the local variables n and m of the object diagram are used while the objects remain anonymous. As discussed for Fig. 4.21, anonymous objects must internally be regarded as existentially quantified. In OCL, the statement TwoAuctions is equivalent to

```
inv:
    forall int n, int m:
      n>0 || m>0 implies
        !exists Auction a, Auction b, Message msg:
          a!=b && a!=msg && b!=msg &&
          a.message[n] == msg &&
          b.message[m] == msg
```

4.4.3 Alternative Object Structures

The disjunction is a suitable means for depicting alternatives. As our application example uses two primary kinds of auctions that are characterized by a rising or falling bidding curve, two classes are provided that realize the rules for these auctions. Each auction possesses exactly one of these two policy classes. Figure 4.27 models these alternatives.

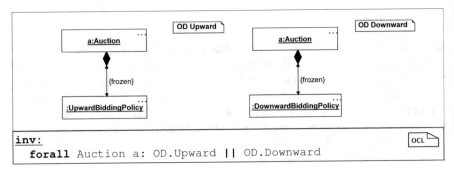

Figure 4.27. Alternative object diagrams

4.4.4 Object Diagrams in a Method Specification

A method specification represents a contract between the calling method and the method which is called: if the caller ensures that the called object is in an appropriate state and provides a context that conforms to the precondition, the calling method ensures that the postcondition is fulfilled after the call. This enables, for example, an alternative description of the method changeCompany defined in Sect. 3.4.3, shown in Fig. 4.28. In this precondition, the new company is assumed to be already present in the system. Contrary to the description in Sect. 3.4.3, the object diagram used here has no illustrative function but is an essential element of the specification.

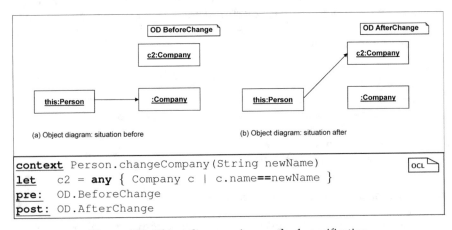

Figure 4.28. Object diagrams in a method specification

An object diagram can, hence, describe a situation in the execution of a software system and, thus, be used as a characterization of both the pre- as well as the postcondition. Similar to the rules of graph grammars [Roz99, EEKR99], two individual but in many details corresponding diagrams are necessary. Graph grammars often allow this characterization within a single diagram by offering additional graphic concepts for depicting the deletion or creation of objects and links. In the proposed form, object diagrams are less expressive but at the same time less overloaded with syntactic concepts. Graph grammars, however, are better suited for certain application forms and can serve as an interesting extension of the introduced usage of object diagrams for specifying methods.

If we use two object diagrams for the pre- and postcondition, it is not necessary to repeat all objects of the precondition in the postcondition. As a result, the postcondition becomes considerably smaller. In the object diagram shown in Fig. 4.28(b), the old company object, for example, could have been omitted. In graph grammars, this would have meant that the company object was to be deleted.

The example in Fig. 4.28(b) also shows the technique applied for binding shared variables in object diagrams. The object this is introduced by the definition of the method context and, thus, is the same for the pre- and postcondition. The objects of both object diagrams labeled c2 are identified by making use of the let construct. This is not the case for the two anonymous objects in the object diagrams BeforeChange and AfterChange. Therefore, these two objects are not the same, although this is suggested by their position in the respective object diagram. While the anonymous object in (a) can still be clearly identified, the anonymous object in (b) can be an arbitrary one (except c2).

A certain deficit of the specification style with pre- and postconditions becomes apparent by this example. In the postcondition, there is no possibility of accessing existentially quantified objects of the precondition. This becomes especially clear when using object diagrams together with anonymous objects. Such an object, thus, has to be, like the object c2, explicitly labeled and determined by the let construct outside both conditions. But this is only possible if the object can clearly be characterized in the let construct. Otherwise, the characterization in the pre- and postcondition must be indicated twice, if necessary.

Figure 4.29 shows an alteration from Fig. 4.28 in which the anonymous objects are labeled c1 and are, thus, identified. So accessing the number of employees of the company is possible.

4.4.5 Object Creation

In Figures 4.28 and 4.29, the behavior for the method changeCompany is specified when a company object c2 already exists. Analogous to the example in Sect. 3.4.3, the creation of a new company object is modeled in Fig. 4.30. Here, we model the creation of the object within the OCL constraint and not in the object diagrams.

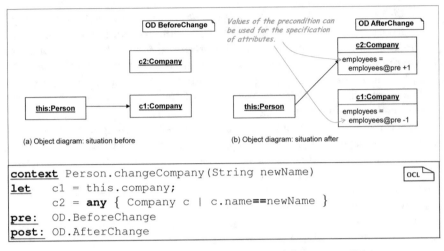

Figure 4.29. @pre in the object diagram of the postcondition

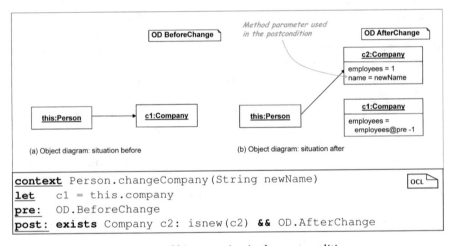

Figure 4.30. Object creation in the postcondition

4.4.6 Validity of Object Diagrams

An object diagram can describe an exemplary situation but can also, as shown above, be applied as an invariant. However, if the structure of an object diagram is not always valid, the invariant can be restricted by an OCL constraint. Typical "scopes of validity" for object diagrams are:

1. Always (invariant)
2. At the beginning of a method call (precondition)
3. After a method call (postcondition)

4. If a variable (usually a "state variable") has a certain state
5. At the beginning of an object's existence (initial structure)

The usage of object diagrams in invariants, pre- and postconditions has already been fully discussed. We restrict the validity of an object diagram by an OCL constraint illustrated in Fig. 4.31. Here, we look at the state of the applets that the user sees in order to participate in auctions. The applet has various states, whereas one of them is the initial state AppStatus.INITIAL.

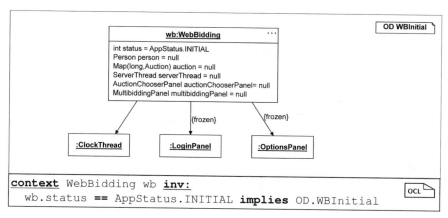

context WebBidding wb inv:
    wb.status == AppStatus.INITIAL implies OD.WBInitial

Figure 4.31. Restriction of an object diagram

The applet is always in the initial state if the user is not logged in. In this state, the user can already adjust general settings such as language and signals via the option panel. However, some other panels are set to null. Accordingly, the user can only access the two panels depicted top left and bottom right in Fig. D.3

For any other state of the applet, another object diagram can be designed to show the structure of this state. Some states also have the same structure or, at least, a clear overlap and, thus, can share and reuse subdiagrams.

4.4.7 Initialization of Object Structures

During their own creation, many objects trigger the creation of further objects and combine these into a complex object structure. Figure 4.31 shows an extract of the structure that exists in the initial state of objects of the class WebBidding. This structure is already created during the creation of WebBidding objects.

These subobjects are created in the constructor. Therefore, the *initial object structure* can be described in the postcondition of the constructor. In applets, however, the creation of the applet object and the initialization are implemented separately. This is why the constructor basically has an empty body and an independent method `init` conducts the initialization. Figure 4.32 describes an extract of the initialization result with some details where also the values of attributes are characterized. For this purpose, parameters are determined with the function `getParameter`, which works as a query and, thus, can be used here.

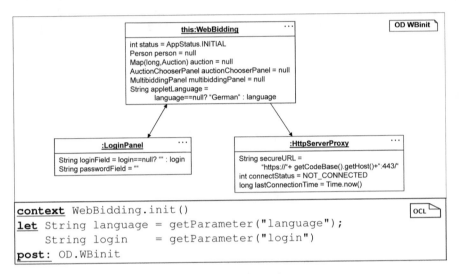

Figure 4.32. Initial object diagram

The object diagram `WBinit` is designed in such a way that each individual attribute can effectively be calculated therein and the link structure can be generated automatically. Attribute values can, e.g., be omitted if, in the class diagram, an initialization value is given for the attribute. Code generation for the creation of initial object structures is, in fact, a helpful technique for efficiently developing object systems. However, this procedure is quickly stretched to its limit if, in the initialization process, already existing object structures are to be incorporated or, as in the auction example, effects on the graphical user interface and the server system cannot be described by an object structure. So, if the description of an initialization or structure change by means of object diagrams is chosen, the decision is to be made whether a complete (and, thus, for code generation suitable) modeling with an object diagram is possible or whether an object diagram rather has illustrative effects. In the latter case, objects can also be depicted incompletely and it is possible to use derived attributes. In Fig. 4.12, for instance, a derived attribute was used in the object `max` that allows inferences to the content of multiple single attributes without directly depicting them.

Depicting new object structures is of particular interest if these objects realize data structures. Thereby, the generation of a new person object with its dependencies can be depicted as in Fig. 4.33. This constructor is used in order to create personal data that are entered via a web form.

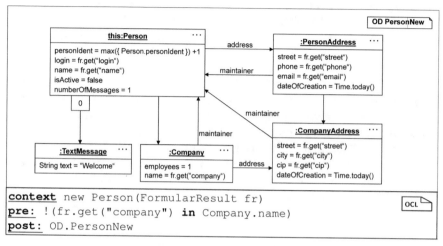

Figure 4.33. Initial object diagram

The object diagram in Fig. 4.33 serves as a template for generating the necessary object structures if a new person signs in. However, this object diagram is only valid if the company is also new. This is ensured by the precondition. Another diagram can be created accordingly to illustrate the situation with an already existing company object.

4.5 Summary

Currently, object diagrams do not receive the attention in the UML standard that they should, although they have been defined as an independent notation since UML 2.0. UML/P upgrades object diagrams and improves the methodical application of object diagrams in the software development process. This includes techniques for:

- Illustrative representation of a situation (snapshot)
- Representation of negative situations
- Usage of an object diagram as an invariant
- Composition of object diagrams
- Representation of alternative possibilities for object structures
- Modeling of initial structures in object creation
- Modeling of defaults for test cases
- Modeling of design patterns

To facilitate precise methodical use of object diagrams, the notation has been introduced and especially the semantics of language concepts in object diagrams discussed in detail. The difference between the object in the system and the *prototypical* object in the object diagram has been developed, and the exemplary character of object diagrams explained.

As a consequence of the restricted expressiveness of object diagrams, we combined object diagrams with the OCL logic. A "logic for object diagrams" arose that not only expands object diagrams by logical statements; Instead, it is possible to depict unsolicited situations, alternatives or compositions of object diagrams with Boolean operations and, hence, increase their expressiveness from exemplary to universally valid statements. With the help of quantifiers, object diagrams parameterized with variables can finally be used also as patterns (similar to the design pattern [GHJV94]).

This methodical usage of object diagrams has been discussed in detail by means of examples to demonstrate the benefit of this chapter.

5

Statecharts

All knowledge is memory.

Thomas Hobbes

Statecharts are an advancement of finite automata for the description of object behavior. Each complex system has steering and controlling parts that can be modeled with Statecharts. The Statechart variant introduced here uses OCL as the constraint language and Java instructions as actions. In the first two sections, fundamental properties of Statecharts are discussed. The next three sections introduce Statecharts as a description technique. We discuss the usage of Statecharts in the context of other UML diagrams to complete the introduction of Statecharts.

© Springer International Publishing Switzerland 2016
B. Rumpe, *Modeling with UML*, DOI 10.1007/978-3-319-33933-7_5

Automata, state transition diagrams, transition systems, as well as State-charts constitute various manifestations of an elementary concept for state-based representation of behavior. While the class and object diagrams described in Chapters 2 and 4 basically focus on the structure of a software system, state transition diagrams in their different manifestations constitute the link between state and behavior of system components. There are various manifestations of automata. Automata can be executable or used for recognizing sequences of characters or messages, describing the state space of an object, or specifying the response behavior to a stimulus. In UML, *Statecharts* are used as a variant of hierarchical automata principally based on the State-charts for embedded systems introduced in [Har87, HG97].

While in the original version [Har87] Statecharts were used for both the structure and the behavior of communicating systems, the function of a Stat-echart in the context of UML is reduced to modeling the objects' behavior. Despite the resulting simplification of a Statechart semantics, these are complex enough to discuss the basics in the form of finite automata first and, then, to introduce Statecharts with all their concepts. The overview given in [vdB94] shows that there are a number of syntactic variants and semantic interpretation possibilities for Statecharts which are adjusted to the respective fields of application. By profiling with suitable stereotypes, Statecharts of UML/P can be used for modeling, code generation, and description of test cases.

In Sect. 5.1, first some fundamental assumptions regarding Statecharts are made, partly simplifying the definition of the syntax and the semantics of Statecharts. It is recommended that the readers who are not familiar with the notation of Statecharts first skip this section and start with the automaton theory in Sect. 5.2, which contains a definition of Statecharts in Figures 5.8, 5.9, and 5.10. The state concept, the kinds of transitions existing, and the describing and procedural actions are introduced in the subsequent Sections 5.3, 5.4, and 5.5. The use of Statecharts in the context of other UML diagrams is discussed in Sect. 5.6. Thereby, we discuss inheritance, the transformation of Statecharts into so-called *simplified Statecharts*, and the mapping to OCL. Appendix C.5 additionally describes the abstract syntax of Statecharts and compares UML/P Statecharts with the UML standard.

5.1 Properties of Statecharts

As already mentioned, there are numerous variants and fields of application for Statecharts. In order to determine not only the notation but also the semantics and the methodical usage of Statecharts precisely enough to benefit software quality, development time, and work effort, it is important to make some fundamental assumptions about the usage of Statecharts. Figure 5.1 contains a list of possible tasks of Statecharts.

Tasks of a Statechart can be (overlaps possible):

- Representation of an object's lifecycle
- Implementation description of a method
- Implementation description of an object's behavior
- Requirements for the (abstract) state space of an object
- Representation of the order of stimuli allowed to occur (sequence of invocation)
- Characterization of the possible or allowed behavior of an object
- Link between state and behavior description

Figure 5.1. Variety of tasks of a Statechart

One of the basic assumptions for using a Statechart is that a Statechart describes only the behavior of a single object. For describing interaction patterns between different objects, sequence diagrams are better suited.

A Statechart describes the response behavior of an object that emerges when a stimulus triggers this object. For now, it is not important whether the stimulus represents a method call, an asynchronous message, a timeout, or something else. However, it is essential that the processing of the stimulus takes place in atomic form, i.e., it is neither interruptible nor hierarchically nested.

Thus, a transition is initiated by a stimulus and then executed without interruption. In doing so, it is assumed that the behavior specified in the transition does not lead to the immediate stimulation of further transitions of the same object. If the stimuli of a Statechart are, for example, method calls, the transition must not lead to further *recursive* method calls on the same object described by the Statechart.

In the case of Statecharts, this required uninterruptibility is also called "run to completion". Some Statechart variants, however, have softened this by allowing compound or prioritized transitions.

Statecharts process their stimuli in sequential order. This means that parallel processing of stimuli does not take place and that, therefore, synchronization between transitions is not necessary. This concept corresponds to the synchronization of object methods using the keyword `synchronized` in Java.

Like any other UML diagram type, a Statechart presents a certain view on an excerpt of the system to be implemented. While an object usually has an infinite state space, a Statechart consists of a not only finite but typically even very small set of diagram states. Hence, the diagram states (often five to ten) necessarily represent an abstraction of the object state space. Depending on the application area of the Statechart, the relation between diagram and object states can be precisely defined by using OCL constraints. The like is true for preconditions and effects of transitions. Therefore, a Statechart can be regarded as an executable implementation or abstract requirement description, depending on the level of detail and the form of representation of these constraints. So the field of application of Statecharts stretches from requirement analysis to the implementation. Statecharts can describe lifecycles of objects as well as detailed object behavior.

One advantage of Statecharts is their intuitive form of representation of the operational behavior description. Due to the additional use of hierarchy, it is possible to structure the state space of the objects described even more intuitively. Unfortunately, such state hierarchy introduces some subtile semantic problems and thus should be applied very carefully and not too extensively. By giving up communication between substatecharts, hierarchically structured states can be semantically dealt with more easily and explained more understandably. Therefore, we do not apply the hierarchy for the composition of subautomata of different objects, as was the case for many original Statechart variants [vdB94, Har87].

5.2 Automaton Theory and Its Interpretation

Basically, the Statecharts used in UML are a form of finite automata extended by hierarchy concepts where outputs may be produced by states and transitions. Let us briefly introduce output-producing Moore and Mealy automata [HU90] and discuss their properties. The finite automaton theory allows this discussion in condensed form as, for example, the input and the output alphabet are not interpreted further. In practical use, these characters of the alphabet are, e.g., replaced by complex method calls with arguments and actions formulated in Java.

The following compact introduction is essentially based on [Bra84, HU90, Rum96].

5.2.1 Recognizing and Mealy Automata

Figure 5.2 contains the definition of *recognizing automata*. A transition always connects a source state with a target state and carries either an input symbol or the symbol ε. The latter transitions are called *spontaneous*, as they do not depend on an input symbol while firing.

The semantics of a recognizing automaton consists of the set of all words of the alphabet E for which there is a path through the automaton starting from an initial state to a final state. Moreover, final states can also be passed through repeatedly. Figure 5.3 contains three recognizing automata. Automaton (a) recognizes whether a binary digit chain ends with 0, while the other two automata (b) and (c) recognize decimal digits with or without a decimal point. The semantics of a recognizing automaton is given by the set of words that are accepted on a path from an initial state to a final state. The two automata (b) and (c) thus have the same semantics even though they differ in their transitions. Besides, automaton (c) contains two nondeterministic

A *recognizing automaton*, also called a *nondeterministic, alphabetic Rabin–Scott automaton (RSA)* or *nondeterministic finite automaton (NFA)*, consists of a quintuple (S, I, t, S_0, F) with the following components:

- A set of *states S*
- An *alphabet I*, also called the *input alphabet*
- A set of *initial states* $S_0 \subseteq S$
- A set of *final states* $F \subseteq S$
- A transition relation $t \subseteq S \times I^\varepsilon \times S$

I^ε is the input alphabet I extended by the empty "sign" ε that is used for spontaneous transitions. Usually, all sets are regarded as finite and are not empty.
A transition is *enabled* if the automaton is in the source state and the corresponding symbol is present or if the transition does not require an input symbol (i.e., if it is spontaneous).

Figure 5.2. Definition of recognizing automata (RSA)

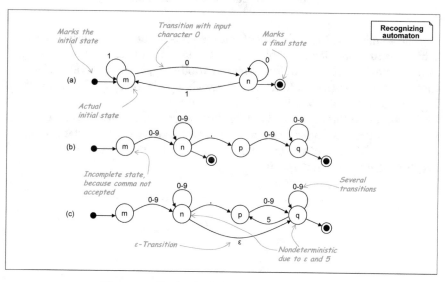

Figure 5.3. Examples for recognizing automata

places that—for example, in the case of the character string 21,0567—allow several paths.

If an automaton is used for modeling object-oriented behavior, the recognition of input sequences plays a minor role. Instead, the output as a reaction to an input element and the destination state reached are considered relevant. The automaton states can, e.g., correspond to the states of the graphical user interface and thus be directly visible to the user of the modeled system. Therefore, the nondeterminism in the automaton discussed in more detail below has a totally different purpose than it does in the recognition of word sets.

According to [Bra84], a Mealy automaton such as the one in Fig. 5.4 is an extension of a recognizing automaton, because it can have an output at each transition. Alternatively, it would also have been possible to extend the recognizing automaton by an output at each state to a Moore automaton. It is known from finite automaton theory that these two extensions do not principally differ in their expressiveness but are convertible into each other.

An alphabetic (nondeterministic and incomplete) *Mealy automaton* is a sextuplet (S, I, O, t, S_0, F) that contains a recognizing automaton (S, I, t, S_0, F) and in addition has:

- An *output alphabet* O
- A transition relation $t \subseteq S \times I^\varepsilon \times O^\varepsilon \times S$ extended by an output

---

Figure 5.4. Definition of Mealy automaton

The semantics of the Mealy automaton consists of the relation describing which input words lead to which output words. If in addition the state space is of interest, as it is in object-oriented modeling, the semantics of an automaton can be extended to the set of possible paths through the automaton. Figure 5.5 contains a Mealy automaton that replaces consecutive sequences of the digit 0 in the input by a single X or several Y. The nondeterminism in the automaton has an effect on the state transitions as well as the produced output. For Mealy automata, final states often do not play a vital role and are, thus, frequently not specified.

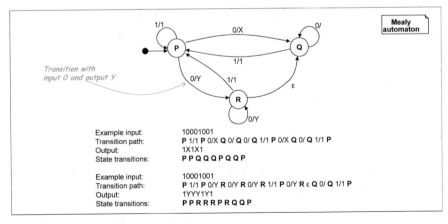

Figure 5.5. Example of Mealy automaton

5.2.2 Interpretation

A formalism, such as the theory of finite automata, concentrates on the representation of structures that are important for the respective analysis. Therefore, it is suited for studying capabilities and restrictions of automaton representations, simplification rules, as well as sequential or alternative compositions. Such a formalism is a closed mathematical structure that abstracts from the real world and can, thus, be applied to many real-world phenomena. In modeling, however, this relation to the real world is of great importance. In order to establish this relation, each concept of a finite automaton has to be interpreted by real-world elements, i.e., within object-oriented systems. A possible interpretation is the following:

- Each *state* of the automaton corresponds to one state of an object.
- An *initial state* is the state of an object that directly eventuates after its creation.
- A *final state* is irrelevant, because of the garbage collection in Java, which removes unreachable objects in each state.
- An *input symbol* is a method call including its arguments.
- An *output symbol* is an action that is executed in the body of a method. It can contain several method calls.
- A *transition* is the execution of a method body.

This interpretation permits transfer of the insights of automaton theory to the state-based modeling of objectoriented systems. However, this is by far not the only possible interpretation. For practical purposes, the set of states as well as the input and output symbols in automata are infinite in this interpretation. These infinite sets are, of course, not suited for representation in a finite, concise diagram. The finite set of diagram states of a Statechart, therefore, needs a better interpretation.

Therefore, we use a two-stage interpretation of a Statechart diagram in analogy to [Rum96, Bro97]. Figure 5.6 illustrates that the finitely many diagram states and transitions of a Statechart are primarily related to an infinite Mealy automaton. This Mealy automaton describes the behavior of an object.

The interpretation of a diagram element by a set of states or a set of transitions introduces some effects that need to be considered when using Statecharts for modeling purposes. We discuss these effects below.

5.2.3 Nondeterminism as Underspecification

Considering, for instance, the interpretation of a single transition, we can see that a large set of target states are possible, even though a concrete object state with a given method call is assumed. Thus, a transition can be highly *underspecified*. This is expressed in the fact that many object state changes that only differ in the object's target states are possible when interpreting a diagram transition (see Fig. 5.6). In automaton theory, this form of underspecification

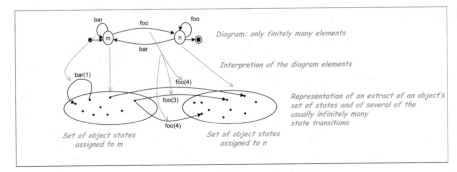

Figure 5.6. Interpretation of a diagram

is called *nondeterminism*. Indeed, this nondeterminism can be of methodical interest, for example, if an object's behavior cannot or should not be specified in full detail. But if this nondeterminism is not wanted, it can be avoided by additional OCL constraints, for example.

Nondeterminism, however, can also occur already in the diagram itself. Several diagram transitions starting from the same source state can process the same input symbol but produce different output symbols. This form of nondeterminism can also be understood in various ways:

1. The developers have not yet decided exactly which transition should be taken. They will either question the users or leave it to the implementation.
2. The automaton is an incomplete representation of the object state, and the information that would be necessary to precisely decide which transition to take has been abstracted in the diagram.
3. The compiler chooses (according to criteria that are not further defined) one of the transitions and ignores all others.
4. In fact, the system is nondeterministic and can choose one transition each time when at this state, depending on external factors or random generators.

The existence of nondeterminism always means a choice. Whether this choice is made by the developer, the user, the compiler or, at least, by the system is not determined. In particular, nondeterminism in the automaton does not necessarily mean a occurring and constantly recurring nondeterministic decision within the system. In contrast, in many systems, especially in Java implementations, nondeterminism can only be realized with additional effort. Instead, this nondeterminism of the automaton can generally be regarded as *underspecification* of the model.

5.2.4 ε-Transitions

ε-Transitions offer a special form of nondeterminism. They represent spontaneous transitions whose trigger is not modeled in the diagram. This also offers a number of possible interpretations:

1. A timer has expired and causes the transition.
2. The automaton provides an incomplete representation of the object's interaction possibilities, and the message leading to this transition has not been modeled. However, its occurrence has effects on the visible state of the object.
3. The transition is a logical consequence of a previous transition and is automatically executed by the system. Thereby, long actions can be broken down into sequences, intersections, and even iterations, and ε-transitions can be interpreted as notational convenience.

In concurrent, time-controlled systems, alternative 1 is of interest, while alternative 2 is used for representation of interface behavior. Alternative 3 can be used for modeling single complex methods. The function of these Statecharts is not to represent the character of a lifecycle but to serve as a control flow diagram.

The interconnection of several ε-transitions into an ε-loop is in principle not forbidden, but it is not helpful either.

5.2.5 Incompleteness

Besides the option of defining several transitions for one situation, there could also be no transition. Then, the automaton is incomplete (for example, see Fig. 5.3 (b)). In state p, it is not described how to react to the input symbol " . " (period). Such *incompleteness* can, for instance, be interpreted in the following ways:

1. The incoming symbol is ignored by not carrying out an action or change of state.
2. A chaotic reaction allows an arbitrary state transition and an arbitrary action. Even a "crash" of the object or the whole system is possible.
3. The object transitions into an explicit error state that can only be left through an explicit reset message.
4. An explicit error message in the mold of "Message not understood" known from Smalltalk is displayed without carrying out a state change.

While alternatives 1, 3, and 4 are typical for dealing with incomplete automata in automatic code generation, the second alternative is methodically interesting. As discussed in [Rum96], the *loose approach* that does not make promises about what is not explicitly represented in the diagram is particularly suited to urge the developer to model soundly. Thus, the modeler cannot only rely on the code generator. Methodically, this approach is also interesting, because adding transitions in order to reduce this incompleteness represents a refinement in the sense of the precision of the described behavior. The same *loose* approach is also used for class diagrams where the incompleteness indicator "..." shows that other classes, methods, or attributes which are not mentioned in the diagram can exist.

However, in order to be able to work with incomplete automata in prototyping, respective defaults should exist for code generators to reasonably realize code for incomplete situations or those underspecified by nondeterminism.

5.2.6 Lifecycle

The possibilities for interpreting the incompleteness of an automaton mentioned in Sect. 5.2.5 are closely related to the way in which an automaton can be interpreted as a description of a lifecycle. As discussed in [EE97], it is possible to understand an automaton as the description of the set of all *possible sequences* of method calls. This describes the external view of a fictional *observer* of an object who determines whether the set of potential call sequences described for that object has been adhered to.

Alternatively, there is also the possibility of regarding an automaton as the set of *possible sequences* of calls. This describes the internal view on an implementation that needs to be able to process the method call sequences specified by the automaton. In a sound implementation, the *implementer* can admit even more call sequences as required by the automaton. The implementers' and observers' views are compatible, as observers behave correctly as callers regarding the modeled permissible call sequences and ideally do not require a robust implementation.

Crucial differences between these two interpretations arise if modifications are applied to automata to, e.g., specialize the behavior or to supplement and inherit it. If an automaton describes guaranteed behavior, transformations, such as the conversions of Statecharts described in Sect. 5.6.2, are only allowed to add and detail behavior. This is only possible in a flexible way if the automaton is understood as underspecified, i.e., with chaos completion as the interpretation. In this sense, an automaton is a description of a *minimal set of lifecycles* of the object, which can be extended.

If the automaton is completed with an error state or if unaccepted method calls are ignored, the automaton describes a *maximal set of lifecycles*. This means that it determines the set of all possible call sequences that do not lead to an error state or to ignoring a method call. The choice of the interpretation of incompleteness is thus a choice of whether the automaton is interpreted as a minimally assured or maximally possible lifecycle.

In both interpretations, however, the behavior is identical for the call sequences described by the automaton, as it is processed by a predefined sequence of transitions.

In a nondeterministic automaton, it is possible to transit into different target states as a reaction to the same input. Because of this, the subsequent behavior can be different. Thus, there are sequences of method calls that can be correctly processed by a sequence of transitions, but that can also lead to incomplete situations. To prevent an object described by an automaton from receiving an illegal input in a certain state, the calling environment has to examine, e.g., through inquiry or internal calculation, whether a call is possible.[1]

5.2.7 Expressiveness

We know that finite automata are restricted in their expressiveness. They are suited to describe *regular sets* but are not able to specify bracket structures such as those appearing in Java expressions, for example. The principal problem is that a finite automaton only has a finite state space, so that opening brackets cannot be counted arbitrarily deeply and, thus, clearly assigned to closing brackets. This restriction known from automaton theory also manifests when using automata for modeling object-oriented systems, especially when methods of an object call other methods of the same object. Recursion does not necessarily have to take place in the same method (*method recursion*); it already suffices if another method of the same object is called directly or indirectly within the method. Such *object recursion* is shown in Fig. 5.7 but can be illustrated even better with the sequence diagrams introduced in Chapt. 6 (see Fig. 6.17).

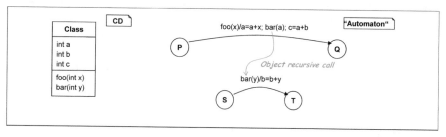

Figure 5.7. Object recursion

---

[1] Objects realizing complex protocols typically contain state components that each contain an abstraction of the state of the communication partners. Thus, both simulate an abstraction of the state space of the communication partner, as far as it is possible for them to do so on the basis of the observed behavior. So, they know in which state each communication partner can be.

Nesting of transitions cannot be adequately represented by the automaton itself. It is, for example, not clear whether the state transition caused by `bar` does lead to the fact that the target state `T` is taken. Generally, the relation of the states `S` and `T` to the state `Q` remains unclear. In order to avoid such problems, suitable restrictions must be made on the usage of Statecharts when modeling object behavior in the case of nested method calls. In [HG97], for instance, object recursion is prohibited.

In case that communication is based on asynchronous messages, finite automata, however, are sufficient. In the example in Fig. 5.7, `bar(a)` only represents the sending of a message but not its processing. This processing only takes place after the current transition is finished, i.e., after reaching the state `Q`. This discussion shows that the underlying communication mechanism plays a role in the assignment of a semantics for Statecharts if objects are allowed to send messages or method calls in recursive form to themselves.

5.2.8 Transformations on Automata

In automaton theory, possibilities for transformation, refinement, and composition of automata have been studied in detail. These transformations, primarily introduced for minimization or removal of nondeterminism and incompleteness in the automaton, have already been used in different variants for modeling object-oriented or embedded systems [Rum96, RK99, KPR97, SPTJ01]. The refactoring techniques [Fow99] that have become prominent in the context of the Extreme Programming approach show the helpfulness of manageable, systematically executed transformation steps on the notations used in the software development process. While refactoring techniques in Java are especially suited for maintaining the behavior, transformation steps on automata can also be used for detailing the behavior. Some of these transformation steps are further discussed in Sect. 5.6.2.

After having examined the basics of Statecharts in this section, the following sections introduce Statecharts in detail and discuss their interpretation in the context of object-oriented modeling. A compact overview of Statechart constructs is summarized in Figures 5.8, 5.9, and 5.10.

5.3 States

Statechart notation is used to describe the behavior of an object on the basis of its state spaces. Hence, states, transitions, and assigned actions are essential elements of a Statechart. The compact definition given in Figures 5.8, 5.9, and 5.10 is now further discussed in the next sections.

According to the UML standard [OMG10a], a *state* is a situation for an object in which the object meets a certain condition and, thereby, awaits an event or executes an internal activity. Typically, an object remains in such

> **State.** A *state* (synonym: *diagram state*) represents a subset of possible *object states*. A diagram state is modeled by a state name and an optional *state invariant, entry-action, exit-action,* and *do-activity*.
>
> **Initial state.** Objects begin their lifecycle in an initial state. Multiple initial states allow the representation of multiple forms of object creation. In a method State-chart, the initial state marks the beginning of the method. The semantics of the Statechart as part of another state is described in Sect. 5.4.2.
>
> **Final state.** A final state describes that the object has fulfilled its duty in this state and is not necessary anymore. However, final states can be left again, if transitions emerge. In a method Statechart, the final state marks the end of the method processing. The semantics of a final state as part of another state is described in Sect. 5.4.2.
>
> **Substate.** States can be nested hierarchically. A *containing state* contains several sub-states.
>
> **State invariant** is an OCL constraint that characterizes for a diagram state which object states are assigned to it. State invariants of different states may generally overlap.

Figure 5.8. Definition of Statechart terms, part 1: states

> **Stimulus** is caused by other objects or the runtime environment and leads to the *execution of a transition*. A stimulus can, e.g., be a method call, a remote procedure call, the receipt of an asynchronously sent message, or a timeout.
>
> **Transition.** A transition leads from a *source state* to a *target state* and contains a description of the *stimulus* as well as the reaction in the form of an *action*. Additional OCL constraints allow one to constrain the enabledness and the reaction of a transition in great detail.
>
> **Enabledness of a Transition.** A transition is *enabled* exactly if the object is in the source state of a transition, the stimulus is correct, and the precondition of the transition is true. If multiple transitions are enabled in the same situation, the Statechart is *nondeterministic*, and it is not defined which transition is chosen.
>
> **Precondition of the Transition.** In addition to the source state and the stimulus, it is possible to restrict a transition's enabledness via an OCL constraint using the attribute and the stimulus values.
>
> **Postcondition of the Transition** (also: *action constraint*). In addition to the operational description of the reaction to a stimulus, a property-oriented restriction of the potential reaction can be given by an OCL constraint.

Figure 5.9. Definition of Statechart terms, part 2: transitions

an *object state* for a certain time. Figure 5.11 shows a single state which the objects of class Auction can have.[2] Apart from the name AuctionOpen, a

---

[2] In this and the following examples, we use mostly the class Auction already known from previous chapters, as it has a complex state concept that is able to demonstrate many Statechart properties.

Action. An *action* is a change of an object's state and its environment described through operational code (for example, Java) or an OCL constraint. A transition typically contains an action.

Entry Action. A state can contain an *entry-action* that is executed if the object enters the state. If actions are described operationally, the entry-action is executed after the transition action. If a property-oriented description is used, the conjunction of both descriptions holds.

Exit-action. Analogous to the *entry-action*, a state can contain an *exit-action*. If operational, the exit-action is executed before the transition action; if described as properties, the conjunction holds.

Do-activity A permanently running activity contained in a state is called a *do-activity*. By different mechanisms such as local threads for timers, its implementation can be executed and simulate parallelism.

Nondeterminism. If there are several alternative transition in one situations that are enabled, this is called *nondeterminism of the Statechart*. Then, the object's behavior is *underspecified*. There are several methodically reasonable possibilities to use and refine underspecification in the software design process.

Figure 5.10. Definition of Statechart terms, part 3: actions

state can have a *state invariant*, an *entry-action*, and an *exit-action*, as well as a *do-activity*.

State names are unambiguous within the diagram.

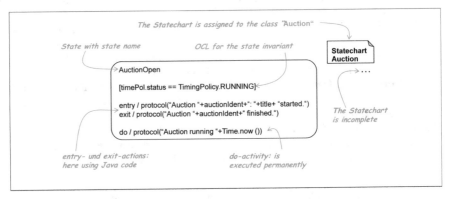

Figure 5.11. A state of the class `Auction` with invariant and actions

5.3.1 State Invariants

As a diagram state corresponds to a set of object states, it is often necessary to describe this set more precisely. For this, the *state invariant* can be used, denoted in the form of an OCL condition. The OCL constraint is formulated in the context of the described object. In Fig. 5.11 that is an object of the class Auction. It is possible to access attributes of the own object but also of dependent objects (i.e., of the object environment). The state invariant, thus, could also have been used in a regular OCL constraint.

It is recommendable to restrict the state invariant by using local attributes and, if needed, attributes of dependent objects, as otherwise a diagram state could change without an explicit stimulus of the modeled object being processed. Usually, such Statecharts only have descriptive character and are suited for modeling tests but not for code generation.

A state invariant can fulfill various tasks:

1. Similar to a contract [Mey97], a transition starting from the state can rely on the fact that the object state fulfills the given condition.
2. Vice versa, this means for a transition ending in this state that it is obliged to establish the state invariant.
3. If, furthermore, a nonvisible, external activity that affects the object can happen on the object environment, while the object is in the state, this activity also has to ensure that the state invariant is not infringed. Such a guarantee is, e.g., necessary if the object has public attributes or if the state invariant accesses the object state of foreign objects.

If, in case of a Statechart, there is the risk of overloading the diagram with information, outsourcing of state elements into a table is recommended as an alternative. Table 5.13 illustrates this for state invariants. According to [Bro98] or [Par93], various forms of tabular representation can also be implemented also for transitions and actions where reasonable.

To understand the state concept in object-oriented modeling, it is helpful to consider its components. The *data state* of an object is determined by its own attributes and possibly attributes of dependent objects. This also includes links to other objects. A second component of the object state is, however, the *control state*, which manifests in the running system through the program counter and the call stack. A state invariant can only specify the data state while the control state remains hidden. Figure 5.12, for example, shows four data states of the class Auction that each have disjoint state invariants.

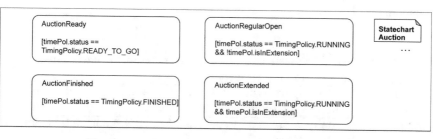

Figure 5.12. Four data states of the class Auction

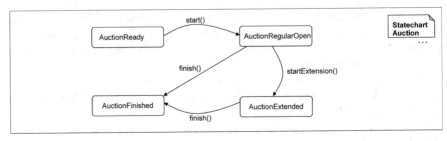

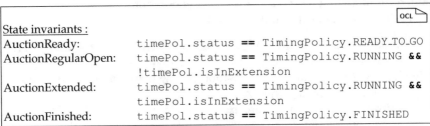

Table 5.13. Tabular representation of states

The control state cannot be modeled in full detail with a Statechart. However, states in a Statechart that describe the process of a single method represent an abstraction of the control state space.

State invariants of data states need not necessarily be disjoint either; For example, the usage of state invariants can be completely neglected if they do not contribute to the representation of the desired information. The Statechart in Table 5.13, for example, has a certain expressiveness in communication and documentation even without describing state invariants.

To distinguish control states from data states, the usage of stereotypes is suitable. For this purpose, Table 5.14 introduces the stereotypes «datastate» and «controlstate».

Stereotypes «datastate» and «controlstate»	
Model element	States of a Statechart.
Motivation	An object state consists of data and control states. This is to be modeled in the Statechart.
Glossary	A state tagged with «datastate» is called a *data state*. «controlstate» tags a *control state*.
Usage condition	Usually, a Statechart consists of only one sort, either data or control states.

(continued on the next page)

(continues Table 5.14.: Stereotypes «datastate» and «controlstate»)

Effect	Attributes and links alone can determine whether an object are located in a state tagged with «datastate». For control states, also the program counter and the stack are relevant.
Example(s)	For an example of data states, see Fig. 5.13. Control states are used in the modeling of internal states of complex methods.
Pitfalls	The state invariant in «datastate» states does not necessarily suffice for identification of the current state. In particular, state invariants can be incomplete or missing and, thus, overlap the invariants of data states in the diagram.
See also	«statedefining» to keep the defining character of the state invariant.
Extendable to	A whole Statechart if it applies to each single state. This is usually the case. Furthermore, for Statecharts that are assigned to classes, «datastate» is assumed as default.

Table 5.14. Stereotypes «datastate» and «controlstate»

A state invariant typically characterizes a property of the state respectively the object in this state. An object, however, can also fulfill the state invariant if it is currently located in another state. This is demonstrated by means of the reliability of persons in Fig. 5.15. A rating that, among other aspects, includes correct behavior in previous auctions is used to distinguish three groups of persons. The stereotype «statedefining» in the state BadPerson leads to the fact that each person with a rating smaller than zero is definitely located in this state. Therefore, this condition is *defining* for the state BadPerson. The condition, in contrast, only has *characterizing* character in the state VIP-Person. Hence, according to the Statechart in Fig. 5.15, there can be persons in the state NormalPerson that also reach a rating higher than 4500. The background of this modeling is the fact that a person only becomes a VIP if this is explicitly decided by, e.g., the auctioneer, while, in the case of a negative rating, the state BadPerson is taken automatically.

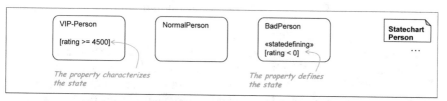

Figure 5.15. Reliability modeled for the class Person

The stereotype «statedefining» is defined in the following Table 5.16.

Stereotype «statedefining»	
Model element	State invariants in the Statechart.
Motivation	Usually, the invariant alone does not define which diagram state an object state belongs to. Thus, the invariant has describing but not *defining* character. This is changed by a stereotype.
Glossary	A state invariant tagged with «statedefining» is called *defining*.
Usage condition	Defining state invariants need to be disjoint. All object states that do not belong to that diagram state necessarily do not fulfill the invariant. The stereotype «statedefining» for a state invariant implies the stereotype «datastate» for the corresponding state and can, thus, only be used for data states. For the purpose of simplification, it is determined that all state invariants have to be of the same kind in a hierarchically composed state. Therefore, it is enough to apply the stereotype «statedefining» to the state invariant at the highest level.
Effect	The question of whether an object is located in the diagram state can be answered precisely by evaluation of the state invariant.
Example(s)	Figure 5.12 has disjoint state invariants and could use the stereotype «statedefining». Figure 5.15 shows a Statechart where not all state invariants have defining character.
Pitfalls	Defining state invariants have to be disjoint. For more complex conditions, this might be hard to ensure.
Also see	«datastate»
Extendable to	A complete Statechart if it applies to each single state invariant.

Table 5.16. Stereotype «statedefining»

Depending on whether the states modeled in the Statechart are control- or data states and whether these are described by defining state invariants, different strategies for implementation of a Statechart are possible. Defining invariants, for example, can be realized by Boolean predicates and used for deriving the state directly from the attributes. If defining state invariants are missing, almost always an additional attribute needs to be used, storing the diagram state explicitly in the object state space.

5.3.2 Hierarchical States

Hierarchy can be used to prevent a state explosion by structuring complex state spaces with it. Additionally, hierarchy is of methodical interest, as it allows one to first define states of the higher level and than refine them later into substates. The use of hierarchies thus allows defining an abstract view of the state space. A hierarchically divided state has, like any other state, a name and can contain a state invariant as well as an entry-action, exit-action, and do-activity. In addition, it contains one or more *substates*. Figure 5.17 shows an alternative representation of the Statechart in Fig. 5.12, where two states have been hierarchically aggregated.

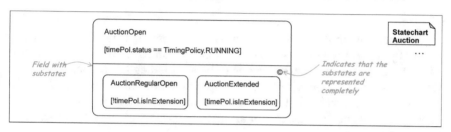

Figure 5.17. Hierarchical decomposition of the state space

The state `AuctionOpen` is structured by two substates `AuctionRegularOpen` and `AuctionExtended`. These substates are denoted separately from the other components of the superstate in their own compartment.

The completeness mark ⓒ determines that the state `AuctionOpen` is partitioned by the two substates. This means that, if the object is located in the state `AuctionOpen`, it is in exactly one of the two substates, and vice versa. If the completeness mark had been omitted or incompleteness mark "..." given, it would be possible that objects of the modeled class take the superstate `AuctionOpen` without being in one of the two substates. This is, e.g., possible if another substate exists but is not explicitly given in the diagram.

One of the advantages of hierarchical decomposition of states is the possibility to note common parts of state invariants in the superstates. This leads to a more compact version of the state invariant for both substates. The actual state invariant of a substate is, hence, the conjunction of all state invariants of its superstates. Accordingly, the two representations shown in Fig. 5.18 are equivalent for states, and use of the more compact form of representation is allowed.[3]

---

[3] The concept of the *equivalence* of two Statecharts is subsequently used to, e.g., introduce a new element of the Statechart notation by relating it to the already known elements. In this sense, some of the equivalences can be regarded as defining. But generally, these equivalences are used in a rather illustrative way and serve for better understandability. Most representations, thus, illustrate only a special case. Figure 5.18, for instance, only describes the case with one substate.

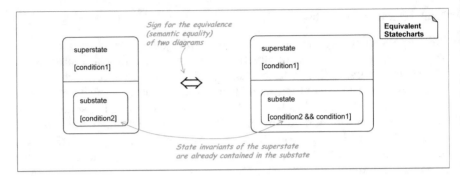

Figure 5.18. State invariant of the superstate also holds for the substate

It is possible that a state invariant is not *satisfiable*. This means that there is no object state where the state invariant evaluates to `true`. As described in Sect. 5.5.2, such a situation needs to be avoided as transitions leading to this state suggest a behavior that the implementation does not even have. In hierarchically structured states, the state invariant must not be considered separately but the conjunction of all state invariants of the substate and its superstates.

A side-effect of the possibility to explicitly take over state invariants from the superstate to the substate and the later discussed options of leading transitions from or to the superstate directly into substates allow for introduction or removal of a hierarchy in the state space where necessary. The equivalence of flat and hierarchical representations is illustrated in the Statechart in Fig. 5.19. Due to this equivalence, hierarchy is mainly a convenience to prevent the explosion of states and transitions.

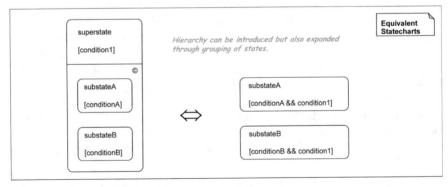

Figure 5.19. Introduction and expansion of hierarchy

Compared with the original Statecharts [Har87] and the UML standard [OMG10a], only the so-called *or-decomposition* of states is used, just like in

ROOM [SGW94]. This form of decomposition allows the hierarchical decomposition of the state space but is not suitable to describe parallelism or concurrency within an object. As today parallelism is immanent in many systems at larger granularity, but sequential processing is the dominant concept within an object, the *and-decomposition* of states for modeling concurrent behavior components is not necessary in UML.[4]

5.3.3 Initial and Final States

As Statecharts mostly model the lifecycle of an object or the process of a method, they require a description to identify diagram states as initial or final states. Figure 5.20 shows how initial and final states are marked.

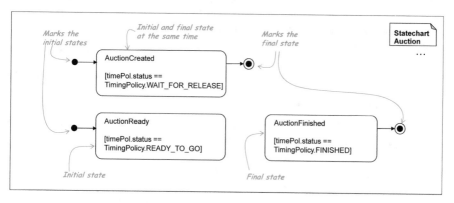

Figure 5.20. Initial and final states

A Statechart may have several initial and final states. States can even be initial and final state at the same time. Figure 5.20 shows that there are two ways to initiate an auction. Normal customers can set up an auction, but it additionally needs to be released. Only an authorized group of good customers are allowed to set up auctions in a directly released state. If an auction is, for example, not released because of a lack of solvency of the person setting up the auction or if the auction is terminated, the lifecycle of the auction object is also terminated. Thus, the black circles and the arrows from or to them do not represent states or transitions themselves, although their representation might create this impression.

The nondeterminism in the Statechart arising from marking several initial states is, as described in Fig. 5.2.2, interpreted as freedom to choose. The developer can either restrict this freedom of choice in the further process of the project or leave all possibilities to the system when implemented with different constructors.

---

[4] This view is consistent with the target language Java, which also prevents parallelism within objects by providing the keyword `synchronized`.

Initial and final states can also be labeled within a hierarchically decomposed state. Then, however, they have another meaning that is discussed in Sect. 5.4.2.

5.4 Transitions

A transition describes an excerpt of the object behavior. The transition can be executed if the object is in the source state of the transition and if the triggering condition is fulfilled. An action is executed and the target state of the transition is taken. This section deals in detail with the stimuli and triggering conditions leading to the execution of a transition. In the next section, actions are discussed. Figure 5.21 shows a Statechart with the state transitions for the class Auction already known from Fig. 5.13. It shows how preconditions for transitions are defined and that transitions can arbitrarily trespass state hierarchies.

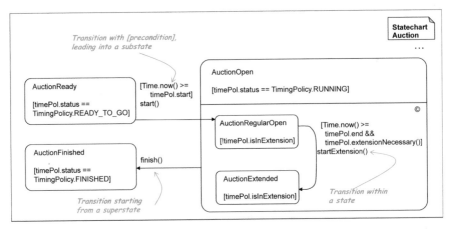

Figure 5.21. Transitions in Auction Statecharts

5.4.1 State Invariants Within the State Hierarchy

The start() transition leads from the state AuctionReady into the substate AuctionRegularOpen. Besides the explicitly given precondition, there is an additional precondition resulting from the source state AuctionReady. The complete precondition for this transition is thus

```
timePol.status == TimingPolicy.READY_TO_GO
&& Time.now() >= timePol.start
```

The transition labeled with `finish()` leading to the closure of an auction has the source state `AuctionOpen`. As this state is completely partitioned by its substates (ⓒ), it is equivalent to instead let two transitions start from the two substates. The two equivalences shown in Figures 5.22 and 5.23 describe this as general rules.

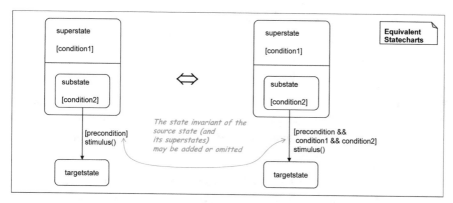

Figure 5.22. Interplay of precondition and state invariant

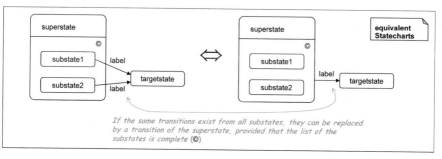

Figure 5.23. Transitions starting from the superstate

5.4.2 Initial and Final States in the State Hierarchy

The transition `start()` described in the Statechart in Fig. 5.21 has the substate `AuctionRegularOpen` as target state. Alternatively, it is possible that this transition only targets the superstate `AuctionOpen`. However, it is then not described in which of the two substates the auction really is after the execution of this transition. Therefore, in Fig. 5.24 it is modeled that an auction runs first in the regular phase when started. This is indicated by using an initial state mark within a hierarchically partitioned state.

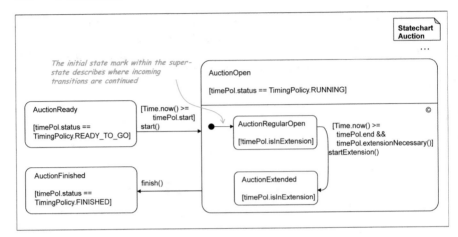

Figure 5.24. Initial state marking the continuation of a transition

The equivalence suggested by Figures 5.21 and 5.24 can generally be expressed as shown in Fig. 5.25. This rule can even be used repeatedly if the initial substate in turn is again refined by substates.

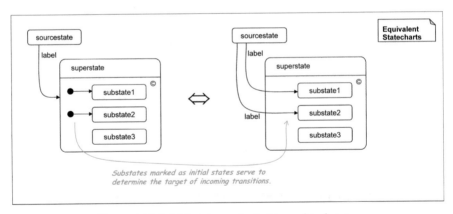

Figure 5.25. Initial state marks in hierarchical states

In a similar manner, it is also possible to use final state marks within hierarchical states. They describe when transitions originating from the superstate may be triggered. Figure 5.26 demonstrates the corresponding rule. However, as the clarity of the Statecharts quickly suffers, it is recommended to use marks for initial and final states not too often. For the same reason, hierarchies should be used carefully in automata.

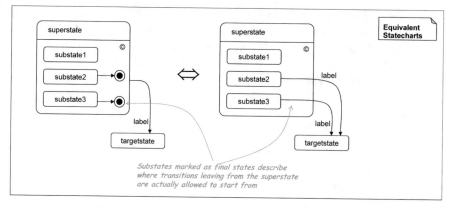

Figure 5.26. Final state marks in hierarchical states

If a superstate does not contain initial states, it is equivalent to the fact that all substates also are initial states. The same holds for missing final states. Figure 5.27 illustrates these equivalences.

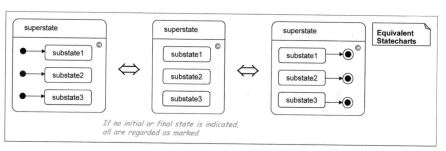

Figure 5.27. Missing initial or final state marks

5.4.3 Stimuli for Transitions

Kinds of Stimuli

As we have now clarified the relation between transitions and the state hierarchy, we discuss in this section which events can cause the firing of transitions. We distinguish five different categories of *stimuli* leading to the firing of a transition:

- A *message* is received
- A *method* is called
- The result of a *return-statement* is returned as an answer to a previous method call
- An *exception* is caught
- The transition occurs *spontaneously*

According to message-based communication known, e.g., from CORBA [OH98] or from distributed architectural models [HRR10, GHK+08], it can be assumed that message management, i.e., buffering and transfer, is realized in an appropriate runtime framework. Thus, it does not make any difference for the receiving object whether a method call is transmitted asynchronously or as a normal method call. Therefore, no distinction is made between these two kinds of stimuli in the Statechart. As a result, we use the kinds of transition stimuli represented in Fig. 5.28.

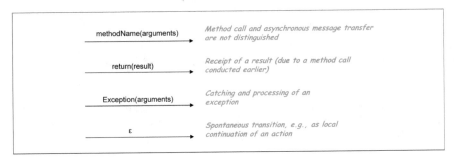

Figure 5.28. Kinds of stimuli for transitions

Object Recursion

In Sect. 5.2.7 it has already been discussed that flat automata are not suitable for depicting recursive call structures. For Statecharts, this problem manifests in the fact that the implementation can execute object-recursive calls but that modeling with Statecharts does not consider this adequately. *Object recursion* always occurs when a method of an object is active and directly or indirectly leads to the call of another method of the same object. Although it is possible to carry out further method calls in procedurally formulated actions (discussed hereinafter) which in turn trigger further transitions, this leads to a number of semantic problems. On the one hand, it is not clear in which state the object really is when the recursive method call starts. It may have already left the source state and reached the target state, or it may be in an undefined intermediate state. On the other hand, it is not clear whether the recursive method leads to further object state alterations so that the target state represented in the Statechart does not correspond to the actually reached object state. To avoid this problem but explicitly allow the object recursion that is often used especially in design patterns [Pre95], we use the observation motivated from practice that methods of an object can mostly be separated into two levels:

- The top-level methods serve for realization of primary functionality. If an object contains a state space that fits the Statechart, these methods depend on the object's state concept and are responsible for the state transitions of the object. These methods do not call each other but only rely on the helper methods of the lower level. An object's helper methods mainly serve for processing of core functionality, such as for the calculation of a value. Classic helper methods are queries and `get`/`set` methods.
- Helper methods are principally independent of the state of an object defined in the Statechart and can, thus, be arbitrarily used by top-level methods and call each other recursively.

Top-level methods of an object can be determined by an explicit statement (e.g., by using a suitable stereotype) or by extraction of the methods that are explicitly used as stimuli in a Statechart. By means of a data flow analysis based on the program code, it can be determined whether these methods really do not carry out an object recursion.[5] We, hence, assume that in practice methods which depend on or change the state of the object do not participate in object recursion.

5.4.4 Enabledness

As we have defined the stimuli for transitions and how transition preconditions can be combined along the state hierarchy, we can now precisely define when a transition is *enabled*. For this, the following conditions must be fulfilled:

1. The object needs to be in an object state that corresponds to the source state of the transition.
2. Either the transition is spontaneous and does not need a stimulus, or the stimulus that is necessary for the transition has occurred. The values given in the stimulus description (for instance, method parameters) correspond to the actual values of the received stimulus. Each variable used in the stimulus description is assigned to the actual value in the stimulus.
3. The precondition which is evaluated over the object state and the parameters of the received stimulus holds.

It can happen that a precondition cannot be fulfilled in any situation. In this case, the transition is pointless, as it never fires.

Even if a transition is enabled, this does not necessarily mean that it is also executed. It is possible that several transitions are enabled at the same

---

[5] A top-level method is definitely entitled to call itself or a top-level method of *another* object. This method recursion can, for example, be used in a linearly linked object list without leading to object recursion. As this depends on the current object structure, a static data flow analysis is sometimes not able to exclude object recursion, even if this does not take place in the implemented system.

time. This is not prohibited—on the contrary, it is explicitly welcome. To enable developers to delay design decisions and leave some choice either to the implementers or even the implementation at runtime, we already allowed this nondeterminism in Sect. 5.2. *Nondeterminism* in a Statechart usually does not mean that the implementation is nondeterministic. Mostly, the decisions necessary for reducing this nondeterminism are made at the right time. Overlapping enabledness is, thus, basically a form of *underspecification* that can manifest in different variants. Figure 5.29 shows two allowed situations of overlapping transition scopes.

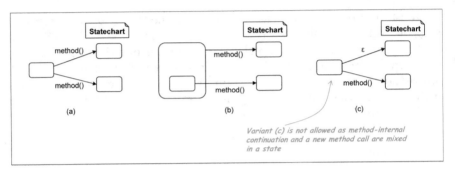

Figure 5.29. Situations of overlapping transition scopes

In both cases (a) and (b), both alternatives are possible and can lead to very different overall behavior of the modeled object, depending on the kind of action executed or the further behavior of the target state. There are several possibilities to remedy underspecification, such as the one shown in Fig. 5.29. Besides the obvious option of canceling one of the two transitions, there is the possibility of transferring the two overlapping transition scopes into disjoint transition scopes by strengthening the precondition.

Another way to remedy underspecification which is especially suitable for transitions of different hierarchy levels, as represented in Fig. 5.29(b), is the usage of priorities. In contrast to classical Statecharts [Har87] and the form of Statecharts adapted to object-oriented systems [HG97], no implicit priorities are used, i.e., neither is the internal transition preferred against the external one nor vice versa. We can, thus, allocate priorities using a stereotype of the form «prio=4», which has an integer value. However, due to compatibility with present Statechart variants, the usage of a stereotype of the form «prio:inner» or «prio:outer» is reasonable to give internal or external transitions priority. Figure 5.30 illustrates the effect of these two stereotypes. Table 5.31 introduces both stereotypes.

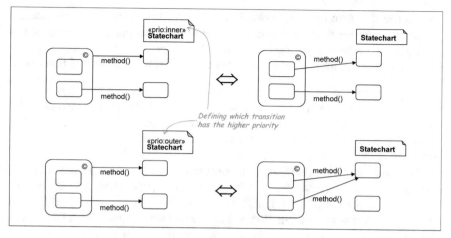

Figure 5.30. Stereotypes for defining priorities

Stereotypes «prio:inner» and «prio:outer»	
Model element	Statechart. See Fig. 5.30 for how to apply.
Motivation	If transitions with overlapping enabledness exist whose source states are located on different hierarchy levels, the inner or outer transitions can be prioritized.
Effect	Nondeterminism due to the described situation is reduced. The effect of both stereotypes is illustrated in Fig. 5.30.

Table 5.31. Stereotypes «prio:inner» and «prio:outer»

5.4.5 Incomplete Statechart

In the previous section, situations with multiple, simultaneously enabled transitions were discussed. However, it is also possible that there is no transition enabled to handle an incoming stimulus. Such a Statechart is called *incomplete*. Analogous to automata (Sect. 5.2.5), various interpretations of this situation exist:

1. The stimulus is ignored, and if applicable, an "alert" is displayed.
2. A default error handling is executed. For example, an exception can be thrown and the normal program execution can be interrupted, resulting in an error state. Alternatively, the error can be logged and handled in a robust way.

3. As the diagram does not contain explicit information about what needs to be done with the incoming stimulus in the respective state, it is not possible to determine the behavior of the object.
4. Thus, everything is possible, as we have underspecification at this point.

As discussed in Sect. 5.2.6, the lifecycle of an object can be interpreted in different ways. In the first two interpretations, the lifecycle is regarded as the *maximal possible* one, while in the last interpretation it is understood as the *minimally ensured* one. This becomes a crucial difference, especially for the transformations discussed in Sect. 5.6.2.

The first two interpretations of incompleteness are useful if the Statechart serves as an implementation. In fact, ignoring nonprocessible stimuli is only a special case of explicit error handling. If there is consistent error handling, it can be modeled as an entry-action in a dedicated state tagged with the stereotype «error». The stereotype «error» is used if explicit transitions for handling errors are not wanted, for example, for the sake of clarity. Figure 5.32 illustrates a possible application.

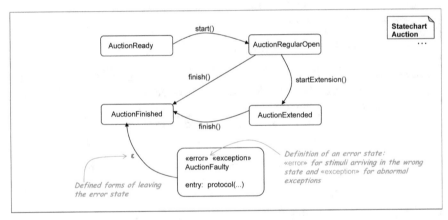

Figure 5.32. Stereotype «error» for error handling

However, using an explicit error state as in Fig. 5.32 has the drawback that only one universal and uniform error handling is possible. Hence, a return to the state that caused the error cannot be modeled. Alternative error handling can use stereotypes, such as «completion:ignore», either for the whole Statechart or for single states. For pragmatic reasons, we also distinguish normal error situations, in which the enabledness for a stimulus is missing, from the receipt of an exception. Thus, the stereotype «exception» is available for dealing with exception stimuli. It is the only stereotype for handling occurrences of explicit exceptions.

Statecharts defined and refined during the development process can temporarily be incomplete without the intention of specifying error handling through their incompleteness. Furthermore, Statecharts can intentionally be incomplete, e.g., if they are used for the definition of tests. The semantics of Statecharts intended for tests says that, if a Statechart describes a behavior, it has to be fulfilled by the object. Otherwise, if the Statechart does not make a statement, the object is completely free in its action. Thus, the third of the aforementioned possibilities of interpreting incompleteness is the best one for the usage of Statecharts in tests. This behaviorial freedom for implementations can be specified for a whole Statechart with the stereotype «completion:chaos». Tables 5.33, 5.34, and 5.35 introduce the three newly mentioned stereotypes for dealing with incompleteness in Statecharts.

Stereotype «error»	
Model element	State. For an example, see Fig. 5.32.
Motivation	If a Statechart is incomplete, a uniform error handling can be conducted by introducing an error state.
Glossary	A state tagged with «error» is called *error state*.
Usage condition	In a Statechart, only one state may be marked with «error». This cannot be a substate, but it can have explicit incoming transitions and substates.
Effect	If there is no transition that can process a stimulus, a transition to the triggered error state processes the stimulus. Exception stimuli are not handled by this stereotype.
See also	«exception», «completion:chaos», and «completion:ignore».

Table 5.33. Stereotype «error»

Stereotype «exception»	
Model element	State. See Fig. 5.32 for an example.
Motivation	The stereotpye «error» handles stimuli in situations without enabledness, but it does not handle exceptions. This can be achieved with the stereotype «exception»
Glossary	A state tagged with «exception» is called an *exception error state*.

(continued on the next page)

(continues Table 5.34.: Stereotype ≪exception≫)

Usage condition	In a Statechart, only one state may be tagged with ≪exception≫. This cannot be a substate, but it can have explicit incoming transitions and substates. The stereotype ≪exception≫ is used independently from the stereotype ≪error≫ and ≪completion:…≫.
Effect	If no other transition can process an exception stimulus, a transition into the exception error state is conducted to process the exception.
See also	≪error≫, ≪completion:chaos≫, and ≪completion:ignore≫.

Table 5.34. Stereotype ≪exception≫

Stereotypes ≪completion:ignore≫ and ≪completion:chaos≫	
Model element	Statechart.
Motivation	There are various possible interpretations for an incomplete Statechart. By using one of these stereotypes, the developer can explicitly choose the desired interpretation.
Usage condition	Both stereotypes exclude each other as well as the simultaneous use of an error state (≪error≫).
Effect	Statecharts tagged with ≪completion:ignore≫ ignore stimuli they cannot process. This is suitable for a robust implementation. Statecharts tagged with ≪completion:chaos≫ allow arbitrary freedom in processing of otherwise unhandled stimuli. This is suited for specification and tests. Exceptions are not handled with these stereotypes.
Pitfalls	Both variants are used to clarify the interpretation of incompleteness. For practical issues other than prototyping, robust treatment of unspecified situations is particularly reasonable, say in an error state.
See also	≪error≫ and ≪exception≫

Table 5.35. Stereotypes ≪completion:ignore≫ and ≪completion:chaos≫

The interpretations dealing with incomplete Statecharts suggested in this section can also be modeled by an explicit completion of the transitions, as known from automaton theory, for example in a Statechart tagged with «completion:ignore», all incomplete states need to be supplemented with loops. These loops start and end in the same state, process all stimuli that are not processed by other transitions, but do not change the state or produce an output.

When using an error state, these transitions must instead end in the marked error state.

In a chaos completion with the stereotype «completion:chaos», a lot more transitions could have to be introduced, as they can lead from each incomplete state to all states of the Statechart. The actions of these transitions have arbitrary freedom. They can freely change the state of the modeled objects, restricted only by the target state and their environment, set up new objects, etc. Nonterminating actions are also not excluded in a chaos completion.

While the first two forms of completion are indeed reasonable for the implementation, due to the explosion of transitions, it is obvious that a chaos completion is only a conceptual mechanism for clarifying the meaning of a Statechart but should not be considered for an implementation.

5.5 Actions

The description of the behavior of a Statechart only becomes complete when adding *actions*. Actions describe the reaction to the receipt of a stimulus in a certain state. They are added to the state as an entry- and exit-action, or to the transition as a reaction. According to the philosophy of UML/P, two types of action descriptions are allowed. The *procedural form* allows the use of assignments and control structures, and the *descriptive action form* allows us to characterize the effect of an action without defining how this action is actually realized.

Both types of action description complement each other and allow the usage of the best-suited technique. In some cases, it is easier to describe an action by procedural instructions and, hence, specify its implementation. Unfortunately, procedural instructions too often lead to needless overengineering, as they anticipate implementation details. Therefore, it is an advantage in many situations to use either the descriptive form or a combination of both forms.

5.5.1 Procedural and Descriptive Actions

In contrast to a descriptive condition, the advantage of using a procedural code snippet is that it can be used directly for code generation. In comparison, descriptive conditions can often be formulated in a more abstract way and allow a certain freedom in the implementation. The combination of both action forms allows us to define the action by procedural code and to describe its desired effect by a condition.

A method Statechart typically has only actions that are modeled by Java code. Such a Statechart is suited for the direct realization into a complete implementation. As UML/P has Java as its target language, the usage of an independent "action language," such as the one discussed in [OMG01a], is not necessary. Instead, code snippets directly formulated in Java can be used. The idea of an "action language" adapted to this task has only restricted value, as it must also be a complete programming language. Thus, it offers only a small advantage in contrast to an existing programming language such as Java, by using a syntactical form adapted to a UML-like syntax. On the contrary, the "action language" requires its own translators and libraries. Hence, the approach of regarding UML as a language family [CKM+99] and including elements of the target language directly into the used UML version is a desirable alternative.

Therefore, we allow arbitrary Java code snippets as actions. They can access attributes of the modeled object and the arguments of the processed stimulus. Modification of the object state and the state of other objects of the environment is explicitly allowed. If the processed stimulus is a method call with a result, the action has to terminate with a return-statement. In order to avoid that the Statechart appearing overloaded, actions can be attached to the Statechart, e.g., in tabular form, as already done in a similar way for preconditions in Table 5.13.

An action described by code does not offer freedom for omission of implementation details which the modeler does not want to state yet. Therefore, Statecharts offer as a second form of action the possibility of giving postconditions in the form of OCL statements to allow characterization of a certain bandwidth of behaviors without defining how these must actually be implemented. A postcondition formulated in OCL is also called an *action condition*. Its character is similar to that of the postcondition of method specifications discussed in Sect. 3.4.3. We will see in Sect. 5.6.3 that transitions processing a method call as a stimulus can actually be translated into a specification in the pre- and postcondition style. As discussed there, Statecharts with action conditions are not directly suitable for code generation. Instead, they assist with the abstract modeling of behavior during the design process and the modeling of tests. While it is generally not possible to automatically establish an action condition, they can be checked well and errors recognized automatically.

The action condition of a transition may access the arguments of the processed stimulus, the attributes of the modeled object, and if applicable, local variables defined in the instruction part of the action. In particular, attributes can thereby be used in the state before and after execution of the transition. With $a==a@pre$, for example, we can model that an attribute may not change.

Figure 5.36 contains an extract a Statechart for the class `Auction` which shows a transition with a procedural action description and a postcondition. If the class `TimingPolicy` is implemented correctly, the postcondition already results from the action instructions. Thus, the postcondition here has illustrative character and can be used particularly for tests.

Figure 5.36. Transition with procedural and descriptive action

Postconditions can not only be formulated as a redundant addendum to action instructions but also supplement them. In this way, one part of the behavior can be modeled procedurally while the other part can be characterized in a descriptive form by an OCL constraint. Subsequently, we also discuss the treatment of actions in hierarchical states and the interaction between a characterizing condition and the procedural implementation.

A descriptive characterization of the action by means of a postcondition has the disadvantage (discussed in Sect. 3.4.3) that further modifications of variables which are not explicitly mentioned in the condition are not excluded either. Here, we also use the pragmatic approach that, in an implementation or an extension of the Statechart towards code generation, the implementer gets the freedom to decide which changes to attributes are additionally necessary. Statecharts whose postconditions only describe a part of the changes made by the implementation are nevertheless perfectly suited for tests. They can be used to describe and test the behavior of the implementation regarding a certain aspect.

5.5.2 State Actions

As Fig. 5.11 shows, there is also the possibility of adding an *entry-* and *exit-action* as well as a *do-activity* to each state. These actions can be described procedurally or by an OCL constraint, too. The entry-action of a target state is executed in combination with the transition action and often has the function of opening connections, signaling state changes, conducting log outputs, or carrying out changes on the user interface.

Exit-actions are used in a very similar manner, namely to accomplish operations that are necessary when leaving the state. This could be the closing of a connection or a file as well as further log outputs. As both entry- and exit-actions are each executed in the context of the execution of a transition, these actions are primarily a writing shortcut. Figure 5.37 shows that entry-actions can alternatively be moved to incoming transitions and exit-actions to outgoing transitions. Figure 5.37 represents the case of procedural actions where the actions are composed sequentially.

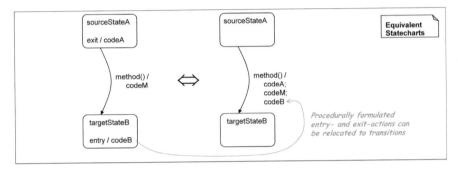

Figure 5.37. Entry- and exit-action as convenient shortcuts

Sequential Composition for Code

The rule shown in Fig. 5.37 allows one to move entry- and exit-actions to transitions and, thus, remove them from states, but this only holds if all concerned transitions are treated uniformly.

This procedure can also be used for entry- and exit-actions in hierarchical states. Figure 5.38 shows the transfer of procedural actions to transitions. This rule also demonstrates in which order entry- and exit-actions are executed in hierarchical states. The execution order of these actions corresponds to the order of the leaving or entering of states of the executed transition, respectively.

Logical Conjunction for Action Conditions

If the actions of a Statechart are specified by OCL action conditions, the logical conjunction is used instead of the sequential composition. Figure 5.39 shows how in this case conditions can be shifted from the states into the transitions. In this transformation, the syntactic correctness certainly needs to be maintained as in all other transformations. In particular, if two local variables accidentally have the same name, renaming becomes necessary.

According to the definition in Sect. 5.4.4, the enabledness of a transition exclusively depends on the source state, the stimulus, and the precondition. However, there are enabled transitions that lead to a target state whose state invariant is not fulfilled, which have an unfulfillable postcondition, or where

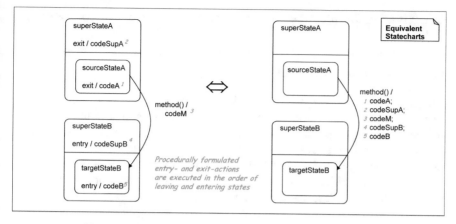

Figure 5.38. Entry- and exit-actions in hierarchical states

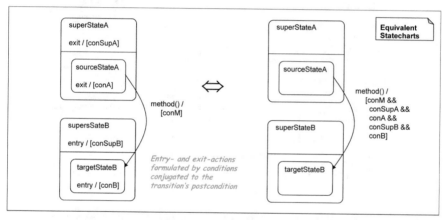

Figure 5.39. Conditions as entry- and exit-action in states

a state invariant and postcondition contradict each other. This problem occurs in case of a predicative description of actions and cannot be automatically recognized. On the one hand, we can avoid this by using forms for the postcondition and the state invariant that ideally make statements about orthogonal parts of the state space. On the other hand, we can ensure this by choosing a suitable precondition stating that such a transition is enabled only if the postcondition can be fulfilled. Accordingly, a transition's enabledness could additionally be determined by the fact that a transition is executable, i.e., the postcondition and target state invariant can be fulfilled. However, generally, an unaccomplishable postcondition should be avoided, as a useful meaning cannot (easily) be assigned to such a Statechart [Rum96]. If used in a software development process and not directly recognized as such, rectification is advisable after their recognition, at the latest, e.g., in corresponding tests.

Piecewise Action Conditions

The interpretation of state actions illustrated in Fig. 5.39 is adequate for purely predicatively described Statecharts. However, if a Statechart has a mixed form of procedural and predicative action descriptions, an alternative interpretation is advisable to meet the sequential processing character of the actions. Figure 5.40 illustrates this interpretation. With the use of the ocl statement for OCL assertions, the piecewise fulfillment of the conditions relevant for a transition can be specified.

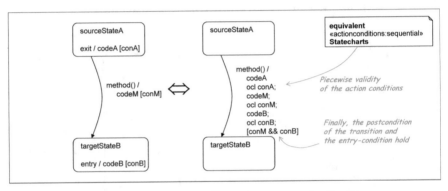

Figure 5.40. Code and conditions in entry- and exit-actions

By using the stereotype «actionconditions:sequential» in Fig. 5.40, we basically prevent that the condition conA used in the exit-action also has to hold at the end of the transition. This condition can instead be invalidated, e.g., by the transition action.

The stereotype «actionconditions:sequential» is defined in Table 5.41.

Stereotype «actionconditions:sequential»	
Model element	Statechart. For example, see Fig. 5.40.
Motivation	The exit condition of a source state can be invalidated through the action of the transition. Therefore, transitions in Statecharts which are tagged with the stereotype «actionconditions:sequential» are interpreted according to Fig. 5.40.

(continued on the next page)

(continues Table 5.41.: Stereotype ≪actionconditions:sequential≫)

Effect	As illustrated in Fig. 5.40, the condition of the exit-action already holds after the execution of this exit-action. In this way, the following transition action can already rely on this condition but also invalidate it. The same applies for hierarchically nested states.
Example	If the conditions of the entry- and exit-action of a state are in contradiction to each other, for instance by an attribute value being supposed to take on different values, there can only be transition loops in this form of interpretation.
Pitfalls	In a Statechart, the combination of descriptive conditions and procedural code should be used with caution. Depending on the purpose of a Statechart, it is often sufficient to use one of the two forms.

Table 5.41. Stereotype ≪actionconditions:sequential≫

Considering the entry- and exit-actions, the state invariants discussed in previous sections, have been neglected so far. A state invariant must always hold when the object is in that state. In particular a state invariant also holds after the entry-action of a state has been executed and before the exit-action of a state is executed. Hence, state invariants can be inserted at the appropriate place, as demonstrated by the equivalences shown in Figures 5.39 and 5.40.

5.5.3 State-Internal Transitions

While the entry- and exit-actions have to be regarded as part of the incoming and outgoing transitions, *state-internal transitions* are complete and independent transitions where the entry- or exit-actions of the state are not executed. Figure 5.42 shows how a state-internal transition can be understood. State-internal transitions do not leave the state and therefore do not execute entry- and exit-actions. If stateA would not have an entry- and exit-action, the transition could simply be attached directly to stateA instead of introducing a substate.

5.5.4 Do-Activity

If a state represents a situation of the object where an activity prevails, when, for example, a phone rings or a warning message flashes, we can use the do-

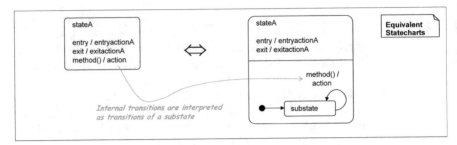

Figure 5.42. State-internal transitions

activity for its modeling. There are two fundamental possibilities of interpretation in a normal Java programming model. One possibility is to implement a do-activity through a parallel thread that is active only in this state. An alternative and preferred method, however, is shown in Fig. 5.43.

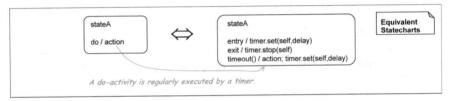

Figure 5.43. Do-activity as time-controlled repetition of an action

In the transformation of Fig 5.43 it has been assumed that a `timer` is available calling the method `timeout()` after the specified amount of time. This is presented as an internal transition that does not leave the state, first executes the action, and then resets the timer.

5.6 Statecharts in the Context of UML

In the previous sections of this chapter, the Statechart notation has been introduced in greater detail and representation possibilities have been demonstrated by means of numerous examples. Using several stereotypes, different variants of Statecharts have been defined and their respective field of application discussed. Possibilities for variation consist, on the one hand, in the semantics of the Statechart elements and, on the other hand, in the interpretation of these elements in the context of object-oriented modeling. In Fig. 5.30, for example, possibilities were presented regarding use of the stereotypes «prio:inner» and «prio:outer» to specify the priority of overlapping transitions as required.

In this section, some basic problems the interpretation of the Statechart that are still unsolved are discussed. Thereby, fundamental characteristics of a transformation into OCL or a programming language and possible transformation techniques (refactoring steps) are explained.

5.6.1 Inheritance of Statecharts

In UML/P, Statecharts are principally attached to classes or methods. Often, OCL constraints and Java code snippets are parts of Statecharts. Thus, Statecharts must always be seen in the context of other artifacts of the software development. In a number of publications [SHJ+94, LW94, LW99, PR94, GKRB96, RK99, KPR97, Rum96, EE97, DL96], different variants have been discussed to show how to specialize Statecharts that describe a class and, thus, allow one to further detail the behavior. This, e.g., includes the *behavioral conformity* from [HG97]. The strategies proposed and used for inheritance differ considerably in some regards. If, for example, a Statechart is intended as an interface description of a class describing the call order of the methods, transitions can be removed because this corresponds to a specialization of the object in the subclass. If, in contrast, a Statechart is intended to describe the implementation, transitions may be added for the inheritance in order to make the behavior of the subclass more robust against errors.

Also, in UML/P, Statecharts have different fields of applications. A Statechart that has been defined for test purposes usually cannot be applied to objects of the subclass, as the subclass has an extended state concept and additional methods. As described above, there are different interpretations in literature for the usage of constructive Statecharts, i.e., Statecharts that are intended for the implementation.

In practice, inheritance of Statecharts is rarely applied—and if so, rather informally—for the refinement of behavior. Mostly, the behavior is only redefined. This means that in practice, state-based behavior of the super- and the subclass are broadly independent of each other if both are modeled by Statecharts. Often the case occurs that only the superclass is modeled by a Statechart while the subclass only redefines the *helper functions*, which do not influence the state concept of the Statechart. So, the Statechart of the superclass is taken over without any change.

A further observation shows that classes described by a Statechart frequently do not have subclasses, as they are conceived as complex steering classes and allow behavioral variability by delegation.

5.6.2 Transformations on Statecharts

With the release of [Fow99], containing transformation techniques for Java code, it has become obvious that transformations on modeling and programming artifacts allow for improvement of the systematics of software development. A systematic transformation in small, composable steps is considerably clearer and, thus, better for planning than "Big Bang"developments and modifications. Modification of architectural aspects of a system modeled by class diagrams often has effects at several places. Therefore, small, systematic, and ideally tool-supported modification steps are ideal. These steps are performed individually and then directly tested for their effect. Hence, as described in [Fow99], refactoring of class diagrams is a fundamental means for incremental improvement of the system.

In contrast, a Statechart models only a small section of the system. It focuses on the modeling of an object's behavior and sometimes also of a strictly limited environment. Modifications in the state model or behavior of individual objects can have considerable effects on the overall behavior of the system. However, regarding Statechart development in practice, single modification steps, such as those introduced in [SPTJ01, RK99, Rum96, Rum97, EHHS00, EH00, Sch98b], do not help to the desired degree. Experience shows that particularly the modification of the state space often enforces such intensive alterations to a Statechart that the initial Statechart has little in common with the new one. For pragmatic reasons, more often it is therefore reasonable to develop a new Statechart instead of deducing it from an old one.

The number of transformation rules necessary to develop a transformation calculus complete enough for practical implementations is also relatively high. This is due to the higher number of model elements that are used in Statecharts and the resulting number of potential combinations. Because of these observations motivated by practical implementations and the discussion above, the definition of a complete calculus for transformation of Statecharts is relinquished. Instead, a set of rules is introduced in this section to serve for the targeted transformation of Statecharts. These rules are partly based on transformations already represented in previous sections in Figures 5.18, 5.19, 5.22, 5.23, 5.25, 5.26, 5.27, 5.30, 5.37, 5.38, 5.39, 5.40, 5.42, and 5.43.

The refactoring techniques for modification of Java code in [Fow99] exclusively serve preservation of the externally visible behavior (see [PR01]). Hence, they focus on improving the design and architecture of the system without changing the functionality and, thus, serve as a basis for later extensions of functionality. However, the motivation for transformation of a Statechart can have other causes. As Statecharts are primarily behavior descriptions, refinement (addition of details) of the behavior described in the Statechart is possibly of the same interest as the preservation of the behavior. As [SPTJ01] shows, modification of the state space with the purpose of refining in accordance with the condition that the behavior does not change can also be of interest. Additionally, it must be distinguished whether the modifications of a Statechart are adaptions only concerning the model, i.e., the presentation, or whether these adaptions change the state space and the behavior of the modeled objects as well. This distinction is important because, in contrast to class diagrams, with Statecharts we have many different possibilities for depicting the same behavior.

Hereinafter, some transformations for Statecharts are presented, serving for, among other goals, preparation of code generation by reducing the concepts used in the Statechart.

Simplification of Statecharts

As Statecharts provide a comprehensive collection of concepts, indicating transformation rules that eliminate single concepts of a Statechart is of interest. As a result, the Statechart becomes less comprehensive in the concepts used and thus more easily accessible for analysis or code generation. In fact, the rules described below can be understood as a first step towards code generation. At the same time, these rules can also be regarded as defining for the concepts they process. The eliminations of the state actions and the state hierarchy presented hereinafter are described by equivalence transformations that can also be used inversely to allow their introduction.

The procedure described below is to a large extent automatable. In steps 12, 15, and 18, however, design decisions can be made or undecidable OCL constraints need to be treated. There, also optimizations for later code generation can be made. Steps 12 and 15 can also be implemented directly by an algorithm, and step 18 can be omitted.

1. **Do-activities** are eliminated according to Fig. 5.43.
2. **Internal transitions** are transformed to real transitions like described in Fig. 5.42. If the state with the internal transition already has substates, internal transitions are added as transition loops solely to already existing states. This means that source the and target state always correspond, because internal transitions do not change the state.
3. **Initial states within hierarchical states** serve for forwarding of transitions whose target state is the hierarchical state to one of the substates. According to Fig. 5.25, these transitions are directly forwarded to substates that are marked as initial states. Then, the marks of the initial states are irrelevant.
4. **Final states within hierarchical states** can be removed in a similar manner according to Fig. 5.26.
5. **Target states with substates.** The remaining transitions that still have target states with substates are all diverted to these substates (and, if necessary, multiplied). The equivalence indicated on the left in Fig. 5.27 is thereby used in combination with Fig. 5.25.
6. **Source states with substates.** In a similar manner, the source states of all transitions are diverted to substates and at the same time multiplied, if applicable. The equivalence from Fig. 5.27 given on the right is applied in combination with Fig. 5.26.
7. **Repetition on several hierarchy levels** can be necessary for steps 3–6 so that all source and target states of all transitions are simple states (i.e., do not have substates anymore). Initial and final states now only exist at the top level.
8. **Exit-actions** are added to the action of the transition leaving the state, according to Figures 5.37 and 5.38. According to Fig. 5.44, if a final state

has an exit-action, it is also conceived as an action of the finalizer.[6] In method Statecharts, a spontaneous transition is used instead of the finalizer. Then, the exit-actions are eliminated.

9. **Entry-actions** are added to the incoming transitions in a similar manner. Entry-actions of initial states are treated according to Fig. 5.45 by introducing a new incoming transition that corresponds to the constructor realizing this entry-action. In a method Statechart, a spontaneous transition is used instead of the constructor. Then, the entry-action is eliminated.

10. **State invariants of hierarchically decomposed states** are added in the substates explicitly, according to Fig. 5.18.

11. **Hierarchically decomposed states** have now become irrelevant and are eliminated according to Fig. 5.19. All initial and final state marks are thereby transferred from the eliminated states to the substates.

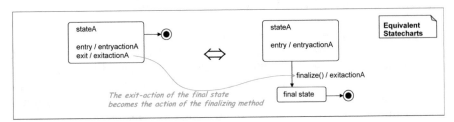

Figure 5.44. Exit-actions in final states

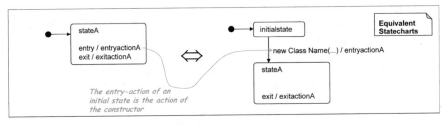

Figure 5.45. Entry-actions in initial states

As result of these transformations, all state actions have been transferred to transitions and all hierarchically decomposed states are eliminated. The remaining atomic states only contain state invariants.

---

[6] The usage of a new final state and this explicit transition with the stimulus `finalize()` corresponds to a variant of the situation known from automaton theory regarding the transformation of Moore to Mealy machines.

Handling of State Invariants

State invariants can be treated in different ways, depending on the meaning of the states. This is why several variants exist for the next step 12, depending on the particular purpose of the Statechart.

For code generation, state invariants can be used as assertions of properties for certain program stages in the system and, thus, directly taken over into the code. This allows use of state invariants as assertions for tests.

However, ensuring that a state invariant is correct is much easier than developing or generating code that ensures that the invariant is fulfilled. Under certain but fairly restricted circumstances, it is possible to produce constructive code from an invariant, especially if the invariant represents a conjunction of equations that can be interpreted as assignments and where the variables on the left are only used after their definition. Such a constructively usable state invariant for the class `WebBidding` (see Fig. 4.32) is for example

```
                                                             OCL
status == AppStatus.INITIAL &&
appletLanguage == (language==null) ? "English" : language &&
statusText== (appletLanguage=="English") ? "Hello" : "Hallo"
```

On the one hand, it can be examined whether a state invariant can be used constructively. However, on the other hand, in general, it cannot automatically be checked whether a state invariant is already fulfilled by the action of the incoming transition and, as a consequence, generation of constructive code is not necessary anymore. This can only be decided by the developers. In order to store the knowledge of, whether the state invariants of a Statechart have already been constructively realized by the actions, in the diagram, a stereotype can be used. This is especially meant for controlling code generation.

In a Statechart attached to a class, state invariants are relevant only at the beginning and end of a method. They are therefore part of a method's pre- and postcondition and of the processing of a message, respectively. One possibility of using these state invariants in the further development is to use them as a pair of OCL pre/postconditions for the definition of a method.

When the Statechart describes an object's lifecycle, the object state is the only place to store the information about the current diagram state of an object. This is why the diagram state of the object needs to be computable from the attributes and links of an object in the object structure. This requires the usage of disjoint state invariants in the implementation. Then it is possible to evaluate the state invariant as a predicate and in doing so to derive the diagram state and the transition to select.

As overlapping state invariants are allowed in Statecharts, it is advisable to convert these into disjoint invariants by an appropriate transformation. Hence, the following rule is proposed as step 12 in the transformation towards simpler Statecharts and offered in two variants:

12. **Tighten state invariants** in order to ensure that the diagram state of an object can be uniquely determined from the object state by evaluating the state invariant such an appropriate transition can be chosen for the arriving stimulus.

So, if a new stimulus arrives at the object, it can be determined solely based on the state invariant which diagram state the object is in and, thereby, which transitions are enabled. In practice, there are different options to realize step 12, of which two are presented here:

12a. **Tighten state invariants** by making statements about further components of the object state. This can, for example, refer to the presence and absence of links, the size of containers, or the values of attributes.

However, tightening a state invariant with the aforementioned step 12a requires the developer to have quite some knowledge about the context of the Statechart. In the realization of Statecharts, these newly introduced disjoint state invariants could be evaluated consecutively until the respective current object state is identified, but in general this is not efficient. An alternative procedure that furthermore has the advantage that it is automatically executable uses an additional attribute for explicitly storing the respective current diagram state:

12b. **Tighten state invariants** by introducing a state attribute, according to Fig. 5.46, that explicitly stores the diagram state of an object.

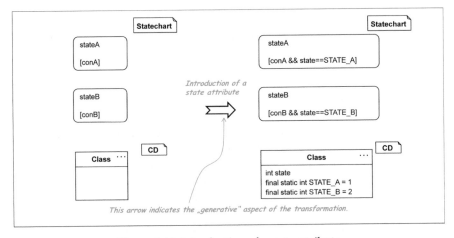

Figure 5.46. Introduction of a state attribute

The transformation in step 12b is clearly directed towards implementation. It is especially efficient because only the attribute state is necessary for determination of the current diagram state and a `casestatement` can be used for the discrimination. In contrast, the original state invariants are not necessary anymore. They can now be used as assertions for tests at the beginning or after the completion of a method processing the respective current stimulus.

In the special case that a Statechart has no explicit state invariants, we can also introduce a state attribute remembering the state.

Adding State Invariants to Transitions

As already discussed for Fig. 5.22, the state invariant of a source state has the same effect as if it were given as a precondition of the transition. The next step 13, thus, transforms the preconditions of all transitions such that the state invariants are explicitly incorporated:

13. **Conjugate state invariants with preconditions,** according to Fig. 5.22, so that the preconditions are represented completely.

By explicit inclusion of state invariants, it becomes easier to recognize incompleteness or overlapping of the firing conditions of transitions. The subsequent steps can therefore be performed more easily.

While the state invariant of a transition's source state is an additional assertion for the transition, a state invariant of the target state is an additional obligation which the transition is responsible for. This obligation can also be made visible in the action condition of a transition by explicit inclusion:

14. **Conjugate state invariants with action conditions,** according to Fig. 5.47, so that the action conditions are represented completely.

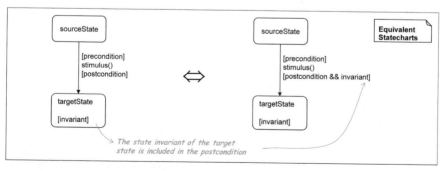

Figure 5.47. Explicitly representing a state invariant in an action condition

Incompleteness of Transition Scopes

We have already discussed various facets of nondeterminism and incompleteness of Statecharts in Sections 5.2 and 5.4.5. We also explained that incompleteness can be interpreted in various ways. For that purpose we introduced the stereotypes «completion:ignore», «completion:chaos», and «error». In all three cases, it is principally possible to complete the Statecharts by adding explicit transitions. This, however, excessively increases the amount of transitions such that a Statechart can practically not be read anymore. For an implementation, such a completion is also not necessary because, for example, in an implementation using a `case` statement, incompleteness can be dealt with by the `default` construct. This is suitable for the stereotypes «completion:ignore» and «error» as both variants offer a precisely determined reaction to arriving stimuli. For the stereotype «exception», we in addition need a `try-catch` statement.

In comparison, the chaos completion (stereotype «completion:chaos») aims at interpreting incompleteness as maximally existing nondeterminism. Thus, it is often methodically reasonable to complete a Statechart by choosing a proper set of transitions instead of executing a chaos completion in order to make the Statechart also react robustly in underspecified cases.

The following step 15a describes the completion of a Statechart marked with «completion:ignore»

15a. **Completion** of a Statechart marked with «completion:ignore» can be achieved by introducing explicit transition loops that contain an empty action or an action condition, that does not change the system state. These loops are added for all potentially incoming stimuli and states for which no transition exists or where the precondition restricts the enabledness of a transition.

As the rule for the performance of step 15a shows, in the worst case there is a transition loop necessary for each combination of state and potential stimulus. Figure 5.48 illustrates how such a completion can be achieved in an exemplary Statechart with two transitions for the same stimulus. Whether the transition added to the state `sourceStateA` in Fig. 5.48 is actually necessary can in the general case only be determined manually due to the generally not automatically recognizable satisfiability of OCL conditions. In this case, it needs to be decided whether the state invariant `invariantA` is already covered by the existing transitions `precon1 || precon2`. Only if this is the case is the newly added transition redundant and its precondition never fulfilled. So, it needs to be checked if the following is true:

```
invariantA implies (precon1 || precon2)                          OCL⬎
```

If this holds, the following can be concluded for the precondition of the new transition:

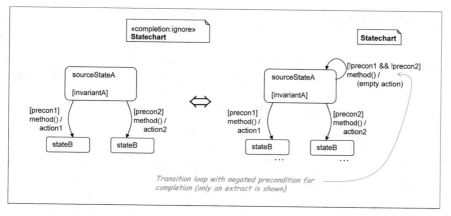

Figure 5.48. Transition loop for the part that is not enabled

```
invariantA && (!precon1 && !precon2)  <=>  false
```
OCL

The completion of a Statechart with an error state is conducted in a similar way:

15b. **Completion** of a Statechart with a state marked with «error» is done analogously to step 15a. All added transitions, however, target the error state. The error state is also completed.

The following rule for step 15c allows us to explicitly add a suitable, self-chosen set of transitions instead of the full set of transitions that implicitly exists when using chaos completion. In particular, we have complete freedom of choice for the reaction to an incoming stimulus.

15c. **Completion.** Statecharts marked with «completion:chaos» are completed by introducing transitions whose preconditions and stimuli are determined as in the previously given steps. However, there is the freedom of choosing a suitable target state and action for each transition. The nondeterministic addition of transitions with overlapping firing conditions is also possible (but only overlapping within the new transitions).

The completion of exception behavior can be conducted in the same way as in step 15b.

16. **Exception completion.** If a state marked with «exception» is given, transitions marked with stimulus `Exception` are added analogously to step 15b, targeting the exception error state. The exception error state is also completed.

Reducing Nondeterminism

Irrespective of whether step 15 has been executed in one of the three variants of completing Statecharts, nondeterminism can occur in the resulting Statechart in several forms. Causes and effects of nondeterminism in Statecharts have already been discussed in detail in Sect. 5.4. There are two essential reasons for dealing with nondeterminism in Statecharts:

1. Nondeterminism interpreted as underspecification can be used for postponing irrelevant details during earlier activities of the software development. If we receive additional requirements from the customer or can make further design decisions, we can refine and detail the behavior modeled with the Statechart by reducing nondeterminism.
2. If the program execution is, as in Java (without threads), deterministic, nondeterministic alternatives always needs to be decided when implementing a nondeterministic Statechart into sequentially processed Java code. An automatic selection is often made by using the random order for the evaluation of the translated functions. But by explicitly reducing the nondeterminism, the selection otherwise made by the code generator can be controlled by the developer.

As the sources of nondeterminism in the Statechart are manyfold, there are a number of possible modifications of a Statechart in order to reduce its nondeterminism. If, for example, the Statechart is incomplete and marked with «completion:chaos», the implicit nondeterminism existing due to the incompleteness can be considerably reduced by a change to the stereotype «completion:ignore» or by explicitly introducing an error state with the stereotype «error».

If a transition action is underspecified, this action can be made deterministic by a suitable transformation.

Another source of nondeterminism is the overlapping of firing conditions of different transitions with the same source state and the same stimulus. A simple instrument to reduce this source of nondeterminism is the usage of priorities as outlined in Sect. 5.4.4. However, it is also possible to reduce this form of nondeterminism by tightening the preconditions of the overlapping transitions. The following rule in step 17 describes this technique:

17. **Reducing nondeterminism.** Nondeterminism caused by transitions with overlapping firing conditions is reduced according to Fig. 5.49 by choosing a suitable condition D that has the effect of a discriminator between the two transitions. This technique can be applied pairwise for all transitions with overlapping firing conditions.

The transformation in Fig. 5.49 initially leads to complex-looking preconditions where the discriminator D separates the overlapping conditions. Although it needs to be syntactically correct, the discriminator can be freely chosen. An apt definition of the discriminator can considerably simplify the

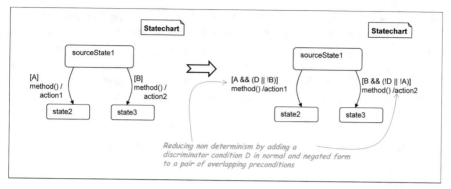

Figure 5.49. Reduction of nondeterminism in overlapping firing conditions

new preconditions. One possibility, for instance, is to use the discriminator `true` which leaves the left transition unchanged and gives it priority over the right transition with the precondition `B&&!A`.

Eliminating Transitions Without Enabledness

Due to the numerous transformation steps performed so far, many transitions have been added or modified. However, especially automatically performed steps may have added transitions that are never enabled. For example, reducing nondeterminism by applying the previously discussed step 17 can restrict a precondition so that an execution of the transition is not possible anymore. This, for example, can happen if the firing condition of one transition includes that of the other. Unfortunately, transitions that are not enabled cannot be recognized automatically. Hence, the next step is an optimization that normally needs to be performed by the developer. Only in exceptional cases will the system itself recognize that a transition has become redundant as its precondition is equivalent to `false`:

18. **Eliminating transitions without enabledness,** as they do not contribute to the system behavior.

Rule 18 is mainly useful in combination with the previous step 17. If two transitions have the same firing condition, the firing condition of one transition can first be reduced to be empty with step 17 and then removed with step 18. In the example in Fig. 5.49, this means that we set A `<=>` B and choose the discriminator `true` and, thus, reduce the precondition of the right transition to `false`.

Removing transitions is generally allowed if one or more alternative transitions exist that overlap the firing condition of the transition to be eliminated. This means that it must be the same stimulus and that the precondition of the transition is subsumed by the preconditions of the alternative transitions, i.e., it is implied by their disjunction. Methodically, the removal of unnecessary transitions details the modeled behavior. It may not seem intuitive that information is actually *added* to the Statechart by *removing* transitions. However, this is exactly the case. After the removal of an alternative, the behavior of the modeled object is described more precisely. Thus, the object behavior is less underspecified as it has fewer alternative ways to behave.

Vice versa, also adding transitions, especially as described in step 15c, can detail the modeled system behavior. The essential difference is that adding transitions is only allowed if there is no alternative in the original Statechart, while the removal of transitions is allowed if alternatives exist.

Eliminating Unreachable States

By applying the transformation steps 17 and 18, states can become unreachable in the diagram. The reachability of a state is defined by using the transitive closure over all enabled transitions starting from the set of initial states. This allows us to detect individual states that are not a destination of a transition. Moreover, it also allows us to detect regions of connected states that can reach each other, but where the region is unreachable from the outside. Step 19 allows removal of these diagram states from the diagram:

19. **Eliminating unreachable diagram states,** as they do not contribute to the system behavior. A state is reachable if it is (1) an initial state or (2) a target state of an enabled transition whose source state is reachable. Transitions with unreachable source states are removed as well.

Result of the Transformation

The described simplification of the Statechart creates a flat structure that only contains transitions that contribute to the described behavior. The states contain disjoint state invariants. All actions have been relocated to transitions. The transitions are complete in the sense that they contain the complete pre- and postcondition and, hence, are directly suited for implementation.

By removing a number of Statechart concepts, the result is more suitable for analysis or code generation. Therefore, a *simplified form of the Statechart* is assumed in the following considerations.

5.6.3 Mapping to OCL

Statecharts serve as a state-based description of object behavior. The behavior of objects is finally realized by the methods that are used as stimuli in the transitions. OCL-based method specifications have been introduced in Sect. 3.4.3, also allowing us to model method behavior. The pre/postcondition style used there for specifying the effect of a method fairly precisely corresponds to the description by a transition if an OCL postcondition is used for

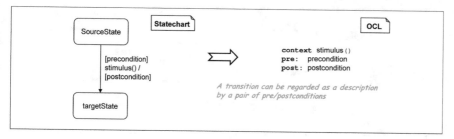

Figure 5.50. A transition as OCL pre/postcondition

modeling the reaction. Hence, the transformation of transitions of the simplified Statechart described in Fig. 5.50 is straightforward.

The transformation shown in Fig. 5.50 creates such a pre/postcondition for each transition. As in a Statechart a number of transitions might contain the same stimulus, so several OCL specifications arise for the same method. The integration of such pairs of OCL specifications has already been discussed in Sect. 3.4.3. There we discussed two basically different forms of combination that also play a role here.

If we transform a deterministic Statechart, i.e., a Statechart whose transitions do not have overlapping firing conditions, we get OCL specifications whose preconditions are pairwise disjoint. The OCL specifications, thus, can be combined by the algorithm described in Sect. 3.4.3 where each precondition acts as a guard for its postcondition. The disjunction of the preconditions ensures that at most one postcondition needs to be fulfilled and, thus, no inconsistencies can arise due to contradicting postconditions.

However, in a nondeterministic Statechart, there are overlapping firing conditions. Transitions with such overlaps cannot be transformed individually into OCL constraints because their combination would lead to inconsistent postconditions. Instead, overlapping transitions are transformed together. Because the state conditions are disjoint in our simplified Statechart, transitions with overlapping transition scopes can start only from the same source state. This form of transformation is shown in Fig. 5.51 by means of two overlapping transitions. Note that, if both preconditions are fulfilled, the freedom of choosing transitions means that afterwards only one postcondition needs to be fulfilled because only one of the transitions fires. This is reflected by the slightly complex form of the postcondition. An application to more than two transitions is possible due to generalization or iterated application of the rule for two overlapping transitions.

The transformation of transition descriptions into OCL method specifications can be applied in two ways. On the one hand, it can be understood as semantic integration of the two UML subnotations, Statecharts and OCL. On the other hand, it also has a practical application. The semantic integration achieved by this transformation shows the relations of both subnotations and maps the semantics of simplified Statecharts to OCL. Together with the

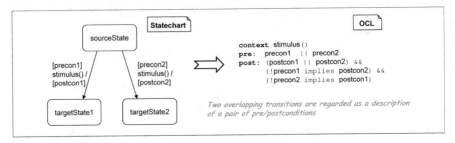

Figure 5.51. Overlapping transitions as OCL pre/postcondition

transformation of general Statecharts into simplified Statecharts already introduced earlier, we now have a coherent transformation chain of Statecharts
in OCL. The meaning of a Statechart can, thus, be derived from the meaning
of OCL. A similar form of semantics definition for flat automata has been
given, e.g., in [Rum96] with the target language Focus [BS01].

If the given transformation is supported by a tool, Statecharts can be
translated into OCL within a project, and the available analysis, simulation,
and code generation techniques can be applied to the generated OCL conditions. This especially enables the application of verification tools available
for OCL to object behavior that has initially been described with Statecharts
and allows one to show certain properties of the modeled object.

5.7 Summary

Statecharts represent an essential link between a system's structure in the
form of state spaces and the classes' behavior. They allow us to structure
the state space hierarchically and define the reaction of objects to incoming
stimuli based on these state hierarchies.

Statecharts are based on the concepts of the Mealy and Moore automata,
which is why fundamental problems, such as nondeterminism, incompleteness, ε-transitions, and expressiveness, were already studied on these automata. We identified the *interpretation* of automaton concepts (input, automaton state, and output) in the "real" world of software development
(method call, object state space, and action) besides automaton theory.

Then we introduced *states, state invariants, transitions, preconditions, stimuli,* and *actions* with procedural and descriptive character.

Especially relevant is the *enabledness of transitions* and the resulting possibilities of treating *nondeterminism* (*underspecification*) and *incompleteness*. The
composition of *entry-, exit-,* and *transition actions* by conjunction, sequential
execution, and piecewise validity has been another crucial point of discussion.

A collection of transformation rules for Statecharts shows on the one hand the semantics of more complex Statechart concepts such as initial and final states in hierarchical states or entry- and exit-actions but also allows on the other hand the transformation of general Statecharts into *simplified Statecharts* that are more suitable for code generation and analysis.

6

Sequence Diagrams

The one just looking sees more
than the one playing the game.

Wilhelm Busch

A sequence diagram represents an exemplary snippet of a software system's process. It models the occurring interactions and activities and can be extended by OCL expressions. This chapter introduces a simplified version of sequence diagrams which are suitable especially for the modeling of tests.

© Springer International Publishing Switzerland 2016
B. Rumpe, *Modeling with UML*, DOI 10.1007/978-3-319-33933-7_6

Sequence diagrams are used for modeling interactions between objects. A sequence diagram describes in which order method calls are executed and when they terminate. Thus, similar to Statecharts, sequence diagrams model behavioral aspects. However, there are some essential differences:

- A sequence diagram focuses on the interaction between objects, but the inner state of an object is not represented.
- Basically, a sequence diagram is *exemplary*. Just like in the object diagram, the represented information can, thus, occur arbitrarily often, multiple times in parallel, or even not at all in the process of a system.
- Due to their exemplary character, sequence diagrams are not suitable for the complete modeling of behavior. They are mainly used for requirements definition and, as shown in this work, test case modeling.

Hence, sequence diagrams are methodically used especially for requirements analysis as well as for test definition for or after implementation. If sequence diagrams are used for modeling a system, they always illustrate specific, desired or undesired situations or erroneous behavior and are therefore suitable as a starting point for test cases.

When used in requirements engineering, developers need to derive a complete implementation from a necessarily finite set of sequence diagrams. A number of proposals extend sequence diagrams in order to systematize this derivation. Control structures are often added that allow alternatives, parallelism, iterations, and *recursive calls* of sequence diagrams. These proposals are discussed, e.g., in [Krü00, Leu95, GRG95, BGH⁺98a, SHB96] and used in different forms in the two essential standards for sequence diagrams. Besides the UML standard [OMG10a], dialects of sequence diagrams are used particularly in the telecommunication, industry in the form of Message Sequence Charts (MSCs) [IT99]. The automaton-based extension in High-Level MSCs also allows the representation of MSC combinations [IT99, Krü00, GGR01]. Another variant of sequence diagrams is Object-MSCs [BMR⁺96] in which activity bars have been introduced. Also the Live Sequence Charts'(LSCs) approach deserves special attention [DH01, HM03, HM08]. It gives sequence diagrams considerably more expressiveness and therefore becomes accessible for complete specifications, simulation of different processes [KHK⁺03], constructive code generation, or verification techniques.

In comparison with the mentioned variants, the form of sequence diagrams introduced in this chapter is kept simple. The reason is, among others, that, in this work, the methodical use of sequence diagrams is rather restricted to modeling of test cases and test drivers. Statecharts can already be used for complete process descriptions. Thereby, a redundant description is avoided. This is based on the experience that it is much more elaborate to create complete descriptions instead of exemplary ones and that, for reasons of developer efficiency, redundancy needs to be avoided. Thus, sequence diagrams are adequate to exemplarily describe system runs.

The following Sect. 6.1 introduces the fundamental concepts of sequence diagrams. Section 6.2 discusses the use of OCL constraints in sequence diagrams. In Sect. 6.3, several different semantics for sequence diagrams are introduced. The developer can choose one by using stereotypes. Additions to sequence diagrams and special cases are discussed in Sect. 6.4. Section 6.5 finally deals with the use of sequence diagrams in the context of other UML diagrams. Additionally to this chapter, Appendix C.6 describes the abstract syntax of sequence diagrams.

6.1 Concepts of Sequence Diagrams

Figure 6.1 describes a sequence diagram that in the following is used as an example explaining the available concepts.

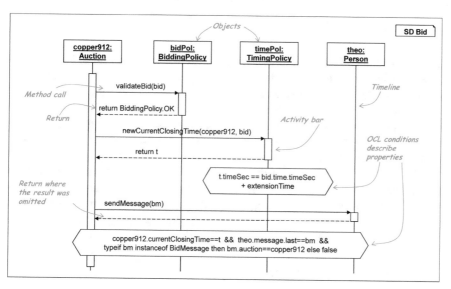

Figure 6.1. Sequence diagram for accepting a bid

The essential concepts occurring in a sequence diagram are briefly explained in Fig. 6.2.

Object, Timeline, and Activity

In a sequence diagram, *objects* are represented next to one another in a row and furnished with a *timeline* pointing downward. Optionally, objects have a name and a type. In contrast to object diagrams, attributes and links are

---

Object An object in the sequence diagram has the same semantics as in the object
diagram (see Fig. 4.1), but it is only shown with name and type. Several objects
of the same type are allowed. Name or type are optional.

Timeline. In a sequence diagram, consecutive events are represented top down.
Each object has a timeline representing the progress of the time for this object.
The timescale shown is not faithful to the time in the system's object. The time-
line, thus, only serves to represent the chronological order of interactions.

Interaction. As discussed in Sect. 5.4.3, an interaction between two objects can be
one of several kinds of stimuli. This includes method calls, returns, exceptions,
and asynchronous messages. Parameters of interactions are optional in a sequence diagram.

Activity bars. For processing a method call, an object is active for a certain time.
The activity bar that can also occur in a nested form in a recursion serves as a
representation for this activity.

Constraint. For a detailed description of properties that hold during a process, OCL
guards can be used.

Figure 6.2. Definitions for sequence diagrams

not represented. Interactions arriving at and leaving from an object are represented in chronological order by reaching the timeline. They could have
been reported in this form by an *observer*.

Basically, also asynchronous messages are permitted as interactions. However, asynchronous communication can be represented only to a limited extent. We simplify sequence diagrams by assuming that messages are not sent
simultaneously and that they do not intersect. This simplification is based
on the usage of sequence diagrams for test purposes where concurrency is
explicitly controlled in order to maintain deterministic test results. This considerably simplifies the modeling with sequence diagrams, but we might not
be able to represent certain phenomena with sequence diagrams that are possible in an implementation. Similar assumptions can be found in other, more
complex MSC dialects [Krü00, BMR+96]. Therefore, the remaining chapter
only further discusses the sequential method call.

An activity bar is used to show when a method of an object is executed.
Usually, activity bars start and end at incoming or outgoing arrows. Activity
bars can be omitted, and we later discuss the ambiguity that can then arise.
For a recursive call, activity bars are represented in a nested form, which is
also discussed later. As a return arrow can also be omitted, an activity bar
may end without an outgoing arrow.

The kinds of possible interactions are represented in Fig. 6.3. Except for
the later discussed recursive call, each interaction is represented by a horizontal arrow. The time spent is neglected.[1]

---

[1] Due to the assumptions described above, this also holds especially for asynchronous messages, which are not differentiated syntactically from normal method
calls. In some dialects, a specific arrow is used for asynchronously sent messages.

At the arrows, method calls, returns, or exceptions are added. These can optionally have arguments. An argument is denoted as a Java expression. If it is a single variable that has not occurred so far, it is defined with its first occurrence. Return information can be omitted completely, as the dashed arrow is already unambiguous. Due to its nature, a return can only occur in the diagram after the corresponding method call.

To avoid information overload, the incompleteness indicator "..." can be used instead of the arguments of the interaction. This has the same effect as if the parameters were omitted completely.

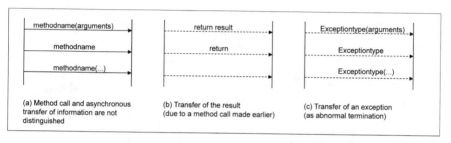

Figure 6.3. Types of interactions in sequence diagrams

Static Methods

If a method is static, it is underlined like in the class diagram. In this case, the arrow ends at a class that is used analogously to an object. This is demonstrated by Fig. 6.4.[2]

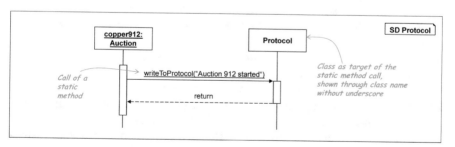

Figure 6.4. Static method in a sequence diagram

---

[2] While objects are underlined as instances, attributes and methods are underlined if they are not assigned to an instance. This is not consistent but corresponds to the rule that elements that are used more often can be described more easily.

Object Creation

If an object is newly created during some interaction, this can be represented by the object's timeline starting at a later point in time. Figure 6.5 shows two typical forms of object creation. Both representations are even equivalent if they are used for certain forms of object creation. Form (b) is then only a more detailed and more implementation-related representation.

A representation for destroying an object is not offered in UML/P, as this is also not possible in the target language Java.

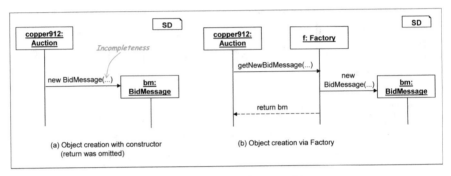

Figure 6.5. Creation of a new object

Stereotypes and Tags

Stereotypes and tags can be used in sequence diagrams as well. The stereotype «match» is introduced in Sect. 6.4 to give the developer the possibility of choosing between different semantics for sequence diagrams.

The stereotype «trigger», for example, can be used to indicate that a method call is the cause for all other interactions of the sequence diagram. Therefore, such a stereotype is especially suited for test drivers, such as those shown in Fig. 6.6, and it can be used only for method calls of objects of the test environment into the tested object structure. Hence, mostly only the first method call is tagged with «trigger». Interactions tagged with «trigger» necessarily lead to the other described interactions. The called objects are not allowed to behave differently. This is a considerably stronger restriction than sequence diagrams without this stereotype would denote.

6.2 OCL in Sequence Diagrams

As Fig. 6.1 shows, conditions that only hold at certain points in time of the process can be added to a sequence diagram. In these OCL constraints, the

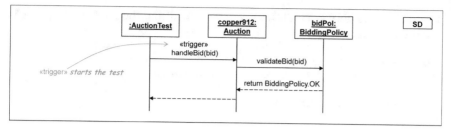

Figure 6.6. Test drivers with starting message

objects and values occurring in the sequence diagram can be related. For this purpose, access to the named objects and the variables used as arguments in method calls is possible. Figure 6.1 contains several such variables. The binding area of each variable stretches from the place of the first occurrence to the overall sequence diagram. This, for example, means that the `Auction` object `copper912` can also be used as a method argument as well as in OCL constraints. In Fig. 6.1, in total the variables `copper912`, `bidPol`, `timePol`, `theo`, `bid`, `t`, and `bm` are available. In both sequence diagrams and object diagrams, anonymous objects are treated as if they had an unambiguous, externally unknown name.

As already discussed, variables such as `bm` and `t` that occur as arguments of a method call or a return for the first time are bound at this place. Their type results from the respective signature that can be read from a class diagram. `bid` is of the type `Bid`, `t` of the type `Time`, and it is known that object `bm` is of the type `Message`.

An OCL constraint can describe occurring objects and parameters as well as a message's effect on an object more precisely, whereas the context results from the sequence diagram. Explicitly stating the context, the bottom constraint in Fig. 6.1 can be represented as follows:

```
context Auction copper912, BiddingPolicy bidPol,
        TimingPolicy timePol, Person theo, Bid bid,
        Time t, Message bm inv:
  copper912.currentClosingTime==t &&
  theo.message.last==bm &&
  typeif bm instanceof BidMesssage then
    bm.auction==copper912
  else false
```

This condition, among other things, requires that `bm` is an object of the type `BidMessage` and then partly checks its content.

The specification of the context shows that access to attributes is possible by qualification with the object. However, if an OCL constraint is exclusively assigned to one timeline, the attributes of this object can directly be accessed, but for better readability, it is reasonable to still use a qualification. Thus, the context of the first OCL constraint in Fig. 6.1 is the following, whereas in contrast to the above mentioned context definition, the `BidMessage bm` is not yet introduced:

```
context Auction copper912, BiddingPolicy bidPol,                    OCL
        TimingPolicy this, Person theo,
        Bid bid, Time t                                inv:
let TimingPolicy timePol = this
in
    t.timeSec == bid.time.timeSec + extensionTime
```

The validity of an OCL constraint refers to the point in time directly after the last occurred interaction or the last occurred activity bar. This means that the OCL constraint must only be satisfied directly after this interaction but not during the overall "period" in which the OCL constraint is embedded. This is illustrated by means of two sequence diagrams in Fig. 6.7.

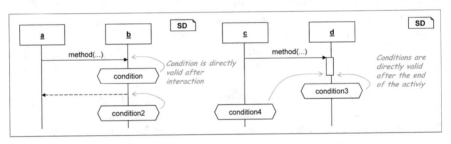

Figure 6.7. Validity of OCL constraints in sequence diagrams

As a sequence diagram models temporal system runs, other than in the OCL method specification, a `@pre` operator is not available. If a previous attribute value must be accessed, this value needs to be stored explicitly in an auxiliary variable. For this purpose, a `let` construct is used that is similar to the OCL construct and that introduces new variables that are accessible only within the sequence diagram. These auxiliary variables are not part of the implementation but exclusively serve for the specification of effects during the process of interactions. Figure 6.8 shows a use of these variables.

6.3 Semantics of a Sequence Diagram

The exemplary character of a sequence diagram has already been referred to. However, for the methodically correct use of sequence diagrams, a precise explanation of the semantics of such an exemplary process and the treatment of incomplete representations is necessary.

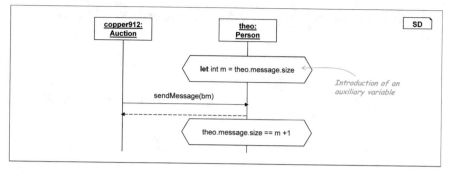

Figure 6.8. Auxiliary variables to store values

Exemplaricity and Incompleteness

Similar to the object diagram, the exemplaricity of a sequence diagram is based on the description of a set of objects that, in this form, can occur in a system arbitrarily often or even not at all. Furthermore, the run itself is exemplary. It can occur arbitrarily often, be concurrent and nested, or not occur at all.

In addition to these forms of *exemplaricity*, a sequence diagram represents an *abstraction* of a process, as it can contain neither all objects of the system nor all occurring interactions. In a sequence diagram, interactions can also be missing. Figure 6.9 can, therefore, represent the same process as Fig. 6.8 on a different abstraction level because different objects are shown.

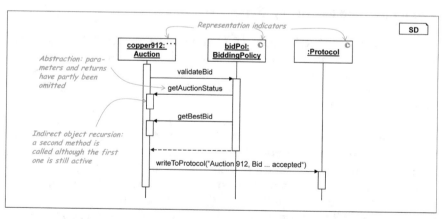

Figure 6.9. Representation with different abstraction level

Formally, the semantics of a sequence diagram can be explained by mapping the diagram's elements to a system run. Figure 6.10 shows such a mapping where the right side uses a representation for the system run that is similar to that of a sequence diagram and that can be understood analogously to Fig. 3.19.

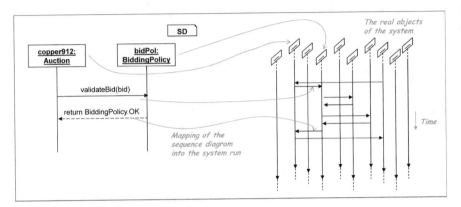

Figure 6.10. Representation of a sequence diagram in a system run

The prototypic objects in the sequence diagram are mapped to real objects, and the shown interactions are mapped to real interactions of the system; the chronological order must be consistent. This form of matching corresponds to the already discussed form of an observer selectively observing objects and protocolling some interactions. With mathematical means, this representation can, e.g., be described as in Figures 6.11 and 6.12.

Ambiguities and Restricting Stereotypes

The matching described in Figures 6.11 and 6.12 allows several assignments. If a method call takes place several times during the observation period, it is ambiguous which actual method call corresponds to the interaction represented in the diagram. The fictive observer has possibly "overlooked" some interactions between the two objects.

However, by using suitable stereotypes, the form of observation can be determined more precisely. The representation indicator "ⓒ" can be used for objects in the sequence diagram to indicate the completeness of the shown interactions. Alternatively, the representation indicator "..." for incompleteness already holds by default but can also be stated explicitly. Figure 6.9 shows the use of these indicators. A "ⓒ" means that the tagged object has no interaction with any other object between the first and last interaction shown in the diagram. This means that the protocol of the fictive observer is complete with regard to the marked object and the represented observation period.

For an object completely observed in this sense, it necessarily holds that a suitable return must be stated for each call. Furthermore, all objects that

A loose **semantics definition for sequence diagrams** is described by mapping the elements of a sequence diagram to the elements of a system run.
The essence of a sequence diagram is given by:

- The set of the prototypic objects $\bar{O}$
- The set of possible interactions $\bar{A}$ in the diagram
- The source of each interaction $\bar{s} : \bar{A} \to \bar{O}$
- The target of each interaction $\bar{t} : \bar{A} \to \bar{O}$
- A sequence of diagram interactions $\bar{d} \in \bar{A}^*$, where multiple occurrence of the same interaction is allowed

The essence of a system run, in analogy, consists of a set of objects Obj, interactions Act, two mappings $s, t : Act \to Obj$ for the source and target of each interaction, and the system run $r \in Act^*$ representing a trace [DR95]. According to [Rum96], the dynamics of object creation can be simulated using a predefined set of existing objects and thus can be ignored here.
Let $Ix_d = \{0..n\}$ be the $n + 1$ indexes of the sequence $d = d_0 d_1 \ldots d_n$ and d_i the element at position $i \in Ix_d$.
The connection is defined by requiring the existence of a mapping $f : \bar{O} \to Obj$ for the objects and a monotonically increasing injection $j : Ix_{\bar{d}} \to Ix_r$ of the indexes of $\bar{d}$ into the indexes of r.
For each index $i \in Ix_{\bar{d}}$ in the sequence diagram the following must hold:

$$s(r_{j(i)}) = f(\bar{s}(\bar{d}_i)),$$
$$t(r_{j(i)}) = f(\bar{t}(\bar{d}_i)).$$

The monotonicity and injectivity of j ensure the chronological order of the representation. A sequence diagram forms an abstraction of the system run, as neither f nor j need be surjective.

Figure 6.11. Loose semantics for sequence diagrams, part 1

The loose **semantics definition of sequence diagrams** from Fig. 6.11 is detailed by the alignment of returns to corresponding calls.
The definition of the essence of sequence diagrams is extended by

- The set of returns and exceptions $\bar{R} \subseteq \bar{A}$
- The assignment of the returns to the respective method calls $\bar{m} : \bar{R} \to (\bar{A} \setminus \bar{R})$

Analogously, the representation of a system run is detailed by returns and exceptions $R \subseteq Act$, and the bijective assignment $m : R \to (Act \setminus R)$. While m is a bijection, due to the incompleteness of a sequence diagram, $\bar{m}$ only needs to be injective.
For each index pair $a, b \in Ix_{\bar{d}}$ it holds that:

$$\bar{d}_b \in \bar{R} \wedge \bar{d}_a = \bar{m}(\bar{d}_b) \ \Rightarrow \ a < b \wedge r_{j(b)} \in R \wedge r_{j(a)} = m(r_{j(b)})$$

Figure 6.12. Loose semantics for sequence diagrams, part 2

directly interact with the observed object need to be shown. This can lead to considerably more detailed diagrams than actually desired. Therefore, further stereotypes are used that allow additional variants of the semantics definition.

The stereotype «match:initial», for instance, is especially well suited for defining testable sequence diagrams, while the interpretation «match:free» corresponds to the default "...". Table 6.13 describes the four variants. More variants that further refine the form of observation are conceivable. Thus, lists of method calls that are completely observed or ignored could explicitly be given, but this would increase the information density of a sequence diagram, making it less readable.

Stereotypes «match:*»	
Model element	Prototypic object in the sequence diagram.
Motivation	Assigning the interactions of a sequence diagram to interactions in the system run is ambiguous, as sequence diagrams can represent abstractions. The defined stereotypes can resolve these ambiguities.
Usage condition	The stereotypes can be stated individually for each object in the sequence diagram.
Effect	Between the first and last interaction, an object tagged with «match:complete» has exactly the interactions with other objects or itself stated in the diagram. Hence, the observation of this object is complete. «match:visible» prohibits omitting interactions with other objects stated in the sequence diagrams but allows that interactions with objects not stated in the diagram are omitted. Therefore, the observation of this object is complete only with regard to the objects visible in the diagram. «match:initial» allows further interactions between the stated objects if these are of another kind, i.e., calls of other methods, for example. Further interactions of the same kind are allowed only after the occurrence of the stated interactions.

(continued on the next page)

(continues Table 6.13.: Stereotypes ≪match:≫)*

	So, the observer tries to carry out an "initial" or early matching. Further interactions of this kind are ignored in the system run as soon as the last one of this kind is checked off in the diagram. Hence, the observer always protocols the first occurrence of the respective interaction and "checks off" the interaction in the sequence diagram. The stereotype ≪match:free≫ represents the default and means that arbitrary omissions are possible in the observation.
Pitfalls	The combination of different stereotypes within a sequence diagram can be used for elegant statements but can also cause confusion.[3]
Extensible	Each stereotype can also be applied to the overall sequence diagram and therefore hold for all objects contained therein.

Table 6.13. Stereotypes ≪match:*≫

A formal definition of the four variants is given on the basis of regular expressions in Fig. 6.14. Here, the overall run of a system is understood as a word, while a sequence diagram is regarded as a regular expression to which a system run has to adhere.

One of the biggest advantages of the equivalence of this formalization to regular expressions is that there are efficient algorithms from the theory of formal languages that can protocol system runs and recognize occurring matches. This is an important prerequisite for using sequence diagrams for tests. However, this efficiency suffers if, in between, values must be assigned to variables and OCL constraints evaluated.

6.4 Special Cases and Extensions for Sequence Diagrams

An analysis of the defined form and semantics for UML/P sequence diagrams shows that, similar to other forms, certain special cases that require a more detailed explanation can arise.

Noncausal Sequence Diagrams

A sequence diagram specifies a chronological order of the messages observed, but it does not necessarily define a *causal order*. As shown in Fig. 6.15, a sequence diagram can especially consist of two disjoint parts. The thus incomplete observation does not show the causal context anymore but only a temporal one of the occurring method calls. Such sequence diagrams are

---

[3] Tricky specifications are often difficult to read and should, thus, be avoided in practice. Sometimes, less elegant specifications should be preferred.

The loose **semantics definition for the stereotypes of the form** «match:*» is based on the foundations from Fig. 6.11. For simplification, let us assume that $\bar{A} \subseteq Act$ and $\bar{O} \subseteq Obj$, that we can ignore arguments of the interactions, and that f, as a consequence, is the identity. Furthermore, let $obj(a) = \{s(a), t(a)\}$.

Without restriction, let each object in $\bar{O}$ be tagged with one of the stereotypes. Let $O_\phi \subseteq \bar{O}$ be the set of the sequence diagram's objects tagged with «match:ϕ».

A system run can be regarded as a *word* over the alphabet of the interactions Act. To build the semantics, a sequence diagram is assigned a *regular expression* which describes valid system runs. This can be used to hereinafter explain the semantics of the «match:*» stereotypes.

The sequence diagram $\bar{d} = a_0 a_1 a_2 \ldots a_n$ consisting of the $n+1$ interactions $a_k \in Act$ can be transformed to a regular expression of the form

$$Sem[a_0 \ldots a_n] = Act^* \, a_0 \, X_1^* \, a_1 \, X_2^* \, a_2 \, \ldots \, X_n^* \, a_n \, Act^*$$

that describes a set of system runs. Before the first and after the last interaction described, the system run is not restricted. The set of possible interactions in X_k depends on the chosen «match:*» stereotypes.

The following interactions are forbidden:

$$A_{complete} = \{a \in Act \mid obj(a) \cap O_{complete} \neq \emptyset\}, \tag{1}$$
$$A_{visible} = \{a \in Act \mid obj(a) \cap O_{visible} \neq \emptyset \land obj(a) \subseteq \bar{O}\}, \tag{2}$$
$$A_{initial,k} = \{a_k, a_{k+1}, \ldots, a_n \mid obj(a_l) \cap O_{initial} \neq \emptyset \text{ for } k \leq l \leq n\}. \tag{3}$$

(1) and (2) describe interactions that must be stated in the sequence diagram and are therefore prohibited in between. (3) identifies interactions that are later stated in the sequence diagram and, thus, would contradict the initial matching.

It holds that $X_k = Act \setminus A_{complete} \setminus A_{visible} \setminus A_{initial,k}$.

The arguments of interactions Act can be taken into consideration by introducing type information. The dynamic assignment of prototypic objects to real objects that is analogous to the object diagram can also be taken into consideration.

Figure 6.14. Semantics of the stereotypes «match:*»

suitable for tests but not for a description from which an implementation is to be developed, as causality plays an essential role for the developer.

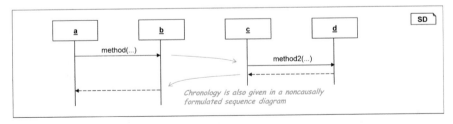

Figure 6.15. Noncausal sequence diagram

A similar phenomenon can be found in Fig. 6.16: it is not stated how control is transferred to object c. Noncausal sequence diagrams can be prohibited by using suitable «match:*» stereotypes.

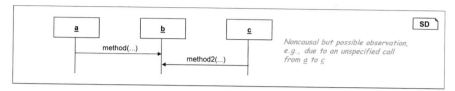

Figure 6.16. Second noncausal sequence diagram

Recursion and Ambiguity

The object recursion already discussed in Sect. 5.2.7 causes complications not only in Statecharts but also in sequence diagrams. We talk of object recursion if, within the execution of a method, another method of the same object is called directly or indirectly. Figure 6.17 shows both forms of calls.

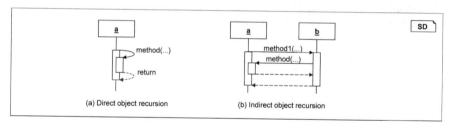

Figure 6.17. Sequence diagrams with object recursion

Normally, activity bars serve to illustrate behavior pattern and can be omitted. In recursive cases however, they allow to resolve ambiguities. In Fig. 6.18(a), neither activity bars nor returns are given, so that the two alternatives 6.18(b) and 6.18(c) are possible. The elimination of ambiguity can, as shown, happen by using activity bars or, in a similar manner, by adding returns.

The source of these ambiguities is the object recursion shown in Fig. 6.17. As such an ambiguity can easily be resolved by using activity bars, we decide that a sequence diagram with such an ambiguity is not well-formed and is rejected by a code generator.

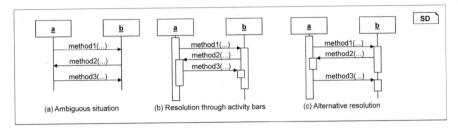

Figure 6.18. Ambiguous sequence diagram

6.5 Sequence Diagrams in UML

Inheritance

A sequence diagram has prototypic objects where optionally name and type are given. The type of an object can be a class with several subclasses or an interface. Correspondingly, the object that is observed in a running system can be from a different class. In this sense, sequence diagrams, thus, take inheritance into account. But due to the used loose semantics for sequence diagrams, the expressiveness for subclasses is also restricted. In fact, a sequence diagram only describes that objects of a certain type can behave according to the described pattern but that they do not have to do so.

But for tests that check a certain behavior pattern for all objects of a type, it is beneficial to give objects from subclasses certain liberties in the behavior, e.g., by assigning the stereotype «match:visible».

Sequence Diagrams and Statecharts

Depending on the development method, there are various options to use Statecharts and sequence diagrams in combination:

1. Statecharts are developed from a set of sequence diagrams.
2. Startecharts and sequence diagrams are used in parallel for different purposes.
3. Sequence diagrams can be derived from Statecharts, thus conforming to them.

In [Krü00, BGK99], for example, a procedure is described to derive automata for the participating objects from a finite set of sequence diagrams. In the form used there, first a word of the automaton's alphabet is derived by dissection of a sequence diagram into the interactions that are relevant for a single object. By manually adding state information, an automaton that accepts these (and further words) can be built from the finite set of words. By further transforming the automaton, they derive a version that can be understood as an operative description of an object which implements the behavior described by sequence diagrams.

A similar procedure is described in [DH01]: an LSC (Live Sequence Chart [HM08, HM03]) is implicitly created by protocolling desired behavior and by building an automaton thereof. Both approaches have in common that they first assume an exemplary specification from which they derive a complete, implementation-related description. With an appropriate adaption, these approaches could also be used for UML/P.

The reverse procedure of deriving sequence diagrams from given Statecharts can be used for two tasks. On the one hand, exemplary and more easily understandable descriptions can be extracted from a given Statechart implementation, and on this basis, the interplay of the participating objects can be analyzed. On the other hand, test cases that check various transition paths of the Statecharts can be derived from the Statechart.

Another alternative is to use Statecharts and sequence diagrams in parallel. In this case, both views of the system have not been derived from each other but developed manually. Thus, it is of interest to check both descriptions for consistency with analytical techniques by regarding a sequence diagram as a word (sequence of interactions) that has to satisfy a Statechart. But when using OCL constraints within both notations, analysis is not necessarily executable. Therefore, it is reasonable to use the Statechart for implementation and sequence diagrams as test cases.

Sequence Diagrams and UML Communication Diagrams

Besides sequence diagrams, the UML standard provides an additional notation which is closely related to the notation of sequence diagrams. *Communication diagrams* represent a subset of a sequence diagram's information but are less focused on the chronological order and more on the cooperation between objects. Figure 6.19 contains the representation of the sequence diagrams from Figures 6.1 and 6.9 as a communication diagram. However, OCL constraints and returns are not represented in the communication diagram.

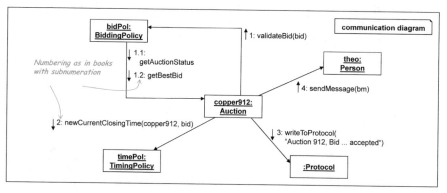

Figure 6.19. Communication diagram

The two-dimensional distribution allows one to accommodate more objects in communication diagrams. The interaction order is not determined by timelines but by numeration. For this, nested calls are marked with ascending lists of numbers. Return values are added to the call. There is no concept analogous to activity bars in communication diagrams. More details regarding communication diagrams can be found in [RQZ07], for example.

Although the information represented in both diagrams is essentially the same, the form of representation and, thus, the way diagrams are dealt with varies considerably. Adding an interaction, for example, is easier in a sequence diagram, because in a communication diagram interactions must be renumbered. Besides, OCL constraints cannot be stated in the simple form for certain points in time, as it is the case for sequence diagrams.

6.6 Summary

In this chapter, a simple form of sequence diagrams, that is suitable for modeling interactions between objects on an exemplary basis, has been introduced. A sequence diagram consists of several objects with one timeline each, between which interactions take place. Method calls, returns, and exceptions are allowed kinds of interactions. OCL constraints can be stated to define object properties at certain "points in time."

With a sequence diagram, desired system runs can, for example, be represented in order to better understand the system that needs to be implemented. Another use for sequence diagrams is the definition of exemplary runs in tests as well as the modeling of test drivers.

As the simple sequence diagrams defined here suffice for this purpose, UML/P leaves out the extensions that can be found in other dialects of sequence diagrams. This also has the interesting advantage that available concepts in sequence diagrams are easy to understand and use. Further literature has already been pointed at in the relevant places in the chapter. Therefore, we once again recommend only the very detailed overview [Krü00] about dialects of sequence diagrams. There, also a chapter about the methodical refinement of sequence diagrams can be found.

7

Further Reading

For those readers who are interested in additional insights, we recommend to look at our additional literature that describes the theoretical underpinning, as well as the application of these concepts in specific domains, and newer forms of use.

Agile Model Based Software Engineering

Can agility and modeling be used in the same project? This question was raised in [Rum04]: "Using an executable, yet abstract and multi-view modeling language for modeling, designing and programming still allows to use an agile development process." Modeling will be used in development projects much more, if the benefits become evident early, e.g with executable UML [Rum02c] and tests [Rum03]. In [GKRS06], for example, we concentrate on the integration of models and ordinary programming code. In this book, respectively [Rum12] and [Rum11], the UML/P, a variant of the UML especially designed for programming, refactoring and evolution, is defined. The language workbench MontiCore [GKR+06] is used to realize the UML/P [Sch12]. Links to further research, e.g., include a general discussion of how to manage and evolve models [LRSS10], a precise definition for model composition as well as model languages [HKR+09] and refactoring in various modeling and programming languages [PR03]. In [FHR08] we describe a set of general requirements for model quality. Finally [KRV06] discusses the additional roles and activities necessary in a DSL-based software development project. In [CEG+14] we discuss how to improve reliability of adaprivity through models at runtime, which will allow developers to delay design decisions to runtime adaptation.

Generative Software Engineering

The UML/P language family defined here is a simplified and semantically sound derivate of the UML designed for product and test code generation.

© Springer International Publishing Switzerland 2016
B. Rumpe, *Modeling with UML*, DOI 10.1007/978-3-319-33933-7_7

[Sch12] describes a flexible generator for the UML/P based on the MontiCore language workbench [KRV10, GKR⁺06]. In [KRV06], we discuss additional roles necessary in a model-based software development project. In [GKRS06] we discuss mechanisms to keep generated and handwritten code separated. In [Wei12] we show how this looks like and how to systematically derive a transformation language in concrete syntax. To understand the implications of executability for UML, we discuss needs and advantages of executable modeling with UML in agile projects in [Rum04], how to apply UML for testing in [Rum03] and the advantages and perils of using modeling languages for programming in [Rum02c].

Unified Modeling Language (UML)

Many of our contributions build on UML/P described in this book are implemented in [Sch12]. Semantic variation points of the UML are discussed in [GR11]. We discuss formal semantics for UML [BHP⁺98] and describe UML semantics using the "System Model" [BCGR09a], [BCGR09b], [BCR07b] and [BCR07a]. Semantic variation points have, e.g., been applied to define class diagram semantics [CGR08]. A precisely defined semantics for variations is applied, when checking variants of class diagrams [MRR11c] and objects diagrams [MRR11d] or the consistency of both kinds of diagrams [MRR11e]. We also apply these concepts to activity diagrams (ADs) [MRR11b] which allows us to check for semantic differences of activity diagrams [MRR11a]. We also discuss how to ensure and identify model quality [FHR08], how models, views and the system under development correlate to each other [BGH⁺98b] and how to use modeling in agile development projects [Rum04], [Rum02c] The question how to adapt and extend the UML in discussed in [PFR02] on product line annotations for UML and to more general discussions and insights on how to use meta-modeling for defining and adapting the UML [EFLR99], [SRVK10].

Domain Specific Languages (DSLs)

Computer science is about languages. Domain Specific Languages (DSLs) are better to use, but need appropriate tooling. The MontiCore language workbench [GKR⁺06], [KRV10], [Kra10] describes an integrated abstract and concrete syntax format [KRV07b] for easy development. New languages and tools can be defined in modular forms [KRV08, Völ11] and can, thus, easily be reused. [Wei12] presents a tool that allows to create transformation rules tailored to an underlying DSL. Variability in DSL definitions has been examined in [GR11]. A successful application has been carried out in the Air Traffic Management domain [ZPK⁺11]. Based on the concepts described above, meta modeling, model analyses and model evolution have been examined in [LRSS10] and [SRVK10]. DSL quality [FHR08], instructions for defining views [GHK⁺07], guidelines to define DSLs [KKP⁺09] and Eclipse-based tooling for DSLs [KRV07a] complete the collection.

Modeling Software Architecture

Distributed interactive systems communicate via messages on a bus, discrete event signals, streams of telephone or video data, method invocation, or data structures passed between software services. We use streams, statemachines and components [BR07] as well as expressive forms of composition and refinement [PR99] for semantics. Furthermore, we built a concrete tooling infrastructure called MontiArc [HRR12] for architecture design and extensions for states [RRW13b]. MontiArc was extended to describe variability [HRR+11] using deltas [HRRS11] and evolution on deltas [HRRS12]. [GHK+07] and [GHK+08] close the gap between the requirements and the logical architecture and [GKPR08] extends it to model variants. [MRR14] provides a precise technique to verify consistency of architectural views against a complete architecture in order to increase reusability. Co-evolution of architecture is discussed in [MMR10] and a modeling technique to describe dynamic architectures is shown in [HRR98].

Compositionality & Modularity of Models

[HKR+09] motivates the basic mechanisms for modularity and compositionality for modeling. The mechanisms for distributed systems are shown in [BR07] and algebraically underpinned in [HKR+07]. Semantic and methodical aspects of model composition [KRV08] led to the language workbench MontiCore [KRV10] that can even develop modeling tools in a compositional form. A set of DSL design guidelines incorporates reuse through this form of composition [KKP+09]. [Völ11] examines the composition of context conditions respectively the underlying infrastructure of the symbol table. Modular editor generation is discussed in [KRV07a].

Semantics of Modeling Languages

The meaning of semantics and its principles like underspecification, language precision and detailedness is discussed in [HR04]. Here, we defined a semantic domain called system model, which is based on a sound mathematical theory. [RKB95, BHP+98] and [GKR96, KRB96]. An extended version especially suited for the UML is given in [BCGR09b] and in [BCGR09a] its rationale is discussed. [BCR07a, BCR07b] contain detailed versions that are applied on class diagrams in [CGR08]. [MRR11a, MRR11b] encode a part of the semantics to handle semantic differences of activity diagrams and [MRR11e] compares class and object diagrams with regard to their semantics. In [BR07], a simplified mathematical model for distributed systems based on black-box behaviors of components is defined. Meta-modeling semantics is discussed in [EFLR99]. [BGH+97] discusses potential modeling languages for the description of an exemplary object interaction, today called sequence diagram.

[BGH$^+$98b] discusses the relationships between a system, a view and a complete model in the context of the UML. [GR11] and [CGR09] discuss general requirements for a framework to describe semantic and syntactic variations of a modeling language. We apply these on class and object diagrams in [MRR11e] as well as activity diagrams in [GRR10]. The second book respectively [Rum12] embodies the semantics in a variety of code and test case generation, refactoring and evolution techniques. [LRSS10] discusses evolution and related issues in greater detail.

Evolution & Transformation of Models

Models are the central artifact in model driven development, but as code they are not initially correct and need to be changed, evolved and maintained over time. Model transformation is therefore essential to effectively deal with models. Many concrete model transformation problems are discussed: evolution [LRSS10, MMR10, Rum04], refinement [PR99, KPR97, PR94], refactoring [Rum12, PR03], translating models from one language into another [MRR11c, Rum12] and systematic model transformation language development [Wei12]. [Rum04] describes how comprehensible sets of such transformations support software development, maintenance and [LRSS10] technologies for evolving models within a language and across languages and linking architecture descriptions to their implementation [MMR10]. Automaton refinement is discussed in [PR94, KPR97], refining pipe-and-filter architectures is explained in [PR99]. Refactorings of models are important for model driven engineering as discussed in [PR03, Rum12]. Translation between languages, e.g., from class diagrams into Alloy [MRR11c] allows for comparing class diagrams on a semantic level.

Variability & Software Product Lines (SPL)

Many products exist in various variants, for example cars or mobile phones, where one manufacturer develops several products with many similarities but also many variations. Variants are managed in a Software Product Line (SPL) that captures the commonalities as well as the differences. Feature diagrams describe variability in a top down fashion, e.g., in the automotive domain [GHK$^+$08] using 150% models. Reducing overhead and associated costs is discussed in [GRJA12]. Delta modeling is a bottom up technique starting with a small, but complete base variant. Features are added (that sometimes also modify the core). A set of applicable deltas configures a system variant. We discuss the application of this technique to Delta-MontiArc [HRR$^+$11, HRR$^+$11] and to Delta-Simulink [HKM$^+$13]. Deltas can not only describe spacial variability but also temporal variability which allows for using them for software product line evolution [HRRS12]. [HHK$^+$13] describes an approach to systematically derive delta languages. We also apply variability to modeling languages in order to describe syntactic and semantic variation points, e.g., in UML for frameworks [PFR02]. And we specified a systematic way to define variants of modeling languages [CGR09] and applied this as a semantic language refinement on Statecharts in [GR11].

State Based Modeling (Automata)

Today, many computer science theories are based on state machines in various forms including Petri nets or temporal logics. Software engineering is particularly interested in using state machines for modeling systems. Our contributions to state based modeling can currently be split into three parts: (1) understanding how to model object-oriented and distributed software using statemachines resp. Statecharts [GKR96, BCR07b, BCGR09b, BCGR09a], (2) understanding the refinement [PR94, RK96, Rum96] and composition [GR95] of statemachines, and (3) applying statemachines for modeling systems. In [Rum96] constructive transformation rules for refining automata behavior are given and proven correct. This theory is applied to features in [KPR97]. Statemachines are embedded in the composition and behavioral specifications concepts of Focus [BR07]. We apply these techniques, e.g., in MontiArcAutomaton [RRW13a] as well as in building management systems [FLP+11].

A

Language Representation with Syntax Class Diagrams

> There is nothing more practical
> than a good theory.
>
> Immanuel Kant

Languages are used for representing and communicating information. There are many different forms of language. This includes textual, diagrammatic, visual, and also audio languages, but what all languages have in common is that they are built on the basis of a vocabulary of basic elements. The basic elements are often called *characters* and are grouped into reasonable and more complex statements, according to the rules defined in a *grammar*. Therefore, a language is usually regarded as the set of *well-formed sentences* that belong to this language [HU90]. This holds for linguistics as well as for computer science. This knowledge forms the basis for an elegant and well-elaborated theory for the representation of textual languages that manifests itself in the Chomsky hierarchy and that is applied in practice as *Extended Backus–Naur Form* (EBNF). Today, EBNF and related approaches are used to represent programming languages such as Java [GJSB05]. Even XML [McL01] and the definition language for XML documents are essentially based on these concepts.

However, the textual form of grammars is not suitable for representing languages such as UML that are almost completely based on diagrams. Due to the nonlinear, two-dimensional structure of diagrams, the representation of such a language is necessarily more complex. A well-elaborated approach is provided by the extension of grammars on graphs, the graph grammars [Nag79, Roz99, EEKR99]. However, this approach wasn't applied for a representation of UML. In part, the reason for this is that the elegance and simplicity of textual grammars could not be retained in graph grammars: but probably graph grammars are not used mainly because the description language of UML in the form of class diagrams is suitable for describing graphical languages as well.

Metamodeling [SRVK10, RA01, CEK01, CEK+00] primarily uses class diagrams as the fundamental notation. A *metamodel* defines the abstract syntax of a graphical notation. Since UML is being standardized, it is common to

© Springer International Publishing Switzerland 2016
B. Rumpe, *Modeling with UML*, DOI 10.1007/978-3-319-33933-7

use a simplified form of class diagrams as the metamodel language. This approach has the advantage that only one language needs to be learned, but at the same time, this approach is vulnerable to circular definitions. Numerous examples such as the successful use of the English language for describing the English grammar or EBNF for defining EBNF show that a circular definition is acceptable for practical purposes. Thus, we use a combination of an EBNF grammar and syntax class diagrams (SCDs) by means of which textual and diagrammatic parts of UML/P notations are defined.

Many of today's systems such as SAP products or plant operating software have to be highly configurable and often need to be able to be supplemented by additional functions/calculations during operation. Exchangeable components such as electronic control units for cars or plugins in extendable architectures must also be configurable after completion of the product. An elegant possibility for configuring the product is the interpretation of dynamically loadable models at runtime. Instead of generating code which is then statically fixed, the model in this case is loaded at the start of or even during the runtime of the production system. However, for this purpose, an explicit representation of the model is necessary. As metamodeling techniques are able to represent the abstract syntax of a model, an explicit configuration with models becomes possible. Models@runtime e.g. in [BBF09, FR07, CEG+14], thus, discuss possible forms of software development.

In the simplest form, dynamically loadable models are used to configure the system. We gain further flexibility but also increased risk if the system itself can manipulate its models by creating new or adapting existing model elements by manipulating its metamodel structure. Such a manipulable architecture is flexible and risky at the same time. This is shown by various applications of reflection and, at the same time, by many software engineering guidelines arguing against reflection. Java provides a reflection application programming interface (API) where inspection and manipulation of objects as well as the class structure are possible. This would be analogous to keeping the metamodel fixed but inspectable while allowing modification of models.

Such explizit representation of models at the runtime of the system enforces integration of parts of the design tools into the runtime system and, thus, blurs the border between design tool and product. Typically, the type system provided by the programming language is a hindrance and needs to be ignored, or a language which does not use a strong type system has to be used. Smalltalk development environments [Gol84] show how this could look. Essential risks are the complexity and the lack of transparency of the system, the lack of understandability of the possible behavior, as well as the lack of testability, maintainability, and further development. However, the system can be used considerably more flexibly, it is easier to configure, and it is better suited for meeting dynamically changing or individual requirements. Some application fields are, for example:

- Interpretation of behavior models as a functional description
- Modeling of the data structure for the adjustment of generic algorithms for storage, display, aggregation, and reporting of data and facts
- Rules concerning diagnostics, constraints, and plausibility
- Definition of user interfaces for screens and smartphones
- Definition of aggregations and reports from datasets
- Definition of automated processes or workflows with human participation

In the UML standard [OMG10a], metamodeling mainly consists of class diagrams that are supplemented by OCL conditions, if necessary. However, by far not all concepts of class diagrams are used. Therefore, in this section, a subset of the concepts provided by class diagrams are identified, and it is proposed to use only this subset for modeling the abstract syntax of a graphic notation. For an explicit distinction between UML class diagrams and the class diagrams used for language definition, the latter are marked with syntactic modifiers. Figure A.1 shows a syntax class diagram that defines a finite automaton.

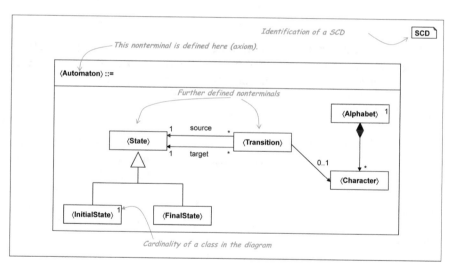

Figure A.1. SCD for finite automaton

Each of the seven classes introduced corresponds to a nonterminal. This is why class names such as ⟨Automaton⟩ are represented in the form of a nonterminal. A syntax class diagram contains a main class, in this case the class ⟨Automaton⟩, that is understood as an axiom. This means that the other six nonterminals introduced in Fig. A.1 are part of the defined automaton. This is shown by the graphic containedness of the additional nonterminals in the main class. Alternatively, it is also possible to represent the composition between the automaton and its components using an association. In Fig. A.2, such an alternative representation for automata is given that, besides an explicit representation of the composition, shows further alternatives to the previous Fig. A.1. Although both syntax class diagrams have different structures, they represent nearly the same information on automata. In Fig. A.2, the only information missing is that only one initial state per automaton is allowed.

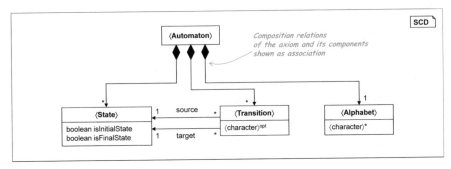

Figure A.2. Alternative SCD for finite automata

Figure A.3 describes single components of syntax class diagrams in detail. Neither methods nor tags such as visibilities are described in syntax class diagrams; In a language description, they are as unimportant as interfaces. However, it is possible to assign a cardinality to the contained classes. As default value, the cardinality * is assumed. The cardinality 1 marks a singleton class.

This cardinality is to be understood as the association cardinality of the implicitly stated association between the axiom and the marked nonterminal. Figure A.2 explicitly shows these associations and their cardinalities.

We regard the terms "nonterminal" and "syntax class" as synonymous and replace them with the term "metaclass" used in metamodeling. It should particularly be mentioned that modifiability is not important in syntax class diagrams. Methods and forms of composition are insignificant because composition mainly affects the lifecycle of participating objects. Also, navigation information only plays a minor role, e.g., in order to depict the reading direction in a reflexive association. The mentioned modeling concepts, hence, are mainly used to increase the readability of the diagram. Readability can additionally be increased by using icons that depict the graphic appearance of a syntax class. Figure A.4 represents such an annotation of Fig. A.1.

A class diagram and, thus, also a SCD describes a set of possible object structures. In case of an SCD such as the one shown in Fig. A.4, each of these object structures describes an automaton. As each object has an object identity, the SCD, however, contains subtle differences from the mathematical definition of automata. Hence, according to the SCD it is possible that different transitions have the same source and target state as well as the same

Class (synonyms: *nonterminal, syntax class, type*) describes a set of similar model elements. Its structure is determined by attributes and associations to other classes.

Attribute (synonyms: *syntax attribute*) describes a property of a model element. An
  attribute principally consists of *name* and *class*. However, when unambiguous,
  the name can be omitted.

Inheritance. The *subclass* inherits its attributes from the *superclass*. The subclass can
  be extended by additional attributes. The instances of the subclass form a *subset*
  of the instances of the superclass.

Association is a binary relation between classes. The *cardinality* restricts this relation. *Association names, role names, composition form,* and *navigation direction* improve readability.

Cardinality (synonyms: multiplicity) is stated for each association end.

Class cardinality describes the number of objects of a class. This cardinality restricts
  the implicit composition from the axiom to the marked nonterminal.

Context conditions describe additional properties that cannot easily or at all be expressed by the SCD.

Model element (synonyms: *element, syntax object, object of the abstract syntax*) is an
  instance of a syntax class.

Figure A.3. Definitions for the syntax class diagram

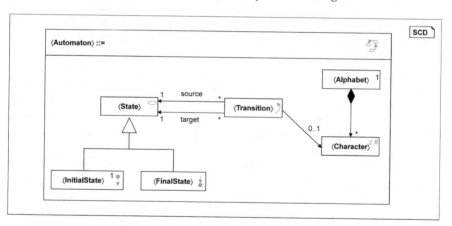

Figure A.4. SCD with illustrating symbols

symbol. In contrast, in mathematical modeling, a transition is typically identified by these three components. A suitable context condition that can, e.g.,
be formulated using OCL allows emulation of the mathematical modeling in
SCDs. Such a context condition is described, for example, in Fig. A.5.

The use of OCL in the context of syntax class diagrams is made visible by
a special marker in the top right. "SOCL" stands for Syntax-OCL, i.e., OCL
is applied to a syntax definition using a syntax class diagram. This allows
use of nonterminals such as ⟨Automaton⟩ and ⟨Transition⟩ as classes and for
navigation purposes. The OCL constraint states that, for each automaton a,

```
context ⟨Automaton⟩ a inv:                                    SOCL
forall t1,t2 in a.⟨transition⟩ :
    t1.source    == t2.source &&
    t1.target    == t2.target    &&
    t1.⟨character⟩ == t2.⟨character⟩
  implies t1 == t2
```

Figure A.5. Automaton transitions are unambiguous

an invariant holds stating that two transitions are identical if they are equal in source state, target state, and input symbol. As is common in OCL, unnamed associations are navigated by using the target class in the given context condition. Hence, the transitions of an automaton a can be assessed by the implicitly given composition relation between the classes ⟨Automaton⟩ and ⟨Transition⟩ by the navigation expression a.⟨transition⟩.

As a syntax class describes a set of model elements, inheritance is a subset relation between those sets. In the example in Fig. A.1, the set of possible states of an automaton is represented by the nonterminal ⟨State⟩. This set has two subsets, represented by ⟨InitialState⟩ and ⟨FinalState⟩. However, it is specified neither whether these partition the total set of states nor whether they are free of overlaps. Such constraints had to be expressed by additional context conditions.

Sometimes it is pragmatic to neglect the representation of a property in the SCD and to describe it by a SOCL condition. Otherwise, the SCD would be overloaded. For programming language grammars, the priorities of infix operators are often represented by an explicit table and not by a context-free grammar. This is a typical example renunciation of representation by an SCD. When using SCDs and SOCL context conditions, there is a large design space for defining languages and representing their syntax in a readable form.

Due to the combination of SCDs with the textual EBNF, further variation possibilities arise; e.g., syntax classes can be represented graphically with associations and attribute lists or by textual productions. However, some conceptional differences need to be taken into consideration when using SCDs and EBNF.

While EBNF strictly distinguishes between the *definition* and the *usage* of a nonterminal, this distinction is not made in the SCD. A production always defines the nonterminal on the left side, while nonterminals in the expression of the right side are only used. A syntax class is defined by the representation in a SCD and, at the same time, used by the connection with other syntax classes in the SCD. Thus, all mentioned syntax classes could formally be regarded as defining. The use of composition structure diagrams of UML could possibly be a remedy by assuming that the occurrence of a class within such a diagram is not defining for this class.

In the SCD in Fig. C.2, we demand that the three nonterminals ⟨Attribute⟩, ⟨Method⟩, and ⟨MethodSignature⟩ exist but do not give a detailed definition. This can be concluded from the omission of any attributes. Therefore, in Fig. C.3 these nonterminals are defined in EBNF.

As a pragmatic rule for combining SCDs and EBNF productions, we, thus, assume that the nonterminals not further detailed in the SCD are defined by EBNF productions or other SCDs. Vice versa, nonterminals used on the right side in EBNF productions can be defined by a SCD. This leads to mutual integration of SCDs with EBNF productions.

As is common in object-oriented modeling and as proposed by the methodology propagated in this book, it is possible to use several class diagrams in order to describe different aspects of systems. This technique can, of course, also be used for syntax class diagrams. Then, a syntax diagram represents a part of the overall language. By merging all syntax class diagrams, a comprehensive representation of the described language arises.

B

Java

> The limits of my language
> are the limits of my world.
>
> Ludwig Wittgenstein

The programming language used in software development considerably influences the developers' effectivity as well as the quality, costs, evolvability, and maintainability of the product. The UML/P methodology introduced in this book uses Java as its target language. To achieve good integration with the modeling language UML/P, elements from the Java grammar are used as far as possible when defining UML/P. Therefore, the reference grammar defined in [GJSB05] for Java 6 is transferred into EBNF in this section.

When using one of the subsequently introduced nonterminals in other chapters, the subscript of the figure in which the nonterminal is defined is added to it. Thus, $\langle\text{Type}_{B.2}\rangle$ refers to the definition of this nonterminal in Fig. B.2.

A representation of Java's lexical elements is left out here and reference is made to [GJSB05], where the form of comments, the "white spaces," the Unicode alphabet used for Java, and the keywords are explained. Especially, the nonterminals $\langle\text{Literal}\rangle$, $\langle\text{Identifier}\rangle$, and $\langle\text{Digits}\rangle$ listed in Fig. B.1 are assumed to be known (see also Appendix A).

$\langle\text{Literal}\rangle$ describes the set of all constants. Among others, it contains numbers and strings. Examples are `34`, `0x3ff`, or `'T'`.

$\langle\text{Identifier}\rangle$ is the set of all names that do not represent keywords. These names start with a letter or an underscore and may contain numbers. Classes, attributes, methods, and other artifacts of Java can be labeled with such names.

$\langle\text{Digits}\rangle$ is a nonempty decimal numerical sequence.

Figure B.1. Basic elements: literal, identifier, and digits

From the 124 nonterminals given in [GJSB05] with relatively simple productions, 62 nonterminals with more complex EBNF productions are com-

© Springer International Publishing Switzerland 2016
B. Rumpe, *Modeling with UML*, DOI 10.1007/978-3-319-33933-7

pressed. In doing so, nearly all nonterminals taken over keep their original semantics. Some nonterminals are newly introduced. Figure B.2 contains types, normal and generic classes, qualified names, and compilation units (files).

$$
\begin{array}{lll}
\langle\text{CompilationUnit}\rangle & ::= & \{~\langle\text{Annotation}\rangle^*~\texttt{package}~\langle\text{Name}\rangle~\underline{;}~\}^{opt} \\
& & \{~\underline{\texttt{import}}~\underline{\texttt{static}}^{opt}~\langle\text{Name}\rangle~\{~\underline{.}~\underline{*}~\}^{opt} \\
& & \underline{;}~\}^*~\langle\text{TypeDeclaration}\rangle^* \\
\langle\text{TypeDeclaration}\rangle & ::= & \langle\text{ClassDeclaration}\rangle \\
& | & \langle\text{InterfaceDeclaration}\rangle \\
& | & \langle\text{EnumDeclaration}\rangle \\
& | & \langle\text{AnnotationTypeDeclaration}\rangle \\
& | & \underline{;} \\
\langle\text{Name}\rangle & ::= & \langle\text{Identifier}\rangle^{1-*}_{\underline{.}} \\[4pt]
\langle\text{BasicType}\rangle & ::= & \underline{\texttt{boolean}}~|~\underline{\texttt{byte}}~|~\underline{\texttt{int}}~|~\ldots \\
\langle\text{Type}\rangle & ::= & \langle\text{BasicType}\rangle \\
& | & \langle\text{Name}\rangle~\langle\text{TypeArguments}\rangle^{opt} \\
& | & \langle\text{Type}\rangle~\underline{[]} \\
& | & \langle\text{TypeVariable}\rangle \\
\langle\text{TypeVariable}\rangle & ::= & \langle\text{Identifier}\rangle~|~\underline{?} \\
\langle\text{TypeArguments}\rangle & ::= & \underline{<}~\langle\text{TypeArgument}\rangle^{1-*}_{\underline{,}}~\underline{>} \\
\langle\text{TypeArgument}\rangle & ::= & \langle\text{Type}\rangle~|~\underline{?} \\
& | & \underline{?}~\underline{\texttt{extends}}~\langle\text{Type}\rangle^{1-*}_{\underline{\&}} \\
& | & \underline{?}~\underline{\texttt{super}}~\langle\text{Type}\rangle^{1-*}_{\underline{\&}} \\
\langle\text{TypeVoid}\rangle & ::= & \langle\text{Type}\rangle~|~\underline{\texttt{void}}
\end{array}
$$

Figure B.2. Types, names, and compilation units

The definition of classes and interfaces is described in Fig. B.3.

The attributes, methods, and constructors contained in class and interface declarations are explained in Fig. B.4.

The form of Java statements is explained in Fig. B.5. Despite the rather compact representation of the grammar that has become possible due to the use of EBNF, the language described here is nearly identical to the original language Java. Minor simplifications have been made to increase the grammar's readability. The grammar, for example, does not specify that at least one `catch` or `finally` needs to be stated in case of a `try` statement. Furthermore, this compact grammar is ambiguous with respect to the known `if-then-else` phenomenon and therefore not directly usable for a parser.

The sublanguage for describing expressions is defined in Fig. B.6. The expression language available in Java is relatively complex, not least due to the possibility of defining and using inner classes as well as initializing arrays. Because of this, the grammar from [GJSB05], on the one hand, has been compactified by a complete outsourcing of operator priorities in Table B.7. On

```
⟨ClassDeclaration⟩   ::= ⟨Modifier⟩* class ⟨Identifier⟩              EBNF
                         ⟨TypeParameters⟩^opt
                         { extends ⟨Type⟩ }^opt
                         { implements ⟨Type⟩_,^{1-*} }^opt
                         ⟨ClassBody⟩
⟨ClassBody⟩          ::= { ⟨ClassBodyDeclaration⟩* }
⟨ClassBodyDeclaration⟩
                     ::= ⟨FieldDeclaration⟩
                       | ⟨MethodDeclaration⟩
                       | static^opt ⟨Block⟩
                       | ⟨ConstructorDeclaration⟩
                       | ⟨TypeDeclaration⟩
⟨Modifier⟩           ::= public | protected | private | static
                       | final | abstract | ...
                       | ⟨Annotation⟩

⟨InterfaceDeclaration⟩
                     ::= ⟨Modifier⟩* interface ⟨Identifier⟩
                         ⟨TypeParameters⟩^opt
                         { extends ⟨Type⟩_,^{1-*} }^opt
                         { ⟨InterfaceBodyDeclaration⟩* }
⟨InterfaceBodyDeclaration⟩
                     ::= ⟨FieldDeclaration⟩
                       | ⟨MethodHeader⟩ ;
                       | ⟨TypeDeclaration⟩

⟨EnumDeclaration⟩    ::= ⟨Modifier⟩* enum ⟨Identifier⟩
                         { implements ⟨Type⟩_,^{1-*} }^opt
                         ⟨EnumBody⟩
⟨EnumBody⟩           ::= { ⟨EnumConstant⟩*_, _,^opt
                         { ; ⟨ClassBodyDeclaration⟩* }^opt }
⟨EnumConstant⟩       ::= ⟨Annotation⟩* ⟨Identifier⟩ ⟨Arguments⟩^opt
                         ⟨ClassBody⟩^opt

⟨TypeParameters⟩     ::= ≤ ⟨TypeParameter⟩_,^{1-*} ≥
⟨TypeParameter⟩      ::= ⟨Identifier⟩ { extends ⟨Type⟩_&^{1-*} }^opt
```

Figure B.3. Classes and interfaces

the other hand, the productions for ⟨Primary⟩ and ⟨Expression⟩ have been restructured.

Annotations are defined in Fig. B.8.

OCL Statement for Assertions

Java offers an `assert` statement that allows to integrate OCL assertions into the code, such that they are checked at runtime. With this, an important step

⟨FieldDeclaration⟩   ::= ⟨Modifier⟩* ⟨Type⟩ ⟨VariableDeclarator⟩$_,^{1-*}$;   EBNF
⟨VariableDeclarator⟩::= ⟨Identifier⟩ []* { = ⟨VariableInitializer⟩ }^{opt}
⟨VariableInitializer⟩ ::= ⟨Expression⟩
              | { ⟨VariableInitializer⟩$_,^*$,^{opt} }

⟨MethodDeclaration⟩
              ::= ⟨MethodHeader⟩ { ⟨Block⟩ | ; }
⟨MethodHeader⟩   ::= ⟨Modifier⟩* ⟨TypeParameters⟩^{opt} ⟨TypeVoid⟩ ⟨Identifier⟩
              ⟨FormalParameters⟩ []* ⟨Throws⟩
⟨ConstructorDeclaration⟩
              ::= ⟨ConstructorHeader⟩ ⟨Block⟩
⟨ConstructorHeader⟩
              ::= ⟨Modifier⟩* ⟨TypeParameters⟩^{opt} ⟨Identifier⟩
              ⟨FormalParameters⟩ ⟨Throws⟩
⟨FormalParameters⟩ ::= (⟨FormalParameter⟩$_,^{1-*}$
              { , ⟨LastFormalParameter⟩ }^{opt})
              | (⟨LastFormalParameter⟩^{opt})
⟨FormalParameter⟩ ::= {final | ⟨Annotation⟩}* ⟨Type⟩ ⟨Identifier⟩ []*
⟨LastFormalParameter⟩
              ::= {final | ⟨Annotation⟩}* ⟨Type⟩ ... ⟨Identifier⟩ []*
⟨Throws⟩   ::= { throws ⟨Type⟩$_,^{1-*}$ }^{opt}

Figure B.4. Attributes, methods, and constructors

Priority	Operator	Associativity	Operand, semantics
13	++, --	Right	Numbers
	+, -, ~, !	Right	Numbers, Boolean(!)
	(type)	Right	Type conversion (cast)
12	*, /, %	Left	Numbers
11	+, -	Left	Numbers, string (+)
10	<<, >>, >>>	Left	Shifts
9	<, <=, >, >=	Left	Comparisons
	instanceof	Left	Type comparison
8	==, !=	Left	Comparisons
7	&	Left	Numbers, Boolean
6	^	Left	Numbers, Boolean
5			Left	Numbers, Boolean
4	&&	Left	Boolean logic
3	||	Left	Boolean logic
2	? :	Right	Choice expression
1	=, *=, /=, %=	Right	Assignment
	+=, -=		
	<<=, >>=, >>>=		
	&=, ^=, |=		

Table B.7. Priorities of the infix operators

⟨Block⟩	::= { ⟨Statement⟩* }
⟨Statement⟩	::= <u>final</u>^{opt} ⟨Type⟩ ⟨VariableDeclarator⟩$_,^{1-*}$ <u>;</u>
	| ⟨TypeDeclaration⟩
	| ⟨Block⟩
	| <u>;</u>
	| ⟨Expression⟩ <u>;</u>
	| <u>switch</u> <u>(</u> ⟨Expression⟩ <u>)</u> { ⟨SwitchPart⟩* }
	| <u>do</u> ⟨Statement⟩ <u>while</u> <u>(</u> ⟨Expression⟩ <u>)</u> <u>;</u>
	| <u>break</u> ⟨Identifier⟩^{opt} <u>;</u>
	| <u>continue</u> ⟨Identifier⟩^{opt} <u>;</u>
	| <u>return</u> ⟨Expression⟩^{opt} <u>;</u>
	| <u>assert</u> ⟨Expression⟩ { <u>:</u> ⟨Expression⟩ }^{opt} <u>;</u>
	| <u>synchronized</u> <u>(</u> ⟨Expression⟩ <u>)</u> ⟨Block⟩
	| <u>throw</u> ⟨Expression⟩ <u>;</u>
	| <u>try</u> ⟨Block⟩ ⟨CatchClause⟩* { <u>finally</u> ⟨Block⟩ }^{opt}
	| ⟨Identifier⟩ <u>:</u> ⟨Statement⟩
	| <u>if</u> <u>(</u> ⟨Expression⟩ <u>)</u> ⟨Statement⟩ { <u>else</u> ⟨Statement⟩ }^{opt}
	| <u>while</u> <u>(</u> ⟨Expression⟩ <u>)</u> ⟨Statement⟩
	| <u>for</u> <u>(</u> ⟨ForInit⟩^{opt} <u>;</u> ⟨Expression⟩^{opt} <u>;</u> ⟨Expression⟩$_,^*$ <u>)</u> ⟨Statement⟩
	| <u>for</u> <u>(</u> ⟨Modifier⟩^{opt} ⟨Type⟩ ⟨Identifier⟩ <u>:</u> ⟨Expression⟩ <u>)</u> ⟨Statement⟩
⟨SwitchPart⟩	::= { <u>case</u> ⟨Expression⟩ <u>:</u> | <u>default</u> <u>:</u> }$^{1-*}$ ⟨BlockStatement⟩*
⟨CatchClause⟩	::= <u>catch</u> <u>(</u> ⟨Type⟩ ⟨Identifier⟩ <u>[]</u>* <u>)</u> ⟨Block⟩
⟨ForInit⟩	::= ⟨Expression⟩$_,^{1-*}$
	| <u>final</u>^{opt} ⟨Type⟩ ⟨VariableDeclarator⟩$_,^{1-*}$

Figure B.5. Block and statement

towards the practical use of invariants has been made. In this section, an additional form of the `assert` statement is suggested, allowing use of OCL expressions and being able to integrate defined and labeled OCL constraints also by referencing them. This statement starts with the keyword `ocl`. Additionally, the `let` construct is taken over from OCL to define local variables which, just as in OCL, are meant for exclusive use in invariants. In Fig. B.9, extensions are introduced by supplementing the nonterminal ⟨Statement⟩ from Fig. B.5 by appropriate statements.

The `ocl` statement defined here only allows the use of OCL expressions, so that the absence of side-effects is ensured. The first argument of the `ocl` statement is the Boolean predicate to be checked. The optional second argument is evaluated if the predicate is false, and its value is printed, e.g., when using it in tests.

		EBNF
⟨Primary⟩	::= (⟨Expression⟩)	
	| ⟨Literal⟩	
	| { ⟨Primary⟩ . }^{opt} ⟨Identifier⟩ ⟨Arguments⟩^{opt}	
	| { ⟨Primary⟩ . }^{opt} this ⟨Arguments⟩^{opt}	
	| { ⟨Primary⟩ . }^{opt} super ⟨Arguments⟩	
	| ⟨Primary⟩ [⟨Expression⟩]	
	| super . ⟨Identifier⟩ ⟨Arguments⟩^{opt}	
	| new ⟨Name⟩ []$^{1-*}$ { ⟨VariableInitializer⟩$_,^*$,^{opt} }	
	| new ⟨Name⟩ { [⟨Expression⟩] }$^{1-*}$ []*	
	| { ⟨Primary⟩ . }^{opt} new ⟨Name⟩ ⟨Arguments⟩ ⟨ClassBody⟩^{opt}	
	| { ⟨Primary⟩ | ⟨TypeVoid⟩ } . class	
⟨PrefixOp⟩	::= ++ | -- | + | - | ~ | !	
	| (⟨Type⟩)	
⟨PostfixOp⟩	::= ++ | --	
⟨Arguments⟩	::= (⟨Expression⟩$_,^*$)	
⟨Expression⟩	::= ⟨PrefixOp⟩* ⟨Primary⟩ ⟨PostfixOp⟩*	
	| ⟨Expression⟩ ⟨InfixOp⟩ ⟨Expression⟩	
	| ⟨Expression⟩ instanceof ⟨Type⟩	
	| ⟨Expression⟩ ? ⟨Expression⟩ : ⟨Expression⟩	
	| ⟨LeftHandSide⟩ ⟨AssignmentOperator⟩ ⟨Expression⟩	
⟨InfixOp⟩	::= * | / | % | + | - | << | >> | >>>	
	| < | > | <= | >= | == | !=	
	| & | ^ | | | && | ||	
⟨AssignmentOperator⟩	::= = | *= | /= | %= | += | -= | <<= | >>=	
	| >>= | &= | ^= | |=	
⟨LeftHandSide⟩	::= ⟨Name⟩	
	| ⟨Primary⟩ { [⟨Expression⟩] | . ⟨Identifier⟩ }	
	| super . ⟨Identifier⟩	

Figure B.6. Expressions in Java

While the first variant of the ocl statement allows direct use of an OCL expression in the first argument, the other two forms refer to an OCL constraint defined elsewhere by using a name. So, OCL constraints can be reused.

An OCL constraint starts with an explicit definition of a context in the form of one or more variables. In this way, a universal quantification over the given variables is made, as explained in Sect. 3.1.1. To resolve this quantification, an explicit assignment of the objects to be checked to the context variables can be made by regarding the OCL constraint as a Boolean predicate that has these objects as arguments. If, for example, the following condition is defined:

$\langle$Annotation$\rangle$	$::=$ <u>@</u> $\langle$Name$\rangle$	EBNF
	$\underline{(}$ $\{$ $\langle$Identifier$_{B.1}\rangle$ $\underline{=}$ $\langle$ElementValue$\rangle$ $\}^*_{,}$ $\underline{)}$	
	$\mid$ <u>@</u> $\langle$Name$\rangle$ $\{$ $\underline{(}$ $\langle$ElementValue$\rangle$ $\underline{)}$ $\}^{opt}$	
$\langle$ElementValue$\rangle$	$::=$ $\langle$Expression$\rangle$	
	$\mid$ $\langle$Annotation$\rangle$	
	$\mid$ $\underline{\{}$ $\langle$ElementValue$\rangle^*_{,}$ $\underline{,}^{opt}$ $\underline{\}}$	
$\langle$AnnotationTypeDeclaration$\rangle$		
	$::=$ $\langle$Modifier$\rangle^*$ <u>@ interface</u> $\langle$Identifier$\rangle$	
	$\underline{\{}$ $\langle$AnnotationTypeElementDeclaration$\rangle^*$ $\underline{\}}$	
$\langle$AnnotationTypeElementDeclaration$\rangle$		
	$::=$ $\langle$TypeDeclaration$\rangle$	
	$\mid$ $\langle$FieldDeclaration$\rangle$	
	$\mid$ $\langle$Modifier$\rangle^*$ $\langle$Type$\rangle$ $\langle$Identifier$\rangle$ $\underline{()}$	
	<u>default</u> $\langle$ElementValue$\rangle$ $\underline{;}$	

Figure B.8. Annotations in Java

$\langle$Statement$\rangle$	$::=$ ...	EBNF
	$\mid$ <u>let</u> $\langle$OCLVarDeclarator$_{C.8}\rangle$ $\underline{;}$	
	$\mid$ <u>ocl</u> $\langle$AssertPredicate$\rangle$ $\{$ $\underline{:}$ $\langle$OCLExpr$_{C.8}\rangle$ $\}^{opt}$ $\underline{;}$	
$\langle$AssertPredicate$\rangle$	$::=$ $\langle$OCLExpr$_{C.8}\rangle$	
	$\mid$ $\langle$Identifier$_{B.1}\rangle$	
	$\mid$ $\langle$Identifier$_{B.1}\rangle$ $\underline{(}$ $\langle$OCLExpr$_{C.8}\rangle^*_{,}$ $\underline{)}$	

Figure B.9. Extension of Java instructions

context Auction a, Person p **inv** NM:
    p **in** a.bidder **implies**
        forall m **in** a.message: m **in** p.message

> OCL

it can be checked with ocl NM(a,theo) whether the messages of an auction have been sent to person theo.

If the context of the OCL constraint is not specified with context but with the keyword import, according to the definition, there is no universal quantification but the specified names are directly imported from the context. This means that the variation of the above OCL constraint

import Auction a, Person p **inv** NM2:
    p **in** a.bidder **implies**
        forall m **in** a.message: m **in** p.message

> OCL

can be used in the statement ocl NM2 about the two variables a and p defined in the Java context without explicitly stating these variables.

Often, previous values of attributes or intermediate results of previous calculations are necessary to check assertions at a certain point in time. At the time of evaluation of an assertion, these may not be available anymore and, therefore, have to be explicitly cached previously.[1] The `let` construct is suited for defining intermediate results that are exclusively used for checking assertions. It introduces an intermediate variable that cannot be used in normal Java code and, therefore, has no effect on the program execution. Like `ocl` instructions, `let` instructions can be omitted in the production system.[2]

According to the semantics of OCL constraints and the OCL `let` construct, exceptions occurring during the evaluation of arguments of these constructs are caught. If the argument of the `ocl` construct evaluates to an exception, this is taken as nonfulfillment of the condition. However, in the `let` statement, the variable is allocated a default value such as `null`.

---

[1] The operator `@pre` is available for attributes and parameters in OCL constraints and designates the respective values at the start of the call.

[2] In Java, such helper variables need to be declared as normal variables and would therefore be usable in the production code.

C

The Syntax of UML/P

> Man is the model of the world.
>
> Leonardo Da Vinci

C.1 UML/P Syntax Overview

Form of the Syntax Definition

A proper description of a language and its semantics is the foundation for a detailed discussion and the introduction of techniques for its use. As discussed in [HR00, HR04], the desired precision of the semantics of a language also depends on the intended readers. As some modifications of the syntax have been made compared with the UML standard, it is necessary to precisely specify the syntactical form of UML/P diagrams. For this purpose, the procedure for representation of combined graphical and textual languages introduced in Appendix A is used.

Using a combination of EBNF and syntax class diagrams (SCDs) for the definition of class diagrams involves some danger of a circular definition. In Appendix A, the resulting problems are discussed and solutions presented. Successful examples such as that EBNF can be used to define itself, or that the English language is also used to define itself (see encyclopedia, dictionary, and grammar) show that a circular definition of a language in itself is no practical problem. By applying a language to itself, a layering into a base language level and a *"meta language level"* arises. In *metamodeling* approaches, the fact that the same language is used on both levels, is utilized to allow a model to access its own metalevel. In total, a metamodel structure that contains up to four layers arises, as in the MOF ("meta object facility" [OMG01b]), whose application to UML surely increases the flexibility of UML but also its complexity and, thus, considerably reduces its understandability. Therefore, we pay particular attention to a strict separation of

© Springer International Publishing Switzerland 2016
B. Rumpe, *Modeling with UML*, DOI 10.1007/978-3-319-33933-7

the language level UML/P and the representation of this language by EBNF and SCD in this approach.

UML/P

UML/P is a syntactically precisely specifiable language, consisting of several types of diagrams and texts that can also be used in an integrated form. Figure C.1 describes the topmost production for UML/P, reflecting this segmentation. Nonterminals that are taken from other figures are tagged with the number of the defining figure, e.g., the nonterminal $\langle ClassDiagram_{C.2} \rangle$ is defined in Fig. C.2.

The artifacts used in UML/P can contain names and, thus, be referenced within other artifacts. In this way, groups of artifacts, for example, can be used in order to define a test case.

			EBNF
$\langle$UML/P$\rangle$	::=	$\langle$UMLPunit$\rangle^*$	
$\langle$UMLPunit$\rangle$	::=	$\langle$ClassDiagram$_{C.2}\rangle$	
	|	$\langle$OCL$_{C.7}\rangle$	
	|	$\langle$ObjectDiagram$_{C.14}\rangle$	
	|	$\langle$Statechart$_{C.16}\rangle$	
	|	$\langle$SequenceDiagram$_{C.19}\rangle$	
	|	$\langle$CompilationUnit$_{B.2}\rangle$	

Figure C.1. Top level of the syntax for UML/P

UML/P described here does not contain a grouping concept like "packages" in Java or UML. Furthermore, other diagram types such as component, communication, use-case, and activity diagrams are not contained in UML/P represented in this book.

C.2 Class Diagrams

This section first defines the core parts of a class diagram, then adds the textual parts, and finally defines stereotypes and tags.

C.2.1 Core Parts of a Class Diagram

The $\langle ClassDiagram \rangle$ language is an important kind of diagram of UML. It is defined in Fig. C.2. It introduces the main nonterminal and a number of further language elements. Including syntax classes such as $\langle Classifier \rangle$ as well as the relation between syntactical elements represented by syntax associations such as implements.

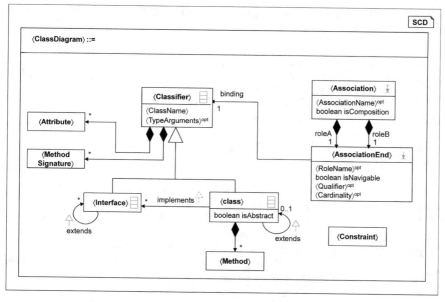

Figure C.2. Syntax of the core parts of class diagrams

The syntax class diagram given in Fig. C.2 is marked with SCD in the top right in order to state that it is not a normal class diagram. A detailed description of SCDs can be found in Appendix A.

It is known from software engineering that there are almost always multiple variants to model information. This also holds for the representation of the internal structure of a language. The structure of class diagrams modeled in Fig. C.2 has been chosen because it is almost compliant with the metamodel given in the UML standard [OMG10a]. Deviations have become possible especially because of simplifications that are partly based on the fact that textual parts of the language are subsequently represented by an EBNF grammar.

As common in language definitions, comments, like that, e.g., shown in Fig. 2.3, are not explicitly included. However, graphical elements are annotatable with comments. Textual comments are also possible and reasonable. As common in Java, textual comments start with // or are included in /* ... */.

C.2.2 Text Parts of a Class Diagram

In Fig. C.2 the nonterminals ⟨MethodSignature⟩, ⟨Method⟩, and ⟨Attribute⟩ have not yet been detailed any further. In addition, several nonterminals have been used as types of syntax attributes that also require definition. ⟨ClassName⟩, for example, is a syntax attribute that is assigned to the syntax class ⟨Classifier⟩. The productions from Fig. C.3 represent these textual parts.[1]

			EBNF
⟨ClassName⟩	::=	⟨Type$_{B.2}$⟩	
⟨AssociationName⟩	::=	/^{opt} ⟨Identifier$_{B.1}$⟩	
⟨RoleName⟩	::=	⟨Modifiers⟩ ⟨Identifier$_{B.1}$⟩	
⟨Qualifier⟩	::=	⟨Identifier$_{B.1}$⟩ | ⟨Type$_{B.2}$⟩	
⟨Cardinality⟩	::=	1 | 0..1 | *	
⟨Visibility⟩	::=	+ | # | = | ?	
⟨Attribute⟩	::=	⟨Modifiers⟩ ⟨VarDeclaration⟩	
⟨Modifiers⟩	::=	/^{opt} { ⟨Visibility⟩ | ⟨Modifier$_{B.3}$⟩ }*	
⟨VarDeclaration⟩	::=	⟨TypeCardinality⟩^{opt} ⟨Identifier$_{B.1}$⟩ []*	
		{ = ⟨Expression$_{B.6}$⟩ }^{opt}	
⟨TypeCardinality⟩	::=	⟨Type$_{B.2}$⟩ { [⟨Cardinality⟩] }^{opt}	
⟨Method⟩	::=	⟨MethodSignature⟩ ⟨Block$_{B.5}$⟩^{opt}	
	|	⟨ConstructorSignature⟩ ⟨Block$_{B.5}$⟩^{opt}	
⟨MethodSignature⟩	::=	⟨Modifiers⟩ ⟨TypeVoid$_{B.2}$⟩^{opt} ⟨Identifier$_{B.1}$⟩	
		⟨FormalParameters$_{B.4}$⟩^{opt} []* ⟨Throws$_{B.4}$⟩	
⟨ConstructorSignature⟩			
	::=	⟨Modifiers⟩ ⟨Identifier$_{B.1}$⟩	
		⟨FormalParameters$_{B.4}$⟩^{opt} ⟨Throws$_{B.4}$⟩	

Figure C.3. Syntax for names and associations

In Java it is customary for class names to begin with upper-case letters. This can be ensured by suitable and automatically verifiable context conditions.

As far as possible and reasonable, the nonterminals in the UML/P grammar were taken over from UML and Java language definitions. To facilitate a smooth connection between UML/P and Java, our productions are mostly defined in analogy to the Java language standard [GJSB05] or the EBNF representation of the Java language standard given in Appendix B.

When comparing the productions in Fig. C.3 with the grammar given in the Java language standard [GJSB05] respectively with its EBNF representation in Appendix B it is striking that in class diagrams some information are optional. While in a programming language, all definitions must essentially be complete, in a modeling language such as UML/P, e.g., type definitions for attributes or parameters as well as the complete parameter list for methods can be missing. For generation of Java code, this information must be

---

[1] Constraint language OCL is examined in Chap. 3.

extracted from other sources, for example, other class diagrams. The possibility of omitting this information in early stages of development allows the modeler to abstractly represent facts suitable for communication purposes and to abstract detailed information if these, at the time of model creation, are still not sufficiently known or consolidated.

The grammar given in Figures C.2 and C.3 basically allows the specification of visibility of attributes and methods in two ways. The rather iconic visibility modifiers "+", "#", "?", and "−" can alternatively be expressed by Java modifiers such as `public`. Further modifiers known from Java, e.g., `final`, have no graphical equivalent in UML. Thus, they are used directly in UML/P. However, it is advised to represent such information only very reluctantly in class diagrams, as class diagrams can thereby seem overloaded very easily. In contrast to a programming language, the absence of information in a modeling language does not automatically imply a realization by default. In principal, models allow abstraction. In class diagrams, abstraction generally manifests itself by omitting detailed information, starting with attribute types, modifiers, attributes, and methods up to whole groups of classes. This means that the modeler is free to decide how much detailed information is represented in the diagrams.

Due to their wide spread use, a detailed explanation of the context conditions of class diagrams is left out here. Examples for context conditions are: In a class, two attributes may not have the same name, all data types used must exist in the UML model, and the number and the type of arguments of method calls must be compatible with the method declaration. Further context conditions arise from using Java as a target language and from the UML standard for class diagrams.

C.2.3 Tags and Stereotypes

Stereotypes and tags are used to classify model elements and assign additional characteristics of various forms to them. Figure C.4 introduces both nonterminals ⟨Stereotype⟩ and ⟨Tag⟩ and shows how stereotypes and tags are used. Furthermore, a template for the definition of stereotypes is introduced in Sect. 2.5.3. Just as in the UML standard, a rather informal, tabular form is provided for the definition of a stereotype. The template is therefore not realized by a precisely specified abstract syntax.

In the previous definitions of the syntax for class diagrams in Figures C.2 and C.3, neither tags nor stereotypes have explicitly been introduced. As tags and stereotypes are rather generic to define additional properties for modeling elements, and as they can be used on all model elements equally, we omit an explicit introduction in the further grammar definitions of UML. Explicitly using the two elements would lead to a less readable overload of the syntax diagrams as well as of the textual grammar. However, we show one syntax diagram with explicit tags and stereotypes as an example in Fig. C.5.

⟨Tag⟩	::= { ⟨TagEntry⟩$_{,}^{*}$ }	EBNF
⟨TagEntry⟩	::= ⟨Keyword⟩ { = ⟨Value⟩ }^{opt}	
⟨Keyword⟩	::= ⟨Identifier$_{B.1}$⟩	
⟨Value⟩	::= ⟨Expression$_{B.6}$⟩	
⟨Stereotype⟩	::= ≪ ⟨Identifier$_{B.1}$⟩ ≫	

Figure C.4. Syntax for tags and stereotypes

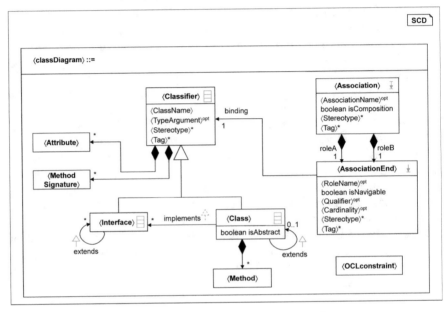

Figure C.5. Syntax of class diagrams with tags and stereotypes

From version 1.4 on, the UML standard provides the possibility of decorating model elements with an arbitrary number of stereotypes. This allows additional convenience when compactly modeling facts, but it should be used with caution. Otherwise, models can become overly complex, similar to what happens with use of multiple inheritance. Textually represented modeling elements can be decorated with stereotypes and tags, too. In the UML standard, stereotypes are generally appended before and tags after a model element. The nonterminals ⟨Attribute⟩ and ⟨MethodSignature⟩ from Fig C.3 are therefore exemplarily extended as follows:

⟨Attribute⟩	::= ⟨Stereotype⟩*	EBNF
	⟨Modifiers⟩ ⟨VarDeclaration⟩	
	⟨Tag⟩*	

⟨MethodSignature⟩ ::= ⟨Stereotype⟩*

⟨Modifiers⟩ ⟨TypeVoid$_{B.2}$⟩^{opt}

⟨Identifier$_{B.1}$⟩ ⟨FormalParameters$_{B.4}$⟩^{opt} [ ]* ⟨Throws$_{B.4}$⟩

⟨Tag⟩*

EBNF

The two representation indicators "©" and "..." introduced in Sect. 2.4 characterize the completeness or incompleteness of a model representation respectively. Similar to stereotypes, they are implicitly added wherever a list of language elements is allowed.

C.2.4 Comparison with the UML Standard

The class diagrams presented in this book differ in some points from the UML standard [OMG10a]. The class diagrams used in UML/P concentrate on aspects significant for an agile development method. Therefore, some concepts less useful for these purposes are not discussed here. Interesting, but only usable in a special context, are, for example, some new constructs such as the subset relation for associations. However, UML/P also provides some extensions especially developed for relevant tasks in this book.

The UML standard [OMG10a] and UML/P vary not only in the language but also in the form of representation, i.e., the language definition. The UML standard at first presents all model elements such as classes, objects, or states as independent units. It describes their properties, restrictions, as well as fields of application and relationships without intensively referring to the embedding of the model element into the graphical representation (diagram). The grouping of the model elements in diagrams, e.g., the class diagram or the Statechart, happens only subsequently. This book, in contrast, pursues, just like many other UML introductions, a diagram-based explanation. Thus, all model elements interesting for class diagrams have been explained in this chapter. The only exception are consistency conditions, which are dealt with separately in Chap. 3.

A comparison of UML/P with the UML standard shows that in UML/P the following model elements are omitted or not integrated in full generality:

- A number of stereotypes, such as «constructor» for tagging constructor methods, have not been introduced explicitly.
- Usually, a class is represented with three *compartments* for the name, the attributes, and the method signatures. In analysis models, further labeled parts are possible, e.g., *responsibilities*.
- Nested classes, as provided for example by Java, can be represented in UML.
- UML offers another compact form for representing an interface in the class diagram. An interface is attached to classes in the form of a small circle if these classes implement the interface.
- *Dependencies* such as the «use» relation for representing syntactic dependency relations are not used in UML/P.

- UML provides parameterized classes and a graphical representation of the parameter binding of such classes.
- UML/P does not require the explicit representation and accessability of the metamodeling level within the language itself. A more detailed discussion of motivation and effects is contained in Appendix A.
- Due to the variety of possibilities to interpret aggregation (see [HSB99]), the introduction of the weak form of aggregation (white diamond) has been omitted and only the strong composition in the form of a black diamond has been explained.
- Associations have been simplified. E.g., cardinalities have been restricted to "1", "0..1", and "*". Association classes and multitier associations have not been introduced. In qualified associations, the qualifier has been restricted to one element, but a mechanism has been added for combining the qualifier with an attribute of the target class. The nonnavigability of an association direction has been omitted, because the necessity for navigability can be directly recognized in code generation by a tool.
- Some tags for the inheritance relation, e.g., {overlapping}, have not been introduced.
- UML/P provides slightly different modifiers such as readonly for attributes.

Many of the mentioned additions could be integrated into UML/P without further ado. Especially, default as well as project- and company-specific stereotypes and tags could easily be transferred, especially when they are meant for documentation purposes.

In contrast to the UML standard, UML/P, however, offers the two representation indicators "©" and "..." that provide the reader of a diagram with additional information on its completeness.

Furthermore, the representation of attributes and method signatures independent from programming languages has been replaced by a version that conforms to Java. UML/P uses "Type attribute" instead of "attribute: Type", and its class names qualified with paths are "path.Class" instead of "Path::Class". This Java conformity has some advantages when turning class diagrams into Java code. In particular, the recognition effect for the reader is increased considerably.

An important property of UML is the modifiability of its model elements with the help of different modifiers, tags, attributes, etc. The programming languages Java and EBNF also offer such mechanisms. Figure C.6 contains a definition of the mechanisms used for this book. The essential sources for the definition are given respectively.

Attribute is a model element with essentially the same meaning in UML class diagrams and Java. See Fig. 2.2. In *attributed grammars*, an *attribute* is a value storage space at an element of the abstract syntax. Attributes are assigned to nonterminals.

Modifiers such as `public` or `final` can be applied to classes, methods, and attributes in UML and Java. Modifiers are an integral part of the language: new modifiers cannot be defined.

Visibility is a modifier that describes the visibility of classes, methods, and attributes. See Fig. 2.2.

Tag (or also: tagged value) can be applied to an arbitrary model element. A tag consists of keyword and value and is arbitrarily definable. See Fig. 2.16.

Stereotype can be applied to an arbitrary model element. Stereotypes are arbitrarily definable. See Fig. 2.16.

Indicator characterizes the representation of a model element with regard to completeness. Indicators are "..." and "©".

Figure C.6. Summarizing definition for modifiers and related mechanisms

C.3 OCL

C.3.1 Syntax of OCL

As OCL is a textual language, the Extended Backus–Naur Form (EBNF) is used for its definition. Compared with OCL in the standard definition [OMG10b], OCL/P presented in this chapter has some significant syntactic differences that can mainly be explained by a syntactic convergence to the target programming language Java and some conceptual improvements. These differences are explained in detail in Sect. C.3.2.

OCL is a language based on the ASCII alphabet. For better readability, keywords such as `forall` are represented in another layout, but special mathematical characters such as $\forall$ are not used. The practice of software development shows that a modeler who is experienced in programming languages faces a considerably smaller hurdle to use a specification language which looks like a programming language.

This hurdle has been further reduced for OCL/P by giving the modeling concepts occurring in both Java and OCL the same syntactic form. Hence, several passages in the following OCL grammar can be explained by referencing the Java grammar given in Appendix B.

OCL constraints can be found in dedicated OCL documents and occur as constraints within other diagrams and as invariants in Java. Therefore, a document type ⟨OCL⟩ for OCL constraints exists in UML/P.

In the UML standard, OCL constraints are also intended for use as annotations for classes and methods within class diagrams. However, practice and also the UML standard itself show that this quickly leads to overloading of the diagrams. Separation of OCL constraints into independent documents or document sections is therefore advisable. The appearance of such documents has already been illustrated by Figures 3.17 and 3.30. Parallel processing of these documents can be well supported by suitable tools such as the editor framework described in [HRR99].

Figure C.7 describes the top level of the OCL grammar. An OCL document consists of a collection of invariants and method specifications. In an OCL document, methods can be marked with tags and stereotypes. In this way it is possible to define auxiliary functions that can be used for describing constraints directly in OCL documents without the need for them to appear in the implementation or in class diagrams.

$\langle \text{OCL} \rangle$ ::= { $\langle \text{Constraint} \rangle$ }$^*_;$ EBNF

$\langle \text{Constraint} \rangle$ ::= $\langle \text{Stereotype}_{C.4} \rangle^*$ $\langle \text{RawConstraint} \rangle$ $\langle \text{Tag}_{C.4} \rangle^*$;

$\langle \text{RawConstraint} \rangle$ ::= $\langle \text{Invariant} \rangle$ | $\langle \text{OperationConstraint} \rangle$

$\langle \text{Invariant} \rangle$ ::= $\langle \text{ClassContext} \rangle^{opt}$ inv $\langle \text{InvariantName} \rangle^{opt}$
: $\langle \text{OCLExpr} \rangle^*_;$

$\langle \text{OperationConstraint} \rangle$
::= context $\langle \text{OperationContext} \rangle$
{ let $\langle \text{OCLVarDeclarator} \rangle^{1-*}_;$ }^{opt}
{ pre $\langle \text{InvariantName} \rangle^{opt}$: $\langle \text{OCLExpr} \rangle^*_;$ }^{opt}
{ post $\langle \text{InvariantName} \rangle^{opt}$: $\langle \text{OCLExpr} \rangle^*_;$ }^{opt}

$\langle \text{ClassContext} \rangle$ ::= { context | import }
{ $\langle \text{ClassOrInterface} \rangle$ $\langle \text{Identifier}_{B.1} \rangle^{opt}$ }$^*_,$

$\langle \text{OperationContext} \rangle$ ::= $\langle \text{OperationSignature} \rangle$ $\langle \text{Throws}_{B.4} \rangle$

$\langle \text{OperationSignature} \rangle$
::= $\langle \text{MethodSignature} \rangle$ | $\langle \text{ConstructorSignature} \rangle$

$\langle \text{MethodSignature} \rangle$ ::= $\langle \text{TypeVoid}_{B.2} \rangle^{opt}$ { $\langle \text{ClassOrInterface}_{B.2} \rangle$. }^{opt}
$\langle \text{Identifier}_{B.1} \rangle$ $\langle \text{FormalParameters}_{B.4} \rangle$ []*

$\langle \text{ConstructorSignature} \rangle$
::= new $\langle \text{ClassOrInterface} \rangle$ $\langle \text{FormalParameters}_{B.4} \rangle$

$\langle \text{ClassOrInterface} \rangle$ ::= $\langle \text{Name}_{B.2} \rangle$ $\langle \text{TypeArguments}_{B.2} \rangle^{opt}$

$\langle \text{InvariantName} \rangle$ ::= $\langle \text{Identifier}_{B.1} \rangle$

$\langle \text{OCLConstraint} \rangle$ ::= $\langle \text{InvariantName} \rangle$ | $\langle \text{OCLExpr} \rangle$ | $\langle \text{Constraint} \rangle$

Figure C.7. OCL constraints

Basically, the constraint language OCL consists of a collection of language concepts for the definition of expressions with Boolean values. Due to this, the nonterminals $\langle \text{OCLExpr} \rangle$ and $\langle \text{OCLPrimeExpr} \rangle$ are accordingly complex.[2]

---

[2] In the Java grammar in Appendix B, the nonterminals $\langle \text{Expression}_{B.6} \rangle$ and $\langle \text{Primary}_{B.6} \rangle$ fulfill an analogous task.

The language of OCL expressions is explained in Fig. C.8. Their productions are constructed analogously to the Java grammar for expressions in Fig. B.6.

$\langle$OCLExpr$\rangle$	::=	$\langle$OCLPrefixOp$\rangle^*$ $\langle$OCLPrimary$\rangle$	EBNF
		| $\langle$OCLExpr$\rangle$ $\langle$OCLInfixOp$\rangle$ $\langle$OCLExpr$\rangle$	
		| $\langle$OCLExpr$\rangle$ `instanceof` $\langle$Type$_{B.2}\rangle$	
		| `if` $\langle$OCLExpr$\rangle$ `then` $\langle$OCLExpr$\rangle$ `else` $\langle$OCLExpr$\rangle$	
		| $\langle$OCLExpr$\rangle$ `?` $\langle$OCLExpr$\rangle$ `:` $\langle$OCLExpr$\rangle$	
		| `typeif` $\langle$Identifier$_{B.1}\rangle$ `instanceof` $\langle$Type$_{B.2}\rangle$	
		`then` $\langle$OCLExpr$\rangle$ `else` $\langle$OCLExpr$\rangle$	
		| $\langle$Identifier$_{B.1}\rangle$ `instanceof` $\langle$Type$_{B.2}\rangle$	
		`?` $\langle$OCLExpr$\rangle$ `:` $\langle$OCLExpr$\rangle$	
		| `let` $\langle$OCLVarDeclarator$\rangle_{;}^{1-*}$ `in` $\langle$OCLExpr$\rangle$	
		| $\langle$CollectionExpr$\rangle$	
$\langle$OCLInfixOp$\rangle$	::=	$\langle$InfixOp$_{B.6}\rangle$ | `<=>` | `implies`	
$\langle$OCLPrefixOp$\rangle$	::=	`+` | `-` | `~` | `!` | `(` $\langle$Type$_{B.2}\rangle$ `)`	
$\langle$OCLVarDeclarator$\rangle$	::=	$\langle$Type$_{B.2}\rangle^{opt}$ $\langle$Identifier$_{B.1}\rangle$ `[]`* `=` $\langle$OCLExpr$\rangle$	

Figure C.8. OCL expressions

In principle, it is possible to directly use Java expressions that are extended by some OCL-specific constructs as constraints. However, besides the operators ++ and -- as well as the assignment, which each have side-effects, in Java expressions there are also constructs for the creation of new objects and arrays that are not applicable in OCL constraints. This could be expressed by suitable context conditions, but it is more reasonable to embed these differences according to Fig. C.9 directly in the grammar in which an own nonterminal $\langle$OCLPrimary$\rangle$ is used, constructed analogously to $\langle$Primary$_{B.6}\rangle$. The last variant of the nonterminal $\langle$OCLPrimary$\rangle$ serves for integration of OCL with object diagrams and is discussed in Chap. 4.

In OCL, containers play an important role. Therefore, the possibilities of defining expressions with containers are summarized in Fig. C.10. The nonterminal $\langle$CollectionExpr$\rangle$ describes quantifiers and other special operations for containers. The nonterminal $\langle$Comprehension$\rangle$ describes the variants for the enumeration of container elements and for their property-oriented description in the form of a comprehension. Besides the already known $\langle$OCLVarDeclarator$\rangle$ for the introduction of a variable in the `let` construct, new variables can be introduced with the nonterminal $\langle$SetVarDeclaration$\rangle$. This form of variable declaration is used to let a variable vary over the elements of a container.

As already mentioned, the grammars of the languages Java and OCL correspond in many aspects with regards to structure and content. The com-

EBNF

| $\langle$OCLPrimary$\rangle$ | ::= | $($ $\langle$OCLExpr$\rangle$ $)$ |

$\langle$OCLPrimary$\rangle$ ::= $($ $\langle$OCLExpr$\rangle$ $)$
  | $\langle$Literal$_{B.1}\rangle$
  | $\{$ $\langle$OCLPrimary$\rangle$ $.$ $\}^{opt}$ $\langle$Identifier$_{B.1}\rangle$
    $\langle$OCLArguments$\rangle^{opt}$
  | $\{$ $\langle$OCLPrimary$\rangle$ $.$ $\}^{opt}$ $\langle$Identifier$_{B.1}\rangle$ @pre
  | $\{$ $\langle$OCLPrimary$\rangle$ $.$ $\}^{opt}$ $\langle$Identifier$_{B.1}\rangle$ $\ast\ast$
  | $\langle$OCLPrimary$\rangle$ $[$ $\langle$OCLExpr$\rangle$ $]$
  | super $.$ $\langle$Identifier$_{B.1}\rangle$ $\langle$OCLArguments$\rangle^{opt}$
  | super $.$ $\langle$Identifier$_{B.1}\rangle$ @pre
  | $\langle$Type$_{B.2}\rangle$ @pre^{opt}
  | this
  | result
  | isnew $($ $\langle$OCLExpr$\rangle$ $)$
  | defined $($ $\langle$OCLExpr$\rangle$ $)$
  | $\langle$Comprehension$\rangle$
  | OD $.$ $\langle$Diagramname$\rangle$ // see Sec. C.4.1

$\langle$OCLArguments$\rangle$ ::= $($ $\langle$OCLExpr$\rangle^{\ast}_{,}$ $)$

Figure C.9. Primitives of the OCL expression language

EBNF

$\langle$CollectionExpr$\rangle$ ::= forall $\langle$SetVarDeclarator$\rangle^{1-\ast}_{,}$ $:$ $\langle$OCLExpr$\rangle$
  | exists $\langle$SetVarDeclarator$\rangle^{1-\ast}_{,}$ $:$ $\langle$OCLExpr$\rangle$
  | any $\langle$OCLExpr$\rangle$
  | iterate $\{$ $\langle$SetVarDeclarator$\rangle$ $;$ $\langle$OCLVarDeclarator$\rangle$
    $:$ $\langle$Identifier$\rangle$ $=$ $\langle$OCLExpr$\rangle$ $\}$

$\langle$Comprehension$\rangle$ ::= $\langle$ContainerType$\rangle^{opt}$ $\{$ $\langle$CollectionItem$\rangle^{\ast}_{,}$ $\}$
  | $\langle$ContainerType$\rangle^{opt}$
    $\{$ $\langle$OCLExpr$\rangle$ $|$ $\langle$ComprehensionItem$\rangle^{\ast}_{,}$ $\}$
  | $\langle$ContainerType$\rangle^{opt}$
    $\{$ $\langle$SetVarDeclarator$\rangle$ $|$ $\langle$ComprehensionItem$\rangle^{\ast}_{,}$ $\}$

$\langle$SetVarDeclarator$\rangle$ ::= $\langle$Type$_{B.2}\rangle^{opt}$ $\langle$Identifier$_{B.1}\rangle$ $[]^{\ast}$ in $\langle$OCLExpr$\rangle$
  | $\langle$Type$_{B.2}\rangle$ $\langle$Identifier$_{B.1}\rangle$ $[]^{\ast}$
$\langle$ContainerType$\rangle$ ::= $\{$ Set $|$ List $|$ Collection $\}$
  $\langle$TypeArguments$_{B.2}\rangle^{opt}$
$\langle$CollectionItem$\rangle$ ::= $\langle$OCLExpr$\rangle$ $\{$ $..$ $\langle$OCLExpr$\rangle$ $\}^{opt}$
$\langle$ComprehensionItem$\rangle$
  ::= $\langle$SetVarDeclarator$\rangle$
  | $\langle$OCLVarDeclarator$\rangle$
  | $\langle$OCLExpr$\rangle$

Figure C.10. Containers in the OCL expression language

monly used and structurally similar nonterminals are summarized in Table C.11.

Corresponding nonterminals	
OCL nonterminal	Java nonterminal
$\langle$OCLArguments$\rangle$	$\langle$Arguments$_{B.6}\rangle$
$\langle$OCLExpr$\rangle$	$\langle$Expression$_{B.6}\rangle$
$\langle$OCLInfixOp$\rangle$	$\langle$InfixOp$_{B.6}\rangle$
$\langle$OCLPrimary$\rangle$	$\langle$Primary$_{B.6}\rangle$
$\langle$OCLPrefixOp$\rangle$	$\langle$PrefixOp$_{B.6}\rangle$
$\langle$OCLVarDeclarator$\rangle$	$\langle$VariableDeclarator$_{B.4}\rangle$
$\langle$OCLVarInitializer$\rangle$	$\langle$VariableInitializer$_{B.4}\rangle$
Nonterminals taken over from Java	
$\langle$FormalParameters$_{B.4}\rangle$	$\langle$Identifier$_{B.1}\rangle$
$\langle$InfixOp$_{B.6}\rangle$	$\langle$Name$_{B.2}\rangle$
$\langle$Literal$_{B.1}\rangle$	$\langle$Type$_{B.2}\rangle$
$\langle$TypeVoid$_{B.2}\rangle$	

Table C.11. Comparison of the grammars of OCL/P and Java

C.3.2 Differences From the OCL Standard

To increase the readability and, thus, the usability of OCL as well as improve the integration with the target language Java, a number of conceptual and syntactical modifications of OCL have been made in contrast to the standard defined in [OMG10b]. The most important modifications are summarized in Table C.12.

Some remarks on the differences described in Table C.12 follow (see superscript indices):

1. The data type String is not regarded as a primitive type in OCL/P but as a normal class. In addition to the modifications of the remaining type names, the available constants and operations are also adjusted to Java.
2. OCL/P has generic types analogous to Java.
3. OCL/P provides only simulated enumeration types. The consolidation of all values of enumeration types in Enumeration in the OCL standard, in contrast, had the disadvantage that further typing information is missing.
4. For pragmatical reasons, the data type Bag for multisets has been omitted. These multisets are not used often, and the explicit necessary conversion to sets can, thus, be left out. Furthermore, the signatures of the container types have been merged with the classes known from Java.

	OCL/P	OCL standard
Primitive types [1]	`boolean, char, int, long, float, ...`	`Integer, String, Boolean, Real, Enumeration`
Generic types [2]	`Class<T`$_1$`, T`$_2$`, ...>`	`-`
Supertype	`Object`	`OclAny`
Meta-datatypes	`-`	`OclType, OclState, OclExpression`
Enumerations [3]	Simulated	`Enumeration`
Containers [4]	`Set<X>, List<X>`	`Set, Sequence, Bag`
Self-reference	`this`	`self`
Logic operators	`&&, ||, ^, !`	`and, or, xor, not`
Comparisons	`==, !=`	`==, <>`
Definedness	`defined(expr)`	Missing
Application [5]	`set.size`	`set->size()`
Type conversion [6]	`(Type)expr`	`expr.oclAsType(Type)`
Type query	`expr instanceof Type`	`expr.oclIsKindOf(Type)`
Set operations [7]	`{ v in set	expr }`	`set.select(expr)`
	`{ expr	v in set }`	`set.collect(expr)`
Quantifiers	`forall v in set: expr`	`set.forall(expr)`
	`exists v in set: expr`	`set.exists(expr)`
	`any v in set: expr`	`set.any(expr)`
sum, iterate [8]	Library	Integrated in language
Operation context	Type Class.operation()	Class::operation() : Type
Variable definition	Type variable	variable : Type
Path name	Path.Class	Path::Class
Comment	`/* ... */, // ...`	`-- ...`

Table C.12. Differences between OCL/P and the OCL standard

Table C.13 shows a comparison for set operators. In OCL/P, some operators of standard Java have been omitted but can be recreated by simply prefixing the negation.

5. The use of OCL operators on container structures starts with `->` in the OCL standard. The reason for this is the syntactical recognizability of the OCL operators. However, this is not necessary as these are already recognized by their names. The operator `instanceof` is provided in combination with `typeif` in order to make an implicit and, thus, secure type conversion, if the argument has the described type.

6. The capabilities of the set and list comprehensions have been extended considerably. They allow generators to define filters and auxiliary variables.

7. The `flatten` operator is not used recursively but only flattens the highest level.

8. With regard to the operators provided, OCL/P is leaner than the OCL standard, as some of the operators have been outsourced to a library.

At the same time, this increases the flexibility of OCL/P because user-specific operators can also be defined.

Beyond the differences given in Table C.12, the following modifications have been made:

- The usage of the `let` construct has been consolidated, and the stereotype «definition» introduced in UML 1.4 has been omitted in favor of the stereotype «OCL».
- In UML/P class diagrams, association classes are not used. Thus, there is no navigation to such classes.
- OCL constraints can already be embedded into a package context by explicitly stating the package name in a class context. Thus, this embedding is not necessary in UML/P.
- Some typing rules have been defined more precisely. In the OCL standard, for example, it has not been specified how heterogeneous enumerations of the form `Set{"text",person}` need to be typed.
- The OCL logic has been adjusted to the capabilities of Java by regarding the interpretation of an undefined value result as `false`. Therefore, the *lifting operator* has been introduced to allow a two-valued logic.

OCL/P	Java	OCL standard
add	add	including
addAll	addAll	union
contains	contains	includes
containsAll	containsAll	includesAll
–	–	excludes
–	–	excludesAll
count	–	count
==	equals	=
isEmpty	isEmpty	isEmpty
–	–	notEmpty
remove	remove	excluding
removeAll	removeAll	–
retainAll	retainAll	intersection
symmetricDifference	–	symmetricDifference
size	size	count
flatten	–	–
asList	–	asSequence

Table C.13. Name comparison of set operators in Java, OCL and OCL/P

C.4 Object Diagrams

The syntactical representation of object diagrams is based on class diagrams from Sect. C.2. Both diagram types consist of a graphical and a textual part that are connected. For object diagrams, the connection with OCL constraints for the realization of the "logic of object diagrams" that also requires an extension of the syntax for OCL diagrams is additionally described.

Thus, this section first describes the graphical part of the abstract syntax of object diagrams, then the textual part, and finally the integration with OCL. For describing the abstract syntax, again the combination of EBNF grammars and syntax class diagrams (SCDs) introduced in Appendix A is used.

In the second part of the section, the conformity of an object diagram with a class diagram is discussed.

C.4.1 Context-Free Syntax

Object diagrams are another form of UML/P diagrams that are summarized by the nonterminal ⟨UMLPunit⟩. Figure C.14 shows the graphical part of the abstract syntax of object diagrams. Besides the nonterminal ⟨ObjectDiagram⟩, other language elements for the representation of prototypic objects and links in the object diagram are introduced therein.

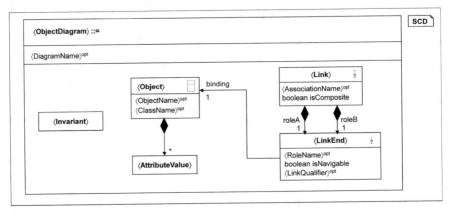

Figure C.14. Syntax of the graphical part of object diagrams

A comparison of the SCDs from Figures C.14 and C.2 shows that there are structural similarities between class and object diagrams. ⟨Object⟩ elements contain, in contrast to the ⟨Class⟩ elements, additional object names but no methods and no information on the inheritance structure between classes. In object and class diagrams, attributes are, in fact, represented in the same way. However, the optional definition of an attribute value has a different meaning, which is why, for object diagrams, the additional nonterminal ⟨AttributeValue⟩ has been introduced. While in the object diagram an attribute value reflects the current state, the optional statement of an attribute value in the class diagram is used for initializing the attribute.

In contrast to ⟨Association⟩ elements, ⟨Link⟩ elements do not contain a cardinality, but instead the qualifier can have a concrete value.

Besides the nonterminals ⟨Object⟩ and ⟨Link⟩, the ⟨Invariant⟩ introduced in Appendix C.3 has also been included in the syntax of object diagrams, which allows the use of OCL invariants for the specification of attribute values in an object diagram.

The concrete syntax of object diagrams introduced in this chapter provides, at two points, alternative representations for the same information that are not distinguished in the abstract syntax. It is possible to represent class attributes by underlining them or adding the modifier `static` in the object diagram. Composition can be represented by links or graphical containedness. Therefore, the two object diagrams from Fig. 4.11 have the same abstract syntax.

Many of the nonterminals used in the syntax diagram from Fig. C.14 have already been introduced for class diagrams or OCL. In particular, these are the nonterminals

⟨Attribute$_{C.3}$⟩   ⟨Invariant$_{C.7}$⟩

⟨ClassName$_{C.3}$⟩   ⟨AssociationName$_{C.3}$⟩

⟨RoleName$_{C.3}$⟩

The nonterminals ⟨DiagramName⟩, ⟨ObjectName⟩, ⟨AttributeValue⟩, and ⟨LinkQualifier⟩ are newly introduced in Fig. C.14, but not further detailed. Thus, the productions given in Fig. C.15 are used for the representation of these textual language elements.

⟨DiagramName⟩	::=	⟨Name$_{B.2}$⟩	EBNF
⟨ObjectName⟩	::=	⟨Identifier$_{B.1}$⟩	
⟨AttributeValue⟩	::=	⟨Attribute$_{C.3}$⟩	
⟨LinkQualifier⟩	::=	⟨Expression$_{B.6}$⟩ | ⟨Identifier$_{B.1}$⟩	

Figure C.15. Syntax for names and links

While object names are simple names, diagram names can be qualified so that a hierarchical package structure for diagrams is possible. The optional qualifier value for links is either an expression describing a concrete value or an attribute name pointing to the value stored in the target object.

Similar to class diagrams, neither comments nor tags or stereotypes have explicitly been included in the abstract syntax of object diagrams. Comments can again be attached to all nonterminals of object diagrams.

Tags and stereotypes can be used for the syntax elements ⟨Object⟩, ⟨Link⟩, and ⟨AttributeValue⟩ and also for ⟨ObjectDiagram⟩, i.e., the whole diagram. By means of some examples, Sect. 4.1.6 has already shown how tags and stereotypes can be used.

The two representation indicators "©" and "..." introduced in Sect. 2.4 are also used for object diagrams and characterize the completeness or incompleteness of the model representation, respectively. Both indicators do not affect the model itself and can, thus, similar to comments, be neglected in the abstract syntax.

OCL Adjustment

The integration of object diagrams with OCL manifests itself at two points in the abstract syntax. The SCD in Fig. C.14 shows that, on the one hand, OCL invariants can be used in object diagrams. On the other hand, an object diagram can directly be used in an OCL expression with OD . *name*. The alternative of the nonterminal ⟨OCLPrimary$_{C.9}$⟩ defined in Appendix C.3 serves this purpose:

⟨OCLPrimary⟩   ::= ...   EBNF
              | OD . ⟨DiagramName⟩

It allows the integration of object diagrams as OCL statements, as multiply shown in this chapter.

C.5 Statecharts

Statecharts are another diagram type of UML/P. Basically, a Statechart is assigned to a class or a method. Therefore, it has the name of the described element. Thus, a Statechart requires its own name only if there are multiple descriptions for the same class or method. This can, for example, be the case for test models. In this section, first the abstract syntax of Statecharts is defined in the usual way by syntax class diagrams introduced in Appendix A and EBNF. The stereotypes introduced in this chapter are summarized in a list together with their semantics and syntactical restrictions. Finally, the differences between UML/P Statecharts and the UML standard are discussed.

C.5.1 Abstract Syntax

The graphical part of Statecharts is specified in the syntax diagram in Fig. C.16.

Each Statechart has an attribute of the kind ⟨ClassName$_{C.3}$⟩ that indicates which class or which interface the Statechart is assigned to. If it is a method Statechart, additionally a method name is specified. The graphic part of Statecharts is structured quite easily. A Statechart consists of a collection of states

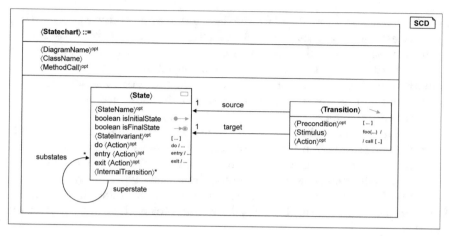

Figure C.16. Syntax of Statecharts

and transitions that each start and end in a state. States are arranged hierarchically.

States as well as transitions have a number of textual parts that, among other aspects, describe constraints and actions. These parts are described in Fig. C.17.

⟨StateName⟩	::=	⟨Name$_{B.2}$⟩
⟨StateInvariant⟩	::=	[⟨OCLExpr$_{C.8}$⟩]
⟨Action⟩	::=	/ ⟨Statement$_{B.5}$⟩* ⟨Postcondition⟩^{opt}
⟨Precondition⟩	::=	[⟨OCLExpr$_{C.8}$⟩]
⟨Postcondition⟩	::=	[⟨OCLExpr$_{C.8}$⟩]
⟨InternalTransition⟩	::=	⟨Precondition⟩^{opt} ⟨Stimulus⟩ ⟨Action⟩^{opt}
⟨Stimulus⟩	::=	ε | ⟨MethodCall⟩ | ⟨Return⟩ | ⟨Exception⟩
⟨MethodCall⟩	::=	⟨Identifier$_{B.1}$⟩ { (...) | ⟨Arguments$_{B.6}$⟩ }^{opt}
⟨Return⟩	::=	return { ... | ⟨Expression$_{B.6}$⟩ }^{opt}
⟨Exception⟩	::=	⟨ExceptionType⟩ { (...) | ⟨Arguments$_{B.6}$⟩ }^{opt}
⟨ExceptionType⟩	::=	⟨Name$_{B.2}$⟩

Figure C.17. Syntax for state and transition components

Statecharts use three kinds of constraints: the state invariant, the pre- and the postcondition. Each is realized as an OCL constraint of the type ⟨OCLExpr$_{C.8}$⟩. Access to attribute values in the original state is only allowed in postconditions using @pre. If a precondition starts with a let construct, the visibility of the thereby locally defined variable is extended to the transition action including the postcondition. In this way, similar to OCL method specifications, local variables can be used more effectively.

Java instructions are used for the description of procedural actions. They can access the attributes of the object and the arguments of the stimulus, which need to be understood as local variables and parameters, respectively. A stimulus initiates a transition. This can either happen spontaneously (marked by ε), by a return of a previously sent query, or by a method call. In the stimulus, it is not distinguished whether the latter arrives as a normal method call or as an asynchronously sent message.

Like in the other diagram types, stereotypes and tags are not explicitly mentioned. However, a number of stereotypes have been introduced that serve for specification of the semantics and, thus, also control code generation and methodical use. Subsequently, these stereotypes are repeated in a shortened form. Generally, for Statecharts as well as for other diagram types, stereotypes and tags can basically be defined for each nonterminal of the syntax.

As common in other graphical UML/P subnotations and as demonstrated in Fig. 2.3, comments are attached to the commented diagram elements.

In Table 5.13, the state invariants have been transferred from the diagram into a separate table. This can also happen in a similar form for transitions and actions in order to avoid overloading the diagram. For this, additional names can be introduced as auxiliary references that establish a connection between a table entry and the described diagram element. Instead of, for example, writing invariants or preconditions directly into the diagram, there is only a name that refers to the respective table entry. Apart from this, these names have no further significance, so this this outsourcing into tables is not made explicit in the abstract syntax.

List of stereotypes for Statecharts	
«datastate»	is applied to *data states*. It can be derived from the attributes and the links of the objects (and dependent objects) whether an object is in such a state.
«controlstate»	is dual to «datastate» and tags *control states*. For control states, program counter and stack are also relevant.
«statedefining»	tags the state invariant of a data state («datastate»). It means that the state invariant exactly describes whether an object is in a state or not. Hence, the state invariant *defines* the state.

(continued on the next page)

(continues Table C.18.: List of stereotypes for Statecharts)

«method»	is applied to a Statechart in order to characterize it as a *method Statechart*. A method Statechart describes a single (possibly complex) method. It only has control states. Besides spontaneous transitions for continuing the method, only `return` is allowed as a stimulus. With it, the result of the method call that was sent in the last transition is awaited. All states of a method Statechart are automatically marked as «controlstate».
«prio:inner»	is applied to a Statechart in order to give priority to transitions whose source states can be found inside the state hierarchy, i.e., substates before superstates. In this way, transitions with overlapping enabledness are dissolved.
«prio:outer»	describes the opposite of «prio:inner»: The outer transitions have priority.
«error»	tags a special state in the Statechart that is interpreted as an error state. The error state is always taken if, in the incomplete Statechart, no other transition is able to process an arriving stimulus. The error state can also, as any other state, have an entry- and exit-action and be left by normal transitions. Alternatives are «completion:ignore» and «completion:chaos».
«exception»	tags a special state in the Statechart that is interpreted as an error state for exceptions. All received exceptions that are not retained target this state. «error», «completion:ignore», and «completion:chaos» do not catch exceptions and, thus, supplement «exception».
«completion: ignore»	is applied to a Statechart in order to represent that arriving stimuli that cannot be processed are ignored. This means that the stimulus does not cause a reaction in the sense of a state alteration.
«completion: chaos»	provides an alternative to «completion:ignore» and «error» that is especially used for specifications. It states that Statecharts tagged with «completion:chaos» can have arbitrary behavior on arrival of stimuli that cannot be processed by a transition. Thus, the possible behavior is left open for a later decision. It is *underspecified*.

(continued on the next page)

(continues Table C.18.: List of stereotypes for Statecharts)

«action-conditions: sequential»	is applied to a Statechart in order to not carry out the composition of action conditions by conjunction. For transitions that enter and leave multiple state levels, several exit- and entry-actions and the transition action may need to be executed. The postcondition in each of these actions needs to be fulfilled at the end of the subaction it is attached to. The next subaction, however, can, in turn, invalidate the postcondition.

Table C.18. List of stereotypes for Statecharts

C.5.2 Comparisons with the UML standard

In contrast to the UML standard [OMG10a], some concepts whose necessity is not evident due to the embedding of Statecharts into UML have been omitted when defining UML/P Statecharts. This, e.g., includes concurrent state regions ("and-states") that make a specification more compact but not more readable. Thus, the identification of possible sequences while "reading" or reviewing Statecharts is considerably aggravated because the reader needs to mentally comprehend these concurrent state spaces. This also holds if the concurrency, as suggested in [HG97], is only of conceptual nature and if it is dissolved in the implementation, for example, by building product automata. For similar reasons, the use of the history mechanism has been left out.

Vice versa, UML/P Statecharts, however, have been extended by *postconditions* in the actions so that a Statechart can be a detailed behavior description as well as an abstract specification of behavior relying on an abstraction of the object states. The form of the introduced postconditions provides a suitable transition to OCL method specifications for the stimuli used in the Statechart.

The differences between UML/P Statecharts and the UML standard are summarized below:

1. Parallel substates have been left out.
2. There is no history mechanism in UML/P.
3. Compared with the *event*-concept of the standard that is described very abstractly, the concepts of *stimuli* and *firing enabledness* have been precisely defined here.
4. Preconditions of transitions are now located at the left side of the stimulus in order to better distinguish them from postconditions.
5. The UML standard does not include descriptively formulated postconditions. Therefore, UML Statecharts are less suitable for specifications but mainly for implementation descriptions.

6. Invariants, preconditions, and actions have been made vitally concrete by embedding OCL expressions and Java instructions.

7. The representation of stimulus parameters has been generalized from name : Type to expressions. This includes concrete values as well as variables that get values assigned thereby and that can be used in preconditions, actions, and postconditions. A type declaration has been left out, as this already results from the signature of the class to which the Statechart is assigned.

8. Concurrent transitions with multiple initial or final states that, thus, simulate concurrency within the Statechart as well as synchronization states have been left out because, generally, objects and therefore their Statecharts do not use concurrency on this level.

9. "Stubbed transitions," i.e., transitions that lead inside a hierarchical state without leading to a concrete substate, have not been included in UML/P because the information expressed therewith is not more precise than if this transition would lead directly to the superstate. If required, such a transition can be tagged by a suitable stereotype.

10. "Junction" and "choice points" represent control states in the processing of transitions and can be defined by states tagged with «controlstate».

Generally, UML/P Statecharts are syntactically and semantically better integrated with other UML/P notations as is the case in the UML standard. The "event" concept has been kept very general in order to be able to subsume the different kinds of stimuli arising from real-time systems as well as from business systems. In the standard, an integration with OCL constraints or a concrete language for the representation of actions is omitted. There, OCL and the Action language [OMG01a] are mentioned as possible languages but no concrete integration is made.

C.6 Sequence Diagrams

C.6.1 Abstract Syntax

The abstract syntax of sequence diagrams is, compared with previous diagram types, unusual as the order of interactions is semantically relevant at each timeline. Figure C.19 contains the abstract syntax for the graphical part. This includes the three main elements ⟨ObjectElement⟩, ⟨ActivityBar⟩, and ⟨SequenceElement⟩. As a superclass, the latter summarizes the different forms of interactions as well as the start and end of activity bars and OCL constraints. ⟨SequenceElements⟩ of a sequence diagram are in linear order and, thus, express the chronological order.

Activity start and end are regarded as independent elements because, as shown in Fig. 6.18(c), activity bars need not necessarily be coupled with interactions, which is why the respective associations are optional.

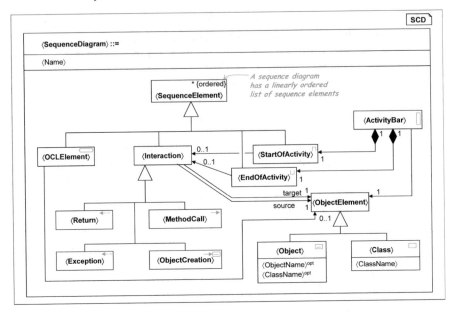

Figure C.19. Graphical part of the syntax of sequence diagrams

The textual part of the syntax is contained in Fig. C.20. It shows the form of OCL constraints and the introduction of auxiliary variables as well as the label of the various interactions. As usual, stereotypes and tags are not explicitly stated in the abstract syntax. The nonterminals $\langle$ClassName$_{C.3}\rangle$, $\langle$MethodCall$_{C.17}\rangle$, $\langle$Return$_{C.17}\rangle$, and $\langle$Exception$_{C.17}\rangle$ have already been introduced for other notations and are reused here.

$\langle$OCLElement$\rangle$	::= $\langle$OCLExpr$_{C.8}\rangle$ _;_	EBNF
	| $\langle$Identifier$_{B.1}\rangle$ _;_	
	| $\langle$Identifier$_{B.1}\rangle$ ($\langle$OCLExpr$_{C.8}\rangle_{,}^{*}$) _;_	
	| <u>let</u> $\langle$OCLVarDeclarator$_{C.8}\rangle_{;}^{1-*}$	
$\langle$Objectcreation$\rangle$	::= <u>new</u> $\langle$Name$_{B.2}\rangle$ { (...) | $\langle$Arguments$_{B.6}\rangle$ }^{opt}	

Figure C.20. Lacking textual part of the syntax of sequence diagrams

The abstract syntax already constitutes some restrictions for the system. The start and end of activity bars need to correspond. In addition, it must hold, for instance, that two activity bars are either disjoint or that one is contained in the other to describe the chronological order that an activity bar associated with an interaction belongs to one of the objects participating in the interaction, that a method call initializes only one activity, etc. It is also relevant that the typing of the arguments and return values is, as far as given, already specified by class diagrams from the context of the sequence diagram.

C.6.2 Comparison with the UML Standard

Basically, UML/P sequence diagrams are a subset of the UML standard [OMG10a]. Several concepts contained in the UML standard such as concurrency, alternatives, repetition, messages with a time delay, or termination of objects are not included in UML/P. Hence, UML/P sequence diagrams are less expressive but optimized for use in modeling of exemplary processes and tests; for example, by distributing the timeline within sequence diagrams, the form of representation of alternatives chosen in the UML standard very quickly leads to unclear models.

By leaving out the representation of asynchronous messages, sequence diagrams can be related with Java implementations relatively canonically. Furthermore, temporal conditions can, like in the UML standard, be added in UML/P by using the tag {time}. This can also be used constructively for specification of times in tests.

In the UML standard [OMG10a], an explicit integration with OCL conditions is missing. In OCL/P, the graphic notation for this has been taken over from the MSC standard [IT99]. In the UML standard, however, there is the possibility to put guards, e.g., [x>0], in front of a method call in order to choose from alternatives.

D

Sample Application: Internet-Based Auction System

> The market is the only democratic judge
> in a modern economy.
>
> Ludwig Erhard, Former German Chancellor

Due to the huge dissemination and high availability of the Internet, commercial applications have gained tremendous economic and cultural significance. A set of these applications are summed up by the term *E-commerce*.

Software systems for supporting cross-company or in-house E-commerce applications are characterized by strong demands to meet the following requirements:

- New or improved functionalities have to be made available very quickly because time-to-market is an essential advantage against competitors who, on the Internet, are only one "click" away.
- Due to the fact that customers easily move to the competition, customer satisfaction needs to be guaranteed, among other things, through high availability and reliability.
- The functionality offered needs to be correct and of high quality.
- Customers and service operators need to have access to multilateral security concepts, as various user groups with highly different objectives participate in one application.

These requirements are not easily compatible and, thus, demand high standards of the software engineering process for E-commerce applications. For a company whose business model is based on the functionality of their applications offered on the Internet, it is indispensable to ensure that the software runs with a high level of reliability and accuracy.

The suggested methodology, thus, notably addresses the requirements mentioned above. The technical implementation of Internet auctions therefore serves especially well as a sample application for this methodology. Subsequently, the sample application described hereinafter is embedded in the E-commerce world. Then, a description of the business application underlying these Internet auctions follows. The sample application is taken from a

© Springer International Publishing Switzerland 2016
B. Rumpe, *Modeling with UML*, DOI 10.1007/978-3-319-33933-7

system that has been running in practice for a while and, thus, demonstrates the capacity of the described methodology for E-commerce applications.

D.1 Auctions as an E-Commerce Application

In about the year 1960, the first software applications for business purposes were developed and deployed in companies. These first-generation applications were largely isolated applications which did not allow data exchange among each other. In the second generation, these applications were interconnected company-wide. Since then, integrated databases have enabled different applications to access the data they require.

In the third generation that has been emerging for some years now, cross-company business transactions are realized.

The initiation and execution of commercial transactions via the Internet as well as electronic payment enable a lot of businesses to change their purchasing and sales channels massively. Internet auctions have been well received by customers as well as for industrial purchases and sales.

In the traditional auction, a single seller faces several potential buyers who outbid each other by placing multiple bids until the top price is reached. Due to the usage of the Internet as an electronic procurement tool, a second auction form has prevailed—the *procurement auction*, also called the *reverse auction*. Here, one buyer faces several potential suppliers who downbid each other in the time frame of the auction until the lowest price is reached.

Figure D.1 shows the result of one of the first and most effective procurement auctions in Germany. The chart displays the view of an *external observer* who, instead of real prices, can see a price scale converted to 100% and who can neither identify the bidders nor distinguish them.

In February 2000, the annual requirement of electricity for the headquarters of a large German bank company was put up for auction among 14 bidders. In two and a half hours, a saving of more than 46% was achieved [Rum02a, Böh00, Dei00]. The auction was conducted using the auction software introduced in this book and operated by our group.

Figure D.1 shows one vertical as well as two horizontal lines in the auction chart. These lines serve for the parameterization of procurement auctions. On the one hand, they allow the purchaser to step back from his wish to purchase when a target price level is not reached (shown by the lower horizontal line). On the other hand, they motivate the bidder not to wait until the last second of the auction but to place their bids early on. Thus, the bidders have the opportunity to react appropriately. The end of the official auction time and, hence, the beginning of the prolongation is indicated by the vertical line.

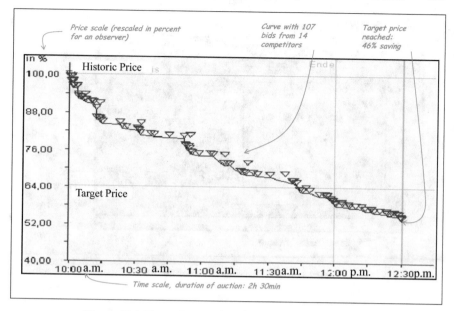

Figure D.1. Example auction of power with 46% saving

D.2 The Auction Platform

An essential part of the auction system is the graphical user interface which enables the bidders to place their bids online. Further participants can follow the auction process with the same graphical user interface but without the possibility to bid actively. As basic technology, Java applets are used. Java technology is well suited because it allows a graphical representation of the results on the user side, facilitates a high interaction rate (refresh time below one second), and still keeps the bandwidth of the communication between auction server and applets small.

The applet offers several subpages for the illustration of different views. As an example, the graphic illustration of an auction process is explained here, and an overview of all available pages of the auction applet is given.

Figure D.2 shows a view that an external guest uses for observing the auction. It contains crucial auction information for the identification of the auction, the date and time of the server, the number of bids placed, the number of active bidders, the allowed increment of bids, the auction's form, and the current bids (here scaled in %). The four auction states `still closed`, `open`, `in prolongation`, and `terminated` show whether bids can be placed. A message bar describes the current connection state and possible messages from the auctioneer to the participants. For bidders, an additional input field for bids is visible that allows bidders to participate in the auction process.

The display is supplemented by a message list that, among other items, contains a precise overview of all bids including when they were placed.

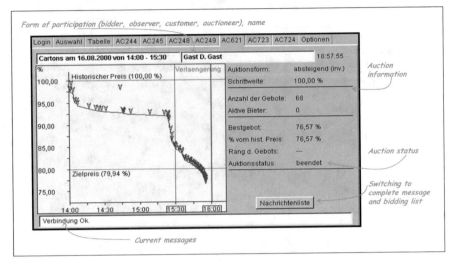

Figure D.2. Representation of an auction

While external observers see all bids in an anonymized way, bidders can identify their own bids against their competitors' bids with a respective symbol. It is possible to provide an internal observer with the same information as a bidder. This is interesting, e.g., when bidders and observers come from the same company.

Thus, a colleague can get access using their own authorization as an observer without the risk that a bidder account is passed on.

The auctioneer can identify the bidder of each bid at any time. The buyer is enabled to do so at the end of the auction.

The auction applet offers a variety of other views that, e.g., serve to give the participant an overview of auctions running in parallel or to enable him to configure the auction applet appropriately. Figure D.3 offers a collection of a part of these views.

Significant elements of a purchase auction are the two price lines marking the historic and the desired target price. Both prices are determined by the purchaser. The historical price characterizes the price the purchaser has paid for the goods up to now and often serves for the bidders as a starting point for their bids. The target price, however, is usually relevant in terms of contractual law. If the target price is reached or undercut, the purchaser is obliged to accept a bid —usually the lowest. Therefore, it is in the bidder's interest to reach the target price. An appropriate bid increment—typically one thousandth of the historical price—prevents bidders from placing bids in arbitrarily small steps.

Usually, an online auction takes place within one to three hours. In order to prevent bids from being mainly placed within the last few seconds, the auction time is divided into an official auction time and a prolongation

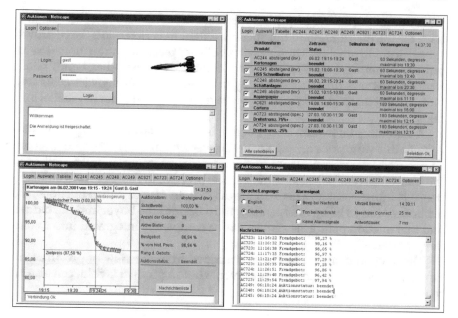

Figure D.3. Different views in the applet

phase. The middle vertical line marks the start of the prolongation phase. If a bid is placed shortly before the end of the official auction time, the auction time is prolonged. Normally, this prolongation has a length of three minutes. Thus, the competitors get the possibility to react to a bid. Continued prolongation of the auction time secures each bidder sufficient time to react and finally leads to the optimal result. If the system is configured such that the initial prolongation time of three minutes is linearly reduced with iterated prolongation, in case of stable increment, a price development similar to a parabola emerges analogous to Fig. D.2.

A number of participants with different interests take part in an auction. Accordingly, the system provides four roles for participation, and the role of observer is divided into three subroles. The *auctioneer* watches the process of the auction, having insight into all relevant data. During the auction, the *purchaser* can only see an anonymized process that first does not allow him to identify the bidders of the bids. Thus, possible subsidiary agreements are excluded. *Bidders* get an anonymized view of the competition but can identify their own bids in the corresponding chart. They also know how many competitors are active. Independent *observers* see anonymized charts, possibly with an additional price scaling to a 100% scale. This view is especially suited for demonstrations in front of a broader audience. Bidders have the additional possibility to invite colleagues as observers, they receive an auction view with bidder information without being able to place bids themselves.

A number of specialized functions, e.g., the combination of several auctions for the distribution of the auctioned item in various slots, have proved to be helpful in practice. Thus, varying delivery places of the auctioned items can, for example, be taken into consideration. On the other hand, goods which sometimes differ considerably in price, quality, or logistics costs and, thus, are not directly comparable, can be related to each other in parallel auctions.

A fundamental feature of an auction is the mutual anonymity of the bidders. In this way, price arrangements between competitors become unlikely. To ensure bidders' confidence in the accuracy of information as well as in the correctness and fairness of the auction process, the auctioneer's independence is indispensable. This also means that, in case of online auctions, the auctioneer has to be an independent third besides the buyer and the bidder, and that auction platforms should not be completely integrated into a company portal.

The auction platform has been described from the view of procurement auctions. Traditional auctions, however, where a product is sold, can also be realized using this auction platform.

References

[AK03]   C. Atkinson and T. Kühne. Model-driven development: a metamodeling foundation. *IEEE Software*, 20(5):36–41, 2003.

[AKRS06] C. Amelunxen, A. Königs, T. Rötschke, and A. Schürr. MOFLON: A standard-compliant metamodeling framework with graph transformations. In A. Rensink and J. Warmer, editors, *Model Driven Architecture – Foundations and Applications: Second European Conference, ECMDA-FA 2006, Bilbao, Spain, July 10-13, 2006*, volume 4066 of *Lecture Notes in Computer Science (LNCS)*, pages 361–375. Springer, 2006.

[Amb98]   S. Ambler. *Process Patterns. Building Large-Scale Systems Using Object Technology*. Cambridge University Press, Sigs Books, 1998.

[Bal99]   H. Balzert. *Lehrbuch der Objektmodellierung. Analyse und Entwurf*. Spektrum Akademischer Verlag. Heidelberg, 1999.

[Bal00]   H. Balzert. *Lehrbuch der Software-Technik. Software-Entwicklung*, 2. Aufl. Spektrum Akademischer Verlag. Heidelberg, 2000.

[BBB$^+$85] F.L. Bauer, R. Berghammer, M. Broy, W. Dosch, F. Geiselbrechtinger, R. Gnatz, E. Hangel, W. Hesse, B. Krieg-Brückner, A. Laut, T. Matzner, B. Möller, F. Nickl, H. Partsch, P. Pepper, K. Samelson, M. Wirsing, and H. Wössner. *The Munich Project CIP, Vol 1: The Wide Spectrum Language CIP-L*. LNCS 183. Springer-Verlag, 1985.

[BBF09]   G. Blair, N. Bencomo, and R.B. France. Models@run.time. *IEEE Computer*, 42(10):22–27, 2009.

[BCGR09a] Manfred Broy, María Victoria Cengarle, Hans Grönniger, and Bernhard Rumpe. Considerations and Rationale for a UML System Model. In K. Lano, editor, *UML 2 Semantics and Applications*, pages 43–61. John Wiley & Sons, November 2009.

[BCGR09b] Manfred Broy, María Victoria Cengarle, Hans Grönniger, and Bernhard Rumpe. Definition of the UML System Model. In K. Lano, editor, *UML 2 Semantics and Applications*, pages 63–93. John Wiley & Sons, November 2009.

[BCR07a]   Manfred Broy, María Victoria Cengarle, and Bernhard Rumpe. Towards a System Model for UML. Part 2: The Control Model. Technical Report TUM-I0710, TU Munich, Germany, February 2007.

[BCR07b] Manfred Broy, María Victoria Cengarle, and Bernhard Rumpe. Towards a System Model for UML. Part 3: The State Machine Model. Technical Report TUM-I0711, TU Munich, Germany, February 2007.

[BD00] B. Bruegge and A. Dutoit. *Object-Oriented Software Engineering: Conquering Complex and Changing Systems*. Prentice Hall, 2000.

[Ber97] K. Bergner. *Spezifikation großer Objektgeflechte mit Komponentendiagrammen*. Dissertation. CS Press, München, 1997.

[Béz05] J. Bézivin. On the Unification Power of Models. *Springer International Journal on Software and Systems Modeling (SoSyM)*, 4(2):171–188, 2005.

[BFG⁺93] M. Broy, C. Facchi, R. Grosu, R. Hettler, H. Hußmann, D. Nazareth, F. Regensburger, O. Slotosch, and K. Stølen. The Requirement and Design Specification Language SPECTRUM, An Informal Introduction, Version 1.0, Part 1. Technical Report TUM-I9312, Technische Universität München, 1993.

[BG98] K. Beck and E. Gamma. Test-Infected: Programmers Love Writing Tests. *JavaReport*, July 1998.

[BG99] K. Beck and E. Gamma. JUnit: A Cook's Tour. *JavaReport*, August 1999.

[BGH⁺97] Ruth Breu, Radu Grosu, Christoph Hofmann, Franz Huber, Ingolf Krüger, Bernhard Rumpe, Monika Schmidt, and Wolfgang Schwerin. Exemplary and Complete Object Interaction Descriptions. In H. Kilov, B. Rumpe, and I. Simmonds, editors, *Proceedings OOPSLA'97 Workshop on Object-oriented Behavioral Semantics*, volume TUM-I9737 of *Technical Report*. TU Munich, Germany, 1997.

[BGH⁺98a] R. Breu, R. Grosu, C. Hofmann, F. Huber, I. Krüger, B. Rumpe, M. Schmidt, and W. Schwerin. Exemplary and Complete Object Interaction Descriptions. *Computer Standards and Interfaces*, 19, 1998.

[BGH⁺98b] Ruth Breu, Radu Grosu, Franz Huber, Bernhard Rumpe, and Wolfgang Schwerin. Systems, Views and Models of UML. In M. Schader and A. Korthaus, editors, *Proceedings of the Unified Modeling Language, Technical Aspects and Applications*, pages 93–109. Physica Verlag, Heidelberg, Germany, 1998.

[BGK99] M. Broy, R. Grosu, and I. Krüger. Verfahren zum Automatischen Erzeugen eines Programms. Deutsches Patent, 19837871, 1999.

[BHP⁺98] Manfred Broy, Franz Huber, Barbara Paech, Bernhard Rumpe, and Katharina Spies. Software and System Modeling Based on a Unified Formal Semantics. In M. Broy and B. Rumpe, editors, *Proceedings of the International Workshop on Requirements Targeting Software and Systems Engineering (RTSE'97)*, volume 1526 of *LNCS*, pages 43–68, Bernried, Germany, October 1998. Springer.

[BMR95] A. Borgida, J. Mylopoulos, and R. Reiter. On the Frame Problem in Procedure Specifications. *IEEE Transactions on Software Engineering*, 21(10):785–789, 1995.

[BMR⁺96] F. Buschmann, R. Meunier, H. Rohnert, P. Sommerlad, and M. Stal. *A System of Patterns. Pattern-Oriented Software Architecture*. John Wiley & Sons, 1996.

[Böh00] R. Böhmer. Sichtbare Hand. Über einen der ersten erfolgreichen Versuche, Zulieferware in Deutschland übers Internet zu ersteigern. *Wirtschaftswoche*, 17.2.(8), 2000.

[BR07] Manfred Broy and Bernhard Rumpe. Modulare hierarchische Modellierung als Grundlage der Software- und Systementwicklung. *Informatik-Spektrum*, 30(1):3–18, Februar 2007.

[Bra84]   W. Brauer. *Automatentheorie: eine Einf"uhrung in die Technik endlicher Auto-maten.* Teubner, 1984.

[Bra04]   G. Bracha. Generics in the Java Programming Language. Technical report, Sun Microsystems, 2004.

[Bre01]   R. Breu. *Objektorientierter Softwareentwurf. Integration mit UML.* Springer Verlag, 2001.

[Bro97]   M. Broy. The Specification of System Components by State Transition Diagrams. TUM-I 9729, Technische Universität München, 1997.

[Bro98]   M. Broy. Pragmatic and Formal Specification of System Properties by Tables. TUM-I 9802, Technische Universität München, 1998.

[BS01]   M. Broy and K. Stoelen. *Specification and Development of Interactive Systems. Focus on Streams, Interfaces and Refinement.* Springer Verlag Heidelberg, 2001.

[BW02a]   A. Brucker and B. Wolff. A Proposal for a Formal OCL Semantics in Isabelle/HOL. In *TPHOLs 2002*, LNCS. Springer-Verlag, Berlin, 2002.

[BW02b]   A. Brucker and B. Wolff. HOL-OCL Experiences, Consequences and Design Choices. In J-M. Jézéquel and H. Hußmann, editors, *«UML»2002 – The Unified Modeling Language: Model Engineering, Concepts and Tools, 5th Intl. Conference.* Springer, LNCS, 2002.

[CAB+94]   D. Coleman, P. Arnold, S. Bodoff, C. Dollin, H. Gilchrist, F. Hayes, and P. Jeremaes. *Object-Oriented Development: The Fusion Method.* Prentice Hall, 1994.

[CEG+14]   B. Cheng, K. Eder, M. Gogolla, L. Grunske, M. Litoiu, H. Müller, P. Pelliccione, A. Perini, N. Qureshi, B. Rumpe, D. Schneider, F. Trollmann, and N. Villegas. Using Models at Runtime to Address Assurance for Self-Adaptive Systems. In N. Bencomo, R. France, B. Cheng, and U. Aßmann, editors, *Models@run.time. Foundations, Applications, and Roadpmaps, State-of-the-Art-Survey*, LNCS 8378, pages 101–136. Springer Verlag, 2014.

[CEK+00]   T. Clark, A. Evans, S. Kent, S. Brodsky, and S. Cook. A Feasibility Study in Rearchitecting UML as a Family of Languages using a Precise OO Meta-Modeling Approach. Technical report, pUML Group and IBM, 2000.

[CEK01]   T. Clark, A. Evans, and S. Kent. The Metamodelling Language Calculus: Foundation Semantics for UML. In H. Hußmann, editor, *Fundamental Approaches to Software Engineering. 4th International Conference, FASE 2001 (Part of ETAPS 2001) Genova, Italy, April 2-6.*, pages 17–31, LNCS 2029, Berlin, 2001. Springer Verlag.

[CGR08]   María Victoria Cengarle, Hans Grönniger, and Bernhard Rumpe. System Model Semantics of Class Diagrams. Informatik-Bericht 2008-05, TU Braunschweig, Germany, 2008.

[CGR09]   María Victoria Cengarle, Hans Grönniger, and Bernhard Rumpe. Variability within Modeling Language Definitions. In *Model Driven Engineering Languages and Systems. Proceedings of MODELS 2009*, volume 5795 of *LNCS*, pages 670–684, Denver, Colorado, USA, October 2009. Springer, Germany.

[Che76]   P. Chen. The Entity-Relationship Model – Toward a Unified View on Data. *ACM Transactions on Database Systems*, 1(1):9–36, 1976.

[CK01]   M. Cengarle and A. Knapp. A Formal Semantics for OCL 1.4. In M. Gogolla and C. Kobryn, editors, *«UML»2001 – The Unified Modeling Language, 4th Intl. Conference*, pages 118–133, LNCS 2185. Springer, 2001.

[CKM⁺99] S. Cook, A. Kleppe, R. Mitchell, B. Rumpe, J. Warmer, and A. Wills. Defining UML Family Members Using Prefaces. In C. Mingins and B. Meyer, editors, *TOOLS Pacific 32*. IEEE Press, 1999.

[CKM⁺02] S. Cook, A. Kleppe, R. Mitchell, B. Rumpe, J. Warmer, and A. Wills. The Amsterdam Manifesto on OCL. In T. Clark and J. Warmer, editors, *Object Modeling with the OCL*, pages 115–149, LNCS 2263. Springer Verlag, Berlin, 2002.

[Dei00] H. Deisenroth. Strombeschaffung über Internet-Online Auktionen. In *35. Symposium Einkauf und Logistik des BME am 25. September 2000 in Berlin*. BME Bundesverband für Materialwirtschaft, Einkauf und Logistik e.V., 2000.

[DeM79] T. DeMarco. *Structured analysis and system specification*. Prentice Hall, 1979.

[DH01] W. Damm and D. Harel. LSCs: Breathing Life into Message Sequence Charts. *Formal Methods in System Design*, 19(1):45–80, 2001.

[DL96] K. Dhara and G. Leavens. Forcing Behavioral Subtyping Through Specification Inheritance. In *18th International Conference on Software Engineering, Berlin, Germany*, pages 258–267. IEEE, 1996.

[DR95] V. Diekert and G. Rozenberg. *The Book of Traces*. World Scientific, Singapore, 1995.

[DSo01] D. DSouza. Model-Driven Architecture and Integration. Opportunities and Challenges. Version 1.1. Technical Report OMG Document ad/2001-03-02, Object Management Group, 2001.

[EE97] J. Ebert and G. Engels. Specialization of Object Life Cycle Definitions. Fachberichte Informatik 19/95, Universität Koblenz-Landau, 1997.

[EEKR99] H. Ehrig, G. Engels, H. Kreowski, and G. Rozenberg. *Handbook of Graph Grammars and Computing by Graph Transformations, Volume 2: Applications, Languages and Tools*. World Scientific, 1999.

[EFLR99] Andy Evans, Robert France, Kevin Lano, and Bernhard Rumpe. Meta-Modelling Semantics of UML. In H. Kilov, B. Rumpe, and I. Simmonds, editors, *Behavioral Specifications of Businesses and Systems*, pages 45–60. Kluver Academic Publisher, 1999.

[EH00] G. Engels and R. Heckel. Graph Transformation and Visual Modeling Techniques. *Bulletin of the European Association for Theoretical Computer Science*, 71, June 2000.

[EHHS00] G. Engels, J.-H. Hausmann, R. Heckel, and S. Sauer. Dynamic Meta-Modeling: A Graphical Approach to the Operational Semantics of Behavioral Diagrams in UML. In A. Evans, S. Kent, and B. Selic, editors, *≪UML≫2000 – The Unified Modeling Language, 3th Intl. Conference*, pages 323–337, LNCS 1939. Springer, 2000.

[FHR08] Florian Fieber, Michaela Huhn, and Bernhard Rumpe. Modellqualität als Indikator für Softwarequalität: eine Taxonomie. *Informatik-Spektrum*, 31(5):408–424, Oktober 2008.

[FLP⁺11] M. Norbert Fisch, Markus Look, Claas Pinkernell, Stefan Plesser, and Bernhard Rumpe. State-based Modeling of Buildings and Facilities. In *Proceedings of the 11th International Conference for Enhanced Building Operations (ICEBO'11)*, New York, NY, USA, October 2011.

[Fow99] M. Fowler. *Refactoring. Improving the Design of Existing Code*. Addison-Wesley, 1999.

[Fow00] M. Fowler. *UML Distilled. A Brief Guide to the Standard Object Modeling Language. Second Edition*. Addison-Wesley, 2000.

[FPR01]   M. Fontoura, W. Pree, and B. Rumpe. *The UML Profile for Framework Architecture*. Addison-Wesley, 2001.

[FR07]   R. France and B. Rumpe. Model-Driven Development of Complex Software: A Research Roadmap. In Lionel C. Briand and Alexander L. Wolf, editors, *International Conference on Software Engineering, ICSE 2007, Workshop on the Future of Software Engineering, FOSE 2007, May 23-25, 2007, Minneapolis, MN, USA*, FOSE, pages 37–54. IEEE Computer Society, 2007.

[GGR01]   J. Grabowski, P. Graubman, and E. Rudolph. HyperMSCs with Connectors for Advanced Visual System Modelling and Testing. In R. Reed and J. Reed, editors, *SDL 2001: Meeting UML, 10th International SDL Forum Copenhagen, Denmark, June 27-29, 2001, Proceedings*. Springer, LNCS 2078, 2001.

[GHG⁺93] J. Guttag, J. Horning, S. Garland, K. Jones, A. Modet, and J. Wing. *Larch: Languages and Tools for Formal Specification*. Springer-Verlag, New York, 1993.

[GHJV94] E. Gamma, R. Helm, R. Johnson, and J. Vlissides. *Design Patterns*. Addison-Wesley, 1994.

[GHK99]   J. Gil, J. Howse, and S. Kent. Constraint Diagrams: A Step Beyond UML. In *Proceedings of TOOLS USA'99*. IEEE Computer Society Press, 1999.

[GHK⁺07] Hans Grönniger, Jochen Hartmann, Holger Krahn, Stefan Kriebel, and Bernhard Rumpe. View-based Modeling of Function Nets. In *Proceedings of the Object-oriented Modelling of Embedded Real-Time Systems (OMER4) Workshop*, Paderborn, Germany, October 2007.

[GHK⁺08] Hans Grönniger, Jochen Hartmann, Holger Krahn, Stefan Kriebel, Lutz Rothhardt, and Bernhard Rumpe. Modelling Automotive Function Nets with Views for Features, Variants, and Modes. In *Proceedings of 4th European Congress ERTS - Embedded Real Time Software*, Toulouse, France, 2008.

[GJSB05] J. Gosling, B. Joy, G. Steele, and G. Bracha. *The Java Language Specification. Third Edition*. Addison-Wesley, 2005.

[GKPR08] Hans Grönniger, Holger Krahn, Claas Pinkernell, and Bernhard Rumpe. Modeling Variants of Automotive Systems using Views. In T. Klein and B. Rumpe, editors, *Modellbasierte Entwicklung von eingebetteten Fahrzeugfunktionen*, volume 2008-01 of *Informatik Bericht*, pages 76–89, Berlin, Germany, March 2008. TU Braunschweig.

[GKR96]   Radu Grosu, Cornel Klein, and Bernhard Rumpe. Enhancing the SysLab System Model with State. Technical Report TUM-I9631, TU Munich, Germany, July 1996.

[GKR⁺06] Hans Grönniger, Holger Krahn, Bernhard Rumpe, Martin Schindler, and Steven Völkel. MontiCore 1.0 - Ein Framework zur Erstellung und Verarbeitung domänspezifischer Sprachen. Informatik-Bericht 2006-04, CFG-Fakultät, TU Braunschweig, Deutschland, August 2006.

[GKRB96] R. Grosu, C. Klein, B. Rumpe, and M. Broy. State Transition Diagrams. TUM-I 9630, Technische Universität München, 1996.

[GKRS06] Hans Grönniger, Holger Krahn, Bernhard Rumpe, and Martin Schindler. Integration von Modellen in einen codebasierten Softwareentwicklungsprozess. In H.C. Mayer and R. Breu, editors, *Proceedings of the Modellierung 2006*, volume 82 of *LNI*, pages 67–81, Innsbruck, Tirol, Österreich, März 2006. Gesellschaft für Informatik.

[Gol84]   A. Goldberg. *Smalltalk 80 - The Interactive Programming Environment*. Addison Wesley, Reading, MA, 1984.

268   References

[GPHS08] C. Gonzalez-Perez and B. Henderson-Sellers. *Metamodelling for Software Engineering*. Wiley Publishing, 2008.

[GPR06]   V. Gruhn, D. Pieper, and C. Röttgers. *MDA: Effektives Software-Engineering mit UML 2 und Eclipse*. Springer Verlag, 2006.

[GR95]   Radu Grosu and Bernhard Rumpe. Concurrent Timed Port Automata. Technical Report TUM-I9533, TU Munich, Germany, October 1995.

[GR11]   Hans Grönniger and Bernhard Rumpe. Modeling Language Variability. In *Proceedings of the 16th Montery Workshop on Modeling, Development and Verification of Adaptive Systems*, volume 6662 of *LNCS*, pages 17–32, Redmond, Microsoft Research, 2011. Springer, Germany.

[GRG95]   J. Grabowski, E. Rudolph, and P. Graubman. Message Sequence Charts: Composition Techniques versus OO techniques. In *Proceedings of the 7th SDL forum*, 1995.

[GRJA12] Tim Gülke, Bernhard Rumpe, Martin Jansen, and Joachim Axmann. High-Level Requirements Management and Complexity Costs in Automotive Development Projects: A Problem Statement. In *Requirements Engineering: Foundation for Software Quality. 18th International Working Conference, Proceedings, REFSQ 2012*, Essen, Germany, March 2012.

[Grö10]   H. Grönniger. *Systemmodell-basierte Definition objektbasierter Modellierungssprachen mit semantischen Variationspunkte*. Aachener Informatik-Berichte, Software Engineering. Shaker Verlag, 2010.

[GRR10]   Hans Grönniger, Dirk Reiß, and Bernhard Rumpe. Towards a Semantics of Activity Diagrams with Semantic Variation Points. In D.C. Petriu, N. Rouquette, and Ø. Haugen, editors, *Model Driven Engineering Languages and Systems, Proceedings of MODELS*, volume 6394 of *LNCS*, pages 331–345, Oslo, Norway, 2010. Springer, Germany.

[Har87]   D. Harel. Statecharts: A Visual Formalism for Complex Systems. *Science of Computer Programming*, 8:231–274, 1987.

[HBvB+94] W. Hesse, G. Barkow, H. von Braun, H. Kittlaus, and G. Scheschonk. Terminologie in der Softwaretechnik - Ein Begriffssystem für die Analyse und Modellierung von Anwendungssystemen. Teil 1: Begriffssystematik und Grundbegriffe. *Informatik Spektrum*, 17/1994:39–47, 1994.

[HG97]   D. Harel and E. Gery. Executable Object Modelling with Statecharts. In *Proceedings of the 18th International Conference on Software Engineering*. IEEE Computer Society Press, 1997.

[HHB02]   R. Hennicker, H. Hußmann, and M. Bidoit. On the Precise Meaning of OCL Constraints. In T. Clark and J. Warmer, editors, *Object Modeling with the OCL*, pages 69–84, LNCS 2263. Springer Verlag, Berlin, 2002.

[HHK+13] Arne Haber, Katrin Hölldobler, Carsten Kolassa, Markus Look, Klaus Müller, Bernhard Rumpe, and Ina Schaefer. Engineering Delta Modeling Languages. In *Proceedings of the 17th International Software Product Line Conference (SPLC'13)*, pages 22–31, Tokyo, Japan, September 2013. ACM.

[HKM+13] Arne Haber, Carsten Kolassa, Peter Manhart, Pedram Mir Seyed Nazari, Bernhard Rumpe, and Ina Schaefer. First-Class Variability Modeling in Matlab/Simulink. In *Proceedings of the Seventh International Workshop on Variability Modelling of Software-intensive Systems (VaMoS'13)*, pages 11–18, Pisa, Italy, January 2013. ACM, New York, NY, USA.

[HKR+07] Christoph Herrmann, Holger Krahn, Bernhard Rumpe, Martin Schindler, and Steven Völkel. An Algebraic View on the Semantics of Model Composition. In D.H. Akehurst, R. Vogel, and R.F. Paige, editors, *Proceedings of the Third European Conference on Model Driven Architecture - Foundations and Applications (ECMDA-FA'07)*, volume 4530 of *LNCS*, pages 99–113, Haifa, Israel, June 2007. Springer, Germany.

[HKR+09] Christoph Herrmann, Holger Krahn, Bernhard Rumpe, Martin Schindler, and Steven Völkel. Scaling-Up Model-Based-Development for Large Heterogeneous Systems with Compositional Modeling. In H. R. Arabnia and H. Reza, editors, *Proceedings of the 2009 International Conference on Software Engineeering in Research and Practice (SERP 2009)*, pages 172–176, Las Vegas, Nevada, USA, July 2009.

[HM03] D. Harel and R. Marelly. *Come, Let's Play: Scenario-Based Programming Using LSCs and the Play-Engine*. Springer, 2003.

[HM08] D. Harel and S. Maoz. Assert and Negate Revisited: Modal semantics for UML Sequence Diagrams. *Springer International Journal on Software and Systems Modeling (SoSyM)*, 7(2):237–252, 2008.

[HR00] D. Harel and B. Rumpe. Modeling Languages: Syntax, Semantics and All That Stuff. Technical Report MCS00-16, The Weizmann Institute of Science, Rehovot, Israel, 2000.

[HR04] David Harel and Bernhard Rumpe. Meaningful Modeling: What's the Semantics of "Semantics"? *IEEE Computer*, 37(10):64–72, October 2004.

[HRR98] F. Huber, A. Rausch, and B. Rumpe. Modeling Dynamic Component Interfaces. In M. Singh, B. Meyer, J. Gil, and R. Mitchell, editors, *TOOLS 26, Technology of Object-Oriented Languages and Systems*. IEEE Computer Society, 1998.

[HRR99] F. Huber, O. Rabe, and B. Rumpe. Frisco OEF - Dokument-basiertes Editor Framework. In S. Maffeis, F. Toenniessen, and C. Zeidler, editors, *Erfahrungen mit Java. Projekte aus Industrie und Hochschule*, pages 333–354. d-punkt Verlag, Heidelberg, 1999.

[HRR10] Arne Haber, Jan Oliver Ringert, and Bernhard Rumpe. Towards Architectural Programming of Embedded Systems. In *Tagungsband des Dagstuhl-Workshop MBEES: Modellbasierte Entwicklung eingebetteterSysteme VI*, volume 2010-01 of *Informatik-Bericht*, pages 13 – 22, Dagstuhl Castle, Germany, February 2010. fortiss GmbH, Germany.

[HRR+11] Arne Haber, Holger Rendel, Bernhard Rumpe, Ina Schaefer, and Frank van der Linden. Hierarchical Variability Modeling for Software Architectures. In *Proceedings of International Software Product Lines Conference (SPLC'11)*, pages 150–159, Munich, Germany, August 2011. IEEE Computer Society.

[HRR12] Arne Haber, Jan Oliver Ringert, and Bernhard Rumpe. MontiArc - Architectural Modeling of Interactive Distributed and Cyber-Physical Systems. Technical Report AIB-2012-03, RWTH Aachen University, February 2012.

[HRRS11] Arne Haber, Holger Rendel, Bernhard Rumpe, and Ina Schaefer. Delta Modeling for Software Architectures. In *Tagungsband des Dagstuhl-Workshop MBEES: Modellbasierte Entwicklung eingebetteterSysteme VII*, pages 1 – 10, Munich, Germany, February 2011. fortiss GmbH.

[HRRS12] Arne Haber, Holger Rendel, Bernhard Rumpe, and Ina Schaefer. Evolving Delta-oriented Software Product Line Architectures. In D. Garlan and R. Calinescu, editors, *Large-Scale Complex IT Systems. Development, Operation and Management, 17th Monterey Workshop 2012*, volume 7539 of *LNCS*, pages 183–208, Oxford, UK, March 2012. Springer, Germany.

[HSB99] B. Henderson-Sellers and F. Barbier. Black and White Diamonds. In *«UML»'99 – The Unified Modeling Language. Beyond the Standard*, pages LNCS 1723, 550–565, Berlin, 1999. Springer Verlag.

[HU90] J. Hopcroft and J. Ullman. *Einführung in die Automatentheorie, Formale Sprachen und Komplexitätstheorie*. Addison-Wesley, 1990.

[Hut07] G. Hutton. *Programming in Haskell*. Cambridge University Press, 2007.

[IT99] ITU-T. *Message Seqeuence Chart (MSC), Recommendation Z.120 (11/99)*. International Telecommunication Union, 1999.

[JJM09] M.A. Jeusfeld, M. Jarke, and J. Mylopoulos. *Metamodeling for Method Engineering*. Cooperative Information Systems. The MIT Press, 2009.

[Jon96] M. P. Jones. *An Introduction to Gofer*, 1996.

[JUn16] JUnit. JUnit Testframework Homepage. http://www.junit.org/, 2016.

[KHK+03] N. Kam, D. Harel, H. Kugler, R. Marelly, A. Pnueli, E. Hubbard, and M. Stern. Formal Modeling of C. elegans Development: A Scenario-Based Approach. In Corrado Priami, editor, *Computational Methods in Systems Biology*, volume 2602 of *Lecture Notes in Computer Science*, pages 4–20. Springer Berlin / Heidelberg, 2003.

[KKP+09] Gabor Karsai, Holger Krahn, Claas Pinkernell, Bernhard Rumpe, Martin Schindler, and Steven Völkel. Design Guidelines for Domain Specific Languages. In M. Rossi, J. Sprinkle, J. Gray, and J.-P. Tolvanen, editors, *Proceedings of the 9th OOPSLA Workshop on Domain-Specific Modeling (DSM'09)*, volume B-108 of *Techreport*, pages 7–13, Orlando, Florida, USA, October 2009. Helsinki School of Economics.

[KPR97] C. Klein, C. Prehofer, and B. Rumpe. Feature Specification and Refinement with State Transition Diagrams. In P. Dini, editor, *Fourth IEEE Workshop on Feature Interactions in Telecommunications Networks and Distributed Systems*. IOS-Press, 1997.

[Kra10] Holger Krahn. *MontiCore: Agile Entwicklung von domänenspezifischen Sprachen im Software-Engineering*. Number 1 in Aachener Informatik-Berichte, Software Engineering. Shaker Verlag, März 2010.

[KRB96] Cornel Klein, Bernhard Rumpe, and Manfred Broy. A stream-based mathematical model for distributed information processing systems - SysLab system model. In E. Najm and J.-B. Stefani, editors, *Proceedings of the first International Workshop on Formal Methods for Open Object-based Distributed Systems*, IFIP Advances in Information and Communication Technology, pages 323–338, Paris, France, March 1996. Chapmann & Hall.

[Krü00] I. Krüger. *Distributed System Design with Message Sequence Charts*. Doktorarbeit, Technische Universität München, 2000.

[KRV06] Holger Krahn, Bernhard Rumpe, and Steven Völkel. Roles in Software Development using Domain Specific Modelling Languages. In J. Gray, J.-P. Tolvanen, and J. Sprinkle, editors, *Proceedings of the 6th OOPSLA Workshop on Domain-Specific Modeling 2006 (DSM'06)*, volume TR-37 of *Technical Report*, pages 150–158, Portland, Oregon, USA, October 2006. Jyväskylä University, Finland.

[KRV07a] Holger Krahn, Bernhard Rumpe, and Steven Völkel. Efficient Editor Generation for Compositional DSLs in Eclipse. In J. Sprinkle, J. Gray, M. Rossi, and J.-P. Tolvanen, editors, *Proceedings of the 7th OOPSLA Workshop on Domain-Specific Modeling (DSM'07)*, volume TR-38 of *Technical Reports*, Montreal, Quebec, Canada, October 2007. Jyväskylä University, Finland.

[KRV07b] Holger Krahn, Bernhard Rumpe, and Steven Völkel. Integrated Definition of Abstract and Concrete Syntax for Textual Languages. In G. Engels, B. Opdyke, D.C. Schmidt, and F. Weil, editors, *Proceedings of Model Driven Engineering Languages and Systems (MODELS'11)*, volume 4735 of *LNCS*, pages 286–300, Nashville, TN, USA, October 2007. Springer, Germany.

[KRV08] Holger Krahn, Bernhard Rumpe, and Steven Völkel. Monticore: Modular Development of Textual Domain Specific Languages. In R.F. Paige and B. Meyer, editors, *Proceedings of the 46th International Conference Objects, Models, Components, Patterns (TOOLS-Europe)*, volume 11 of *LNBIP*, pages 297–315, Zurich, Switzerland, July 2008. Springer, Germany.

[KRV10] Holger Krahn, Bernhard Rumpe, and Stefen Völkel. MontiCore: a Framework for Compositional Development of Domain Specific Languages. *International Journal on Software Tools for Technology Transfer (STTT)*, 12(5):353–372, September 2010.

[Lan05] K. Lano. *Advanced Systems Design with Java, UML, and MDA*. Elsevier, 2005.

[Lan09] K. Lano. *Model-Driven Software Development With UML and Java*. Cengage Learning EMEA, 2009.

[Leu95] S. Leue. Methods and Semantics for Telecommunication Systems Engineering. PhD Thesis, Universität Bern, 1995.

[LRSS10] Tihamer Levendovszky, Bernhard Rumpe, Bernhard Schätz, and Jonathan Sprinkle. Model Evolution and Management. In *MBEERTS: Model-Based Engineering of Embedded Real-Time Systems, International Dagstuhl Workshop*, volume 6100 of *LNCS*, pages 241–270, Dagstuhl Castle, Germany, October 2010. Springer, Germany.

[LW94] B. Liskov and J. Wing. A Behavioral Notion of Subtyping. *ACM Transactions on Programming Languages and Systems*, 16(6):1811–1841, November 1994.

[LW99] B. Liskov and J. Wing. Behavioral subtyping using invariants and constraints. CMU CS-99-156, School of Computer Science, Carnegie Mellon University, 1999.

[MC99] L. Mandel and M. Cengarle. On the Expressive Power of the Object Constraint Language OCL. In *FM'99, World Congress on Formal Methods*, LNCS 1708. Springer-Verlag, Berlin, 1999.

[McL01] B. McLaughlin. *Java und XML. Deutsche Ausgabe*. O'Reilly, 2001.

[Mey97] B. Meyer. *Object-Oriented Software Construction*. Prentice Hall, Englewood Cliffs, NJ, 1997.

[MMPH99] P. Müller, J. Meyer, and A. Poetzsch-Heffter. Making Executable Interface Specifications More Expressive. In C. Cap, editor, *JIT '99 Java-Informations-Tage 1999*, Informatik Aktuell. Springer-Verlag, 1999.

[MMR10] Tom Mens, Jeff Magee, and Bernhard Rumpe. Evolving Software Architecture Descriptions of Critical Systems. *IEEE Computer*, 43(5):42–48, May 2010.

[MPH00] P. Müller and A. Poetzsch-Heffter. Modular Specification and Verification Techniques for Object-Oriented Software Components. In G. Leavens and M. Sitaraman, editors, *Foundations of Component-Based Systems*. Cambridge University Press, 2000.

[MRR11a] Shahar Maoz, Jan Oliver Ringert, and Bernhard Rumpe. ADDiff: Semantic Differencing for Activity Diagrams. In *ESEC/FSE '11: Proceedings of the 19th ACM SIGSOFT Symposium and the 13th European Conference on Foundations of Software Engineering*, pages 179–189, Szeged, Hungary, 2011. ACM.

[MRR11b] Shahar Maoz, Jan Oliver Ringert, and Bernhard Rumpe. An Operational Semantics for Activity Diagrams using SMV. Technical Report AIB-2011-07, RWTH Aachen University, Aachen, Germany, July 2011.

[MRR11c] Shahar Maoz, Jan Oliver Ringert, and Bernhard Rumpe. CD2Alloy: Class Diagrams Analysis Using Alloy Revisited. In *Proceedings of Model Driven Engineering Languages and Systems (MODELS'11)*, volume 6981 of *LNCS*, pages 592–607, Wellington, New Zealand, October 2011. Springer.

[MRR11d] Shahar Maoz, Jan Oliver Ringert, and Bernhard Rumpe. Modal Object Diagrams. In *Proceedings of the 25th European Conference on Object-Oriented Programming (ECOOP'11)*, volume 6813 of *LNCS*, pages 281–305, Lancaster, UK, July 2011. Springer.

[MRR11e] Shahar Maoz, Jan Oliver Ringert, and Bernhard Rumpe. Semantically Configurable Consistency Analysis for Class and Object Diagrams. In *Proceedings of Model Driven Engineering Languages and Systems (MODELS'11)*, volume 6981 of *LNCS*, pages 153–167, Wellington, New Zealand, October 2011. Springer.

[MRR14] Shahar Maoz, Jan Oliver Ringert, and Bernhard Rumpe. Verifying Component and Connector Models against Crosscutting Structural Views. In *36th International Conference on Software Engineering (ICSE 2014)*, pages 95–105, Hyderabad, India, 2014. ACM New York.

[MTHM97] R. Milner, M. Tofte, R. Harper, and D. MacQueen. *The Definition of Standard ML (Revised)*. MIT Press, Cambridge, 1997.

[Nag79] M. Nagl. *Graph-Grammatiken: Theorie, Implementierung, Anwendungen*. Vieweg, Braunschweig, 1979.

[OH98] R. Orfali and D. Harkey. *Client/Server Programming with Java and CORBA*. John Wiley & Sons, 1998.

[OMG99] OMG Analysis and Design Task Force. White Paper of the Profile Mechanism. Version 1.0. Technical Report OMG Document ad/99-04-07, Object Management Group, 1999.

[OMG01a] OMG. Action Semantics for the UML. Response to OMG RFP ad/98-11-01. Technical Report OMG Document ad/2001-08-04, Object Management Group, 2001.

[OMG01b] OMG. Meta Object Facility (MOF) Specification. Technical Report 1.3.1, formal/01-11-02, Object Management Group (OMG), Sept. 2001.

[OMG03] OMG. MDA (Model Driven Architecture) Guide Verion 1.0.1. Technical Report OMG Document omg/2003-06-01, Object Management Group, 2003.

[OMG04] OMG. Enterprise Collaboration Architecture (ECA) Specification. Technical Report OMG Document formal/04-02-01, Object Management Group, 2004.

[OMG09] OMG. UML Profile for MARTE: Modeling and Analysis of Real-Time Embedded Systems. Technical Report OMG Document formal/2009-11-02, Object Management Group, 2009.

[OMG10a] OMG. OMG Unified Modeling Language: Infrastructure Specification, Superstructure Specification; formal/2010-05-03, formal/2010-05-05. Technical report, Object Management Group (OMG), May 2010.

[OMG10b] OMG. OMG Unified Modeling Language: Object Constraint Language 2.2; formal/2010-02-01. Technical report, Object Management Group (OMG), February 2010.

[Par93]   D. Parnas. Predicate Logic for Software Engineering. *IEEE Transactions on Software Engineering*, 19(9), September 1993.

[PFR02]   Wolfgang Pree, Marcus Fontoura, and Bernhard Rumpe. Product Line Annotations with UML-F. In G.J. Chastek, editor, *Proceedings of the Second International Conference on Software Product Lines (SPLC'02)*, volume 2379 of *LNCS*, pages 188–197, San Diego, California, USA, August 2002. Springer.

[PH97]   A. Poetzsch-Heffter. Specification and Verification of Object-Oriented Programs. Habilitation Thesis, Technische Universtität München, January 1997.

[PM06]   R. Petrasch and O. Meimberg. *Model-Driven Architecture: Eine praxisorientierte Einführung in die MDA*. dpunkt.verlag, 2006.

[PR94]   B. Paech and B. Rumpe. A new Concept of Refinement used for Behaviour Modelling with Automata. In *FME'94, Formal Methods Europe, Symposium '94*, LNCS 873. Springer-Verlag, Berlin, October 1994.

[PR99]   J. Philipps and B. Rumpe. Refinement of Pipe And Filter Architectures. In *FM'99, LNCS 1708*, pages 96–115, 1999.

[PR01]   J. Philipps and B. Rumpe. Roots of Refactoring. In K. Baclavski and H. Kilov, editors, *Tenth OOPSLA Workshop on Behavioral Semantics. Tampa Bay, Florida, USA*. Northeastern University, 2001.

[PR03]   Jan Philipps and Bernhard Rumpe. Refactoring of Programs and Specifications. In Kilov, H. and Baclavski, K., editor, *Practical Foundations of Business and System Specifications*, pages 281–297. Kluwer Academic Publishers, 2003.

[Pre95]   W. Pree. *Design Patterns for Object-Oriented Software Development*. Addison-Wesley, 1995.

[RA01]   G. Reggio and E. Astesiano. A Proposal of a Dynamic Core for UML Meta-modelling with MML. Technical Report DISI-TR-01-17, DISI - Universita di Genova, 2001.

[RG02]   M. Richters and M. Gogolla. OCL: Syntax, Semantics and Tools. In T. Clark and J. Warmer, editors, *Object Modeling with the OCL*, pages 42–68, LNCS 2263. Springer Verlag, Berlin, 2002.

[Ric02]   M. Richters. *A Precise Approach to Validating UML Models and OCL Constraints*. Doktorarbeit, Universität Braunschweig, 2002.

[RK96]   Bernhard Rumpe and Cornel Klein. Automata Describing Object Behavior. In B. Harvey and H. Kilov, editors, *Object-Oriented Behavioral Specifications*, pages 265–286. Kluwer Academic Publishers, 1996.

[RK99]   B. Rumpe and C. Klein. Automata Describing Object Behavior. In *Object-Oriented Behavioral Specifications*, pages 265–287. Kluwer Academic Publishers, Norwell, Massachusetts, 1999.

[RKB95]   Bernhard Rumpe, Cornel Klein, and Manfred Broy. Ein strombasiertes mathematisches Modell verteilter informationsverarbeitender Systeme - Syslab-Systemmodell. Technischer Bericht TUM-I9510, TU München, Deutschland, März 1995.

[RLNS00]   K. Rustan, M. Leino, G. Nelson, and J. Saxe. ESC/Java user's manual. Technical Note 2000-02, Compaq Systems Research Center, Palo Alto, CA, 2000.

[Roz99]   G. Rozenberg. *Handbook of Graph Grammars and Computing by Graph Transformations, Volume 1: Foundations*. World Scientific, 1999.

[RQZ07]   C. Rupp, S. Queins, and B. Zengler. *UML 2 glasklar*. Carl Hanser Verlag, 3rd edition, 2007.

[RRW13a] Jan Oliver Ringert, Bernhard Rumpe, and Andreas Wortmann. From Software Architecture Structure and Behavior Modeling to Implementations of Cyber-Physical Systems. *Software Engineering 2013 Workshopband*, LNI P-215:155–170, May 2013.

[RRW13b] Jan Oliver Ringert, Bernhard Rumpe, and Andreas Wortmann. MontiArcAutomaton: Modeling Architecture and Behavior of Robotic Systems. In *Workshops and Tutorials Proceedings of the 2013 IEEE International Conference on Robotics and Automation (ICRA'13)*, pages 10–12, Karlsruhe, Germany, May 2013.

[Rum96] B. Rumpe. *Formale Methodik des Entwurfs verteilter objektorientierter Systeme.* Herbert Utz Verlag Wissenschaft, 1996.

[Rum97] B. Rumpe. Formale Methodik des Entwurfs verteilter objektorientierter Systeme. In *Ausgezeichnete Informatikdissertationen 1997*, pages 118–134. Teubner Stuttgart, 1997.

[Rum02a] B. Rumpe. Online Auctions (lessons learned from strategic E-Business consulting). In *Issues & Trends of Information Technology Management in Contemporary Associations, Seattle*, pages 682–686, Hershey, London, 2002. Idea Group Publishing.

[Rum02b] B. Rumpe. «Java»OCL Based on New Presentation of the OCL-Syntax. In T. Clark and J. Warmer, editors, *Object Modeling with the OCL*, pages 189–212, LNCS 2263. Springer Verlag, Berlin, 2002.

[Rum02c] Bernhard Rumpe. Executable Modeling with UML - A Vision or a Nightmare? In T. Clark and J. Warmer, editors, *Issues & Trends of Information Technology Management in Contemporary Associations, Seattle*, pages 697–701. Idea Group Publishing, Hershey, London, 2002.

[Rum03] Bernhard Rumpe. Model-Based Testing of Object-Oriented Systems. In de Boer, F.S. and Bonsangue, M. and Graf, S. and de Roever, W.-P., editor, *Proceedings of the International Symposium on Formal Methods for Components and Objects (FMCO'02)*, volume 2852 of *LNCS*, pages 380–402, Leiden, Netherlands, November 2003. Springer.

[Rum04] Bernhard Rumpe. Agile Modeling with the UML. In M. Wirsing, A. Knapp, and S. Balsamo, editors, *Proceedings of the Radical Innovations of Software and Systems Engineering in the Future. 9th International Workshop (RISSEF'02)*, volume 2941 of *LNCS*, pages 297–309, Venice, Italy, October 2004. Springer.

[Rum11] Bernhard Rumpe. *Modellierung mit UML.* Springer Berlin, 2te edition, September 2011.

[Rum12] Bernhard Rumpe. *Agile Modellierung mit UML: Codegenerierung, Testfälle, Refactoring.* Springer Berlin, 2te edition, Juni 2012.

[RWH01] B. Reus, M. Wirsing, and R. Hennicker. A Hoare Calculus for Verifying Java Realizations of OCL-Constrained Design Model. In *FASE 2001, ETAPS, Genova*, LNCS 2029, pages 300–316. Springer Verlag, 2001.

[Sch98a] S. Schiffer. *Visuelle Programmierung. Grundlagen und Einsatzmöglichkeiten.* Addison-Wesley, 1998.

[Sch98b] P. Scholz. *Design of Reactive Systems and their Distributed Implementation with Statecharts.* Doktorarbeit, Technische Universität München, 1998.

[Sch00] W. Schwerin. Models of Systems, Work Products, and Notations. In *Proceedings of Intl. Workshop on Model Engineering, ECOOP, France.* Tech. Report, 2000.

[Sch02]   A. Schürr. A New Type Checking Approach for OCL Version 2.0? In T. Clark and J. Warmer, editors, *Object Modeling with the OCL*, pages 21–41, LNCS 2263. Springer Verlag, Berlin, 2002.

[Sch12]   Martin Schindler. *Eine Werkzeuginfrastruktur zur agilen Entwicklung mit der UML/P*. Number 11 in Aachener Informatik-Berichte, Software Engineering. Shaker Verlag, 2012.

[SE99a]   S. Sauer and G. Engels. Extending UML for Modeling of Multimedia Applications. In M. Hirakawa and P. Mussio, editors, *Proc. 1999 IEEE Symposium on Visual Languages, Tokyo, Japan*, pages 80–87. IEEE Computer Society, 1999.

[SE99b]   S. Sauer and G. Engels. UML-basierte Modellierung von Multimedianwendungen. In J. Desel, K. Pohl, and A. Schürr, editors, *Modellierung '99, Karlsruhe*, pages 155–170. Teubner, Stuttgart, 1999.

[SGW94]   B. Selic, G. Gulkeson, and P. Ward. *Real-Time Object-Oriented Modeling*. John Wiley and Sons, 1994.

[SHB96]   B. Schätz, H. Hußmann, and M. Broy. Graphical Development of Consistent System Specifications. In *FME'96, Industrial Benefit and Advances in Formal Methods*, LNCS 1051. Springer-Verlag, Berlin, 1996.

[SHJ⁺94] G. Saake, P. Hartel, R. Jungclaus, R. Wieringa, and R. Feenstra. Inheritance Conditions for Object Life Cycle Diagrams. In *Formale Grundlagen für den Entwurf von Informationssystemen*, GI-Workshop, Tutzing 24.-26. Mai 1994 (GI FG 2.5.2 EMISA). Institut für Informatik, Universität Hannover, May 1994.

[SPHP02] B. Schätz, A. Pretschner, F. Huber, and J. Philipps. Model-Based Development. Technical report TUM-I0204, Technische Universität München, 2002.

[SPTJ01] G. Sunye, D. Pollet, Y. Le Traon, and J.-M. Jezequel. Refactoring UML Models. In M. Gogolla and C. Kobryn, editors, «*UML*»*2001 – The Unified Modeling Language, 4th Intl. Conference*, pages 134–148, LNCS 2185. Springer, 2001.

[SRVK10] Jonathan Sprinkle, Bernhard Rumpe, Hans Vangheluwe, and Gabor Karsai. Metamodelling: State of the Art and Research Challenges. In *MBEERTS: Model-Based Engineering of Embedded Real-Time Systems, International Dagstuhl Workshop*, volume 6100 of *LNCS*, pages 57–76, Dagstuhl Castle, Germany, October 2010. Springer, Germany.

[Sta73]   H. Stachowiak. *Allgemeine Modelltheorie*. Springer Verlag, Wien, 1973.

[vdB94]   M. von der Beeck. A Comparison of Statecharts Variants. In H. Langmaack, W.-P. de Roever, and J. Vytopil, editors, *Formal Techniques in Real-Time and Fault-Tolerant Systems (FTRTFT'94)*, volume LNCS 863, pages 128–148. Springer-Verlag, 1994.

[vO01]   D. von Oheimb. Hoare Logic for Java in Isabelle/HOL. *Concurrency and Computation: Practice and Experience*, 13(13):1173–1214, 2001.

[Völ11]   Steven Völkel. *Kompositionale Entwicklung domänenspezifischer Sprachen*. Number 9 in Aachener Informatik-Berichte, Software Engineering. Shaker Verlag, 2011.

[Wei12]   Ingo Weisemöller. *Generierung domänenspezifischer Transformationssprachen*. Number 12 in Aachener Informatik-Berichte, Software Engineering. Shaker Verlag, 2012.

[WK98]   J. Warmer and A. Kleppe. *The Object Constraint Language*. Addison Wesley, Reading, Mass., 1998.

[WKS10]   I. Weisemöller, F. Klar, and A. Schürr. Development of Tool Extensions with MOFLON. In H. Giese, G. Karsai, E. Lee, B. Rumpe, and B. Schätz, editors, *Model-Based Engineering of Embedded Real-Time Systems: International Dagstuhl Workshop, Dagstuhl Castle, Germany, November 4-9, 2007*, LNCS 6100, pages 337–343. Springer Verlag, 2010.

[ZPK+11] Massimiliano Zanin, David Perez, Dimitrios S Kolovos, Richard F Paige, Kumardev Chatterjee, Andreas Horst, and Bernhard Rumpe. On Demand Data Analysis and Filtering for Inaccurate Flight Trajectories. In D. Schaefer, editor, *Proceedings of the SESAR Innovation Days*, Toulouse, France, November/December 2011. EUROCONTROL.

Index

© Springer International Publishing Switzerland 2016
B. Rumpe, *Modeling with UML*, DOI 10.1007/978-3-319-33933-7

Printed in the United States
By Bookmasters